BIBLICAL PRINCIPLES

concerning issues
of importance
to Godly Christians

"Behold, I lay in Zion for a Foundation, a stone, a tried stone, a precious cornerstone, a sure foundation . . . Judgement also will I lay on the line, and righteousness to the plummet" (Isa. 28:16, 17).

Plymouth Rock Foundation
Plymouth, Massachussetts
1984

PUBLISHED BY THE PLYMOUTH ROCK FOUNDATION
PLYMOUTH, MA
PRICE: $4.95

ISBN 0-942516-0

MANUFACTURED IN THE UNITED STATES OF AMERICA

TABLE OF CONTENTS

1

ABORTION

BACKGROUND BRIEFING Abortion, murder of a pre-born child, is *number one killer in US* (cardiovascular diseases are second). "In the US it is statistically confirmed that the most dangerous place for anyone to be, with regard to the preservation of one's life, is in the womb of one's mother."[1] *Abortion is a major business in US:* about *5,500 abortuaries in nation; Fortune* magazine estimates their take is more than half-billion dollars a year. *That does not include revenue from sale of aborted babies' bodies.*

Estimated some *1.3 million babies aborted in 1983* (not including number of those unreported—about another 260,000)[2]. About 25% of women having abortions are "repeats"—have had one or more priors. Abortuary centers report women who have abortions are generally young, unmarried and not likely to have ever given birth to live infant.[3]

Kansas was first state to legalize abortion on demand to time of birth. (In 1967, *then-Governor Ronald Reagan* signed California "Therapeutic Abortion Act" into law. It permitted abortion in case of rape, incest, if birth might impair physical or mental health of mother, or if there were a risk child would be born deformed. Loophole was "mental health"; certification of that came easily from many psychiatrists: thus, between 1967 and 1973, hundreds of thousands of abortions were commited in California under in the name of "mental health.")

National floodgates were opened on Jan. 22, 1973. US Supreme Court (*Roe v. Wade*) held woman has right to do as she chooses with her body, preborn child is not "legally" a person, has no legal rights until birthed. On same day, in *Doe v. Bolton*, Court held babies may be aborted (killed) until day they are to leave womb. Decisions made it Constitutionally impossible for any State to prohibit abortion at any time during pregnancy.[4] Since then, *some 15 million pre-born babies have been slaughtered* by curette or syringe.[5] A modern-day holocaust. That's an average of 4,000 each and every day during the decade 1973-83; *that's one abortion every 40 seconds.*

THE COURT'S BLOODY RECORD[6]

Roe v. Wade and *Doe v. Bolton* just first in a chain of decisions by US Supreme Court that paved way for 15 million abortions, 1973-1983.

1976—Planned Parenthood v. Danforth: preborn babies may be killed against will of father or grandparents. *1977—Maher v. Roe:* States cannot obstruct abortion but are not required to fund it. *1979—Colautti v. Franklin:* Physicians not required to assist babes who survive abortion. *1979—Bellotti v. Baird:* Babies of teenage mothers may be murdered without parental consent. *1980—McRae v. H.E.W.:* govt. does not have to fund abortions. *1983—Akron v. Akron:* (a) Unconstitutional to require informed consent (i.e. advise mother of what occurs in womb during abortion process, or to list alternatives.) (b) to require 24-hour waiting period, (c) Courts may overrule parents who refuse consent for teenage daughter's abortion.

Human sacrifice on the altar of nihilistic humanism continues. About three abortions to every live birth in District of Columbia. The ratio of birth to abortions in New York city is about one-to-one. Michael R. Gilstrap, in *The Phineas Report,* suggests *"abortion is an act of religious faith* . . . (for the woman who undergoes an abortion) *it affirms a belief in man as ultimate rather than as created in the image of God.* It is a commitment to an alien faith that rivals Christianity at the most fundamental levels."[7]

Advocates of right to abortion on demand insist it is woman's right to terminate unwanted pregnancy; that it is part of her freedom of choice, part of freedom of control over her own body; that abortion is just one method of contraception (that latter argument is taught in many high school [even elementary] "Sex Education" classes).

Supporters of abortion include several *religious denominations* (American Baptists, United Methodists, United Presbyterian Church, Episcopal Church and Lutheran Church of America. The *Religious Coalition for Abortion Rights* is housed in the Methodist Building on Capitol Hill, Washington, D.C.) Spokesman for those and other churches have made public statements that "continuance of pregnancy is *not* a moral necessity." Federal Judge John F. Dooling, Jr., cited their statements when arguing that Court's pro-abortion decision was *"in the mainstream of the nation's religious mainstream."*

Biblical Christians and other pro-life advocates do not agree. They assert willful termination of pregnancy and wanton aborting of pre-born child is against God's law. *That it is murder.* That in no other area of society is homicide condoned. Further, they insist, woman should control her body by controlling her self (emotions); that such control *should come before not after the act;* that women have no moral or legal right to murder pre-born baby to avoid the fruit of sin. (Less than 3% of all abortions are performed for reasons of rape or incest.)

Some pro-abortionists argue *it is cheaper to do away with unwanted babies than let them be born to be put on welfare or have them end up in court/prison.* Democrat's Vice Presidential nominee, *Geraldine Ferraro* (Vacarro), agrees: "The cost of putting an unwanted child through the [welfare] system far outweighs the cost [the federal funding] of these [abortion] procedures." And, as for costs of "justice" Rep. Ferraro said during House of Representatives debate on federal funding of abortions: *"It is a simple matter of economics.* Unwanted children so often end up in the criminal justice systems . . . it's very expensive to take care of them."[8]

Pro-abortionists urge termination of pregnancies as way to *ease economic dislocation (poverty),* remedy *sexual promiscuity,* and *build "planned"* and "perfect" *society.* July 1983 journal of *American Academy of Pediatrics* carried article arguing that handicapped children may have less (social) value than dogs or pigs with "superior capacities." In article, Peter Singer asserted:

"Once the religious mumbo-jumbo surrounding the term, 'human' has been stripped away . . . we will not regard as sacrosanct the life of each and every member of our species. . . ."[9]

Thus, anti-life groups would have physicians be "social executioners" according to State blueprint. So much for *Hippocratic Oath* ("I will not give a woman a pessary [vaginal suppository] to produce abortion.") So much for *Declaration of Geneva* ("I will maintain the utmost respect for human life, from the moment of conception.") *In Communist China,* govt. birth control policy permits one child per couple, max of two in rural areas. Women exceeding birth quota face forced abortions.[10] *New York Times* hailed Red China policy as "most effective in implementing birth control and population planning."[11]

Say pro-life forces: (1) such crass *economic determinism* of life, if accepted, *would enforce "Hitlerian concept"*— a continuing holocaust to eliminate those considered *"non-productive"* (the deformed and handicapped, the elderly and the unwanted pre-borns who failed to meet predetermined genetic standards). (2) Commiting abortion to escape fruits of promiscuity *simply adds one sin on top of another.* (3) Issue of public funding of abortion should be resolved by *prohibiting abortion on demand,* and (4) suggestions of either *pre-* or *post-partem* murder reveal *total disregard for sanctity of life* on part of abortionists and planners.

Dr. Bernard Nathanson, a founder of National Abortion Rights League, performed about 5,000 abortions following 1973 *Roe v. Wade* court decision. Dr. Nathanson once vehemently subscribed to and promoted pro-abortion arguments. *He has changed his mind; he now fights against abortions and abortionists.*

As to a woman's right to control her own body, he retorts: "I think everyone should control their own body . . . *BUT we have very sound data which have demonstrated that the fetus is not part of a woman's body.* It is an uneasy tenant . . . immunologically distinct, biologically distinct . . . it is not in fact a part of a woman's body."[12]

As for *key premises of US Supreme Court's 1973 pro-abortion decision,* Dr. Nathanson argues, "Some of the key premises are now so outdated, now so anachronistic that the decision itself has been rendered an anachronism . . . *The times, the new data, the new perceptions, and the new science, cry out for a change in that decision."*[13]

In letter to President Reagan, *26 doctors emphasized scientific methods make clear preborn babies feel pain during abortion.* "Nerves are in place by 6 to 8 weeks after conception . . . chemicals to transmit sensations from nerves through the spinal cord to the brain exist by 12 weeks . . . fetus reacts the same way a full-grown individual would when exposed to something painful, by squirming, thrashing . . . accelerated heartbeat and higher blood pressure."[14]

Dr. Nathanson made public an untrasonic filming of abortion which *shows pre-born baby in womb, thrashing about, trying to avoid suction device tearing off its head.* Viewers saw child dismembered, head crushed, as it is sucked out of womb. *The physician who performed the filmed abortion has never performed another.*[15]

Supreme Court Justice Sandra Day O'Connor has warned (June 15, 1983): *"The Roe framework . . . is clearly on a collision course with itself . . . it has no justi- fication in law or logic."*

"101 USES FOR A DEAD (OR ALIVE) BABY"[16]

A workman in *Wichita, KS*, tossing bags of "pathological waste" into incinerator from *Wesley Medical Center* (owned and operated by United Methodist Church) discovered bags contained bodies of dead babies. For years Medical Center had been sending remains of aborted babies to be burned along with "other trash." . . . *Milwaukee, WI:* Police found four children in parking lot behind *Mill Medical Center* play- ing with plastic jars containing aborted fetuses. "They told the officers they were throwing little people." . . . Not all bod- ies are "trashed." Babies' bodies are sold by the bag, $25 a batch—up to $5,500 a pound. Sales of aborted pre-borns brought *Washington, D.C., General Hospital $68,000,* 1966-1976. Money was used to buy TV sets and cookies for visiting professors . . . In *Richmond, VA,* abortion center used trash compactor to mash 100 babies' bodies which were tied up in plastic bags and tossed in trash bin. Dogs dragged bags away and fought over the contents. . . . In *Cincinnati, OH,* abortuary allowed dense smoke to pour from its chimney. When firemen arrived on scene, they were told, "We're burning babies." . . . *Massachusetts Supreme Court* ruled goldfish could not be awarded as prizes because that would violate State's anti-cruelty laws. Same court upheld mandatory state funding of abortions. . . . In *California,* bab- ies aborted at 6 months were submerged in jars of liquid to see if they could breathe through their skin (they couldn't). . . . An *Ohio* medical research company tested brains and hearts of 100 fetuses as part of a $300,000 pesti- cide contract. . . . Baby placentas are sold to drug compan- ies, 50-cents a piece (for Placenta Plus shampoo). . . . Human collagen from pre-borns (the gelatinous substance found in connective tissue, bone and cartilage) is sold to cosmetic firms for use in beauty products. . . . Dr. Jeronimo Dominguez writes, "On any Monday you can see about 30 garbage bags with fetal material in them along the sidewalks of abortion clinics in *New York.*"

What about political scene?

Democrat's 1984 platform states: "The Democratic Party supports the 1973 Supreme Court decision on abortion rights as the law of the land and opposes any constitutional amendment to restrict or overturn the decision." *Republicans* adopted this: "The unborn child has a fundamental individual right to life which cannot be infringed. We therefore reaffirm our support for a human life amendment to the Constitution."[17]

President Reagan: pro-life. Supports Constitutional amendment to protect pre-born children (*Human Life Bill,* Helms; *Respect Human Life Act,* Hyde-Jepsen).

Vice President George Bush: opposes Constitutional amendment banning abortion; supports federal funding of abortion in case of rape or incest.

Walter Mondale: Supports abortion on demand and federal funding for abortions. As US Senator from Minnesota, had *100% pro-abortion voting record.* "We must not let anyone assault the United States Constitution by eliminating the right of a woman to choose an abortion or some forms of birth control. Without that right her other liberties would be violated."[18]

Vice presidential nominee Geraldine Ferraro (Vacarro): Champions pro-abortion; has consistently promoted and voted for abortion on demand and federal funding of abortion during three terms in US House of Representatives. *On 14 key abortion-related votes in House* (since her election in 1978), *Rep. Ferraro voted pro-abortion on all 14 occasions.* Rep. Ferraro believes women should have free choice in matter of abortions but taxpayers should have no choice but to provide funds for abortions.[19]

CONSIDER THE BIBLICAL PRINCIPLES God's word makes it abundantly clear: *Abortion is murder, the wanton taking of an innocent human life.* Murder is prohibited by The Lord God (*"You shall not commit murder" Ex. 20:13,* see also *Gen. 9:5-7*).

All life is created by The Lord God; all life is under God's law. God, not the State, not the individual, not the parents, is the Lord of life. His will governs; men and nations may deny that fact but neither man nor nation can escape it — *or the consequences for violating it.*

Man is to preserve and protect life. Physicians and surgeons once took an oath to do that (Christian physicians still do). Once the courts were a sanctuary for the sanctity of life.

"If men strive and hurt a woman with child (one who is pregnant) *so that her fruit* (child) *depart from her . . . and if any harm follow* (if the child dies), *then you shall give life for life"* (Ex. 21:21-24). If God requires capital punishment when a fatal miscarriage is caused, surely his judgment for pre-meditated abortion can be no less severe toward those who are party to such murder.

Pro-abortionists claim terminating a pregnancy is not murder because the fetus (they never recognize it is a pre-born child) is not a human life. Thus, the question: *"When does life begin?"*

The Bible has always given the answer: and, the more science learns through study and research, the more if affirms The Scriptures. *Life begins at the moment of conception;* when *zygote* ("genesis" cell) is formed by the fusion of the sperm and the egg, at that point in time life commences.

"Marvelous are Your works, and that my soul knows right well! My substance was not hidden from You when I was made in secret and intricately wrought . . . Your eyes did see my substance, yet being unformed; and in Your book all my members were written, which in continuance were fashioned, when as yet there was none of them" (Ps. 139:14-16).

Consider Matthew Henry's *Commentaries:* Each individual is God's work, according to His divine model; His eternal wisdom formed the plan and mold. As a great mercy, all our members in continuance were fashioned as they were written in the book of God's wise counsel when as yet there was none of them. Thus, who would destroy his handiwork and purpose? At what stage of life's development and span? Six days? Six weeks? Six months, or sixty years?

"Before I formed you in the womb, I knew you; and before you came forth from the womb, I sanctified you, and I ordained you . . . " (Jer. 1:5). God did not sanctify a glob of protoplasm, he sanctified unto His work a living human being of great potential and inesti-

mable worth. *(See Eph. 1:4-5).*

Isaiah testified to the beginning of life: *"Thus says The Lord, your Redeemer, and he Who formed you from the womb: I am The Lord Who makes all things"* (Isa. 44:24).

For further insight into the life of the pre-born child, read luke 1:41, 44. When Mary, the mother of Jesus, visited Elizabeth, pregnant with John, the babe *"leaped in my womb for joy!"* Thus does The Bible tell us what medical doctors now know: pre-born babies feel, experience, react.

And, consider the words of Job (measure them against what we now know about the development of the child — about gestation — in the womb): *"Have You not poured me out as milk, and curdled me like cheese? You have clothed me with skin and flesh, and have fenced me with bones and sinews. You have granted me life and favor, and Your visitation has preserved my spirit"* (Job 10:10-12).

It is God Who has made us, male and female. God, not man, not State, not biochemist or genetic engineers.

It is The Lord God, not the "planners" and social engineers, Who writes the span and sets the stretch of life for each one of His creations. We are instruments of His power and providence through His gift of procreation; evidence of His incredible love *(Gen. 1:27, 28; John 3:16).* The soul that animates the body is His gift *(Gen. 2:7).* The astounding structure of the body — that which the abortionist slashes apart with scalpel, or rips apart with suction pump, or burns to death with saline solution — that body is the product of His omniscience and omnipotence and grace. Into it The Lord God breathes the soul of life that is capable of becoming a temple of The Holy Ghost *(I Cor. 6:19)*.

Mark this well, abortionist: give heed to what you destroy in your gravest of all acts of blasphemy!

And, this, you civil magistrates: you are to be servants (ministers) of God to the people for good *(Rom. 13:1-4)*? How, then, can magistrates (justices, legislators, executives) serve God or His people by decreeing that abortion murder is "legal" when it is in direct violation of God's unchanging law?

Citizens and nations: In a representative form of government, in that nation wherein the people make the final public decisions, *the majority that approve (condone) abortion will be held accountable unto The Lord.* The nation and its people are, in God's sight, *culpable*—accomplices to murder! *(Num. 35:30, 33; Hosea 4; Isa. 59:1-9)*.

> "Churches and other groups opposed to abortion must be prepared to extend practical help to . . . the unmarried woman who is pregnant . . . Merely to say 'you must not have an abortion,' without being ready to involve ourselves in the problem is another way of being inhuman." Francis A. Schaeffer and Everett Koop, M.D., in *Whatever Happened to the Human Race?*

Notes

1. *Campus Life*, July/August, 1982.
2. National Centers for Disease Control, UPI, 10/10/83.
3. *Opus cit.*
4. *Lifelite*, 2/84, as quoted in Salt Shakers Newsletter, March 1984.

5. 1982 World Book.

6. *Lifelite, op. cit.*

7. Michael R. Gilstrap, *Phineas Report*, Geneva Divinity School, May, 1983.

8. *Natnl. Right to Life News*, Aug. 2, 1984, p. 13.

9. *Our Throwaway Society*, Right to Life of Kansas folder.

10. United Press International, Peking, 11/11/82.

11. *A.L.L. About Issues*, American Life Lobby, June 1983, p. 31.

12. Interview with Dr. Bernard Nathanson, *Human Events*, 5.7.83, pp. 13, 14.

13. *Idem.*

14. United Press International, Washington, 2/14/84.

15. Jeffrey Hart, syndicated column, 8/4/84.

16. Excerpted from the article by the same title published in *A.L.L. About Issues*, American Life Lobby, January 1984.

17. "How The Party Platforms Compare," *Human Events*, 9/1/84, pp. 19, 21.

18. "Mondale and Ferraro Support Tax-Funded Abortion on Demand," *National Right To Life News*, 8/2/84, pp. 1, 13.

19. Background Sheet: *Ferraro: A Catholic For Abortion*, American Life Lobby, 7/25/84.

2

CAPITAL PUNISHMENT

BACKGROUND BRIEFING On Sept. 7, 1984, Ernest Dobbert, Jr. electrocuted by the State of Florida for the 1971 first degree murder of his 9-yr-old daughter, Kelly Ann. Dobbert, 46, beat his daughter about the head, burned her hands, beat her in the abdomen until it was swollen as if she were pregnant, held her under water, choked her. He was also convicted of the second-degree murder of his 7-yr-old son, Ryder, who died two months later from constant beatings he had received from his father.

Dobbert was 23rd person to be executed since US Supreme Court, in 1976, lifted ban on capital punishment. In 1967, Court announced it was taking question of capital punishment under advisement. Lower courts then put death penalty "on hold," awaiting high court's decision. In 1972, Supreme Court held death penalty laws of 41 states were unconstitutional on grounds they were applied arbitrarily and in a discriminatory manner. Subsequently, three States enacted *revised* death penalty statutes; these were upheld by Supreme Court. Thirty two States then followed suit and enacted similar laws.

In 1983, 230 inmates were added to death rows in *38 States* that have capital punishment laws. As of Sept. 1984, there were some *1,200* inmates being held under sentence for capital crimes (each had been convicted of murder). Of those condemned to die, 654 are white; 531, black; 67 Hispanic; 9 American Indian, 5 Asian and 2 unknown. Males totalled 1,255; females, 13.

Three rounds of appeal provided every convict before death sentence is executed. Pursuit of those appeals can stretch out for years. (Robert Sullivan, convicted of 1973 shooting of restaurant manager, had his case reviewed *20 times* by appellate courts including *five trips* US Supreme Court. Sullivan was finally electrocuted in Dec. 1983. In another notorious case, child killer Jimmy Lee Gray was sentenced to death for the 1976 sex slaying of 3-year-old Deressa Jean Scales. At the time Gray murdered Deressa Jean, he was on parole after serving seven years of a 20-yr sentence for the murder of his 16-yr-old girlfriend. Gray was put to death *after seven years and 82 judicial reviews by 26 State and Federal judges.*)

Opponents of capital punishment continue campaign to prevent additional executions and seek to outlaw death penalty. However, opinion polls show public strongly favors capital punishment for crimes such as premeditated murder and kidnapping. (At present, no federal laws demand death penalty. Bill before Senate calls for capital punishment for assassination of President, treason, and certain federal crimes such as hi-jacking when it results in death of a person.)

Advocates of death penalty contend capital punishment necessary *to protect public because it serves as a deterrent* to capital crimes. Opponents disagree, say death penalty no deterrent. *Statistics support deterrent argument:* during 10 yrs death penalty was outlawed, number of murders in US *almost doubled* — from 10,000 in '67 to more than 19,000 in 1977. *As executions declined, murders increased:* in 1975, 76 executions, 7,000 murders. In 1960, 56 executions, 8,000 murders. In 1972, no executions, 18,000 murders. And, in 1978, no executions but 19,555 murders; since 1980, 23 executions and more scheduled in 1984 and number of murders (which reached high of 23,000 in 1980) is dropping (is below 19,000 for 1984).

After making study of crime and punishment, Gordon Tullock, Virginia Polytechnic Institute, concluded: *"Eighty percent of the people who seriously think about crime think of punishment as a deterrent* — except for the sociologists and they wrote all the books."

Professor Isaac Ehrlich, Univ of Chicago and an opponent of capital punishment, nevertheless stated his studies indicated that *if death penalty were really enforced eight murders would be prevented for every one executed.* Others who had researched the subject contended Erhlich's data were off by a factor of at least five — *that for each execution at least 50 murderers were deterred.*

Opponents of death penalty claim it is "cruel and unusual" punishment and thus prohibited by Constitution. Courts have held to the contrary. No court has ever deviated from the position taken by the US

Supreme Court in 1890: *"Punishments are cruel when they involve torture or lingering death; but the punishment of death is not cruel within the meaning of that word as used in the Constitution.* It implies something inhuman and barbarous . . ."

Opponents maintain capital punishment is "racist" in that it is applied most often against members of minorities. Study of capital punishment indicates that about *42% of those sentenced to die are black.* But, FBI Uniform Crime code disclosed that *57% of those arrested for willful homicide were black.* Further, statistics show 50% of all murder victims are black. Thus, it is argued, failure to apply death penalty for first degree murder is in fact "racist" since it deprives black community of demonstrable deterrent to homicide.

CONSIDER THE BIBLICAL PRINCIPLES For those who would obey The Lord God, capital punishment is not a matter of choice or opinion poll, or even court decree: *It is God's requirement,* a Biblical mandate. God established the death penalty for willful murder *(Gen. 9:4-6): Whosoever sheds man's blood, by man shall his blood be shed: for in the image of God made He man."* Thus, capital punishment was ordained — and, not just for Noah or Noah's time but "for perpetual generations" *(Gen. 9:12).*

Capital punishment and the manner in which it was to be applied is detailed and reaffirmed many times in The Scriptures *(Ex. 21:12-15; Lev. 25:17-23; Num. 35:9-34; Dt. 21:1-9,* etc.). Some of these sentences may seem harsh, yet it is clear that if they had been continued many of the ills that plague society today would not have arisen. In His perfect justice, The Lord God provided for protection of the lawful from the lawless. In *Acts 25:10-12,* the Apostle Paul makes it clear that he recognizes the continuing validity of the death penalty: *"For if I be an offender, or have committed anything worthy of death, I refuse not to die . . ."*

Importantly, in its application of justice, The Bible carefully and clearly delineates between the crime of willful homicide (premeditated murder) and accidental death (manslaughter). God's word also declares that causing the death of an unborn child (miscarriage or abortion) is murder *(Ex. 21:23).*

Capital punishment is not to be used for personal revenge; it is strictly a matter of divine retribution to be exercised as a requirement from The Lord God. God instructs us (1) the person who willfully takes another's life must pay for that act by forfeiting his own, (2) the death penalty is not to be exercised by an individual or group but by the properly constituted civil authorities, and that (3) this must be done to uphold the sacredness (sanctity) of human life *("in the image of God created He man").*

When The Lord God established capital punishment, he also ordained the institution to enforce it (to bear the sword). That institution is civil government — the corporate body politic *(Gen. 9:5).* The Apostle Paul refers to this power to protect the innocent and to punish the law-breaker in *Rom. 13:4* "(the magistrate) *beareth not the sword in vain; for he is the minister of God, a revenger to execute wrath upon him who does evil."*

The foundation (basis) of civil government is *power* (implied or applied) bestowed upon it by the citizenry. When that power is abused or not used, govt. is weakened and eventually overturned. When that occurs, the individual, the family, the home, and most if not all lawful aspects of society are imperiled. Capital punishment is essential for protection of the innocent and maintenance of a safe and peaceful society. It is part of God's grace, one of His provisions for the protection of His creation, man.

The Bible tells us that murder pollutes the land, and that the only way to cleanse the land is capital punishment *(Num. 35:33-34)*. The Bible also instructs us that those nations that fail to enforce capital punishment will be harshly judged *(Jer. 2:34-37;* Hos. 1:4, 4:1-5). By obeying The Lord God and enforcing the death penalty for capital crimes, the nation cleanses itself of the guilt of innocent blood; conversely, the nation that refuses to obey God and avenge the taking of innocent human life must share the guilt of the murderer *(Dt. 21:7-8)*.

God's word sets forth certain definite rules so that this *ultimate exercise of civil power* — the death penalty — *will not be* abused. Capital punishment is to be enforced *judiciously, impartially, and only after full and proper (and swift) legal proceedings.* Testimony in such cases must be corroborated by *at least two witnesses* and should a witness give false testimony (perjury), thus to jeopardize the accused improperly, *that witness shall be subject to the penalty attached to the crime under consideration.* Finally, capital punishment is not to be enforced in a spirit of maliciousness or revenge (that is forbidden—*Mt. 5:38-44*) but used only as God directed. Thus, we may keep His commandments and statutes so that "It may go well with thee." (*Dt. 19:13, Num. 35:31-34*).

RECOMMENDED REFERENCES: *Neither Cruel Nor Unusual*, Frank Carrington, Arlington House; *Toward A Biblical View of Civil Government*, Robert Duncan Culver, Moody Press.

3

CHILD ABUSE

BACKGROUND BRIEFING *Every 60 seconds in USA a child is abused.* That's an average one victim each and every minute; *more than 500,000 a yr.* And, actual total may be much higher than that. Thousands of children die each yr as a result of abusive treatment. *More than 700 are killed by their own parents.* Child abuse is fifth most-common cause of child death in US. Average age of abused child is *less than 3 yrs.* Average age of abusive mother is 26; of abusive father, 30.

Physical violence is not only form of abuse: can be *physical neglect* (starvation, filthy conditions), *verbal abuse, emotional deprivation* (child starved for affection) —and, *sexual abuse.*

Estimated that a child is sexually abused every two minutes. Some experts admit that number could range *as high as 1 million a yr.* National studies report that one out of every five victims of sexual abuse is *less than 7 yrs. old.*

Experience indicates that only about 2% of sexual molestations against *pre-school* children are ever reported. In many cases child is warned not to tell under threat of harm to child or a loved one; in other cases, children won't tell because abuse was commited by someone they love (incest accounts for large number of child abuse cases.) And, when children do tell, many adults refuse to believe, think child is fantasizing.

Most shocking case recently: sexual abuse of about *400 3-, 4-, and 5-yr-old children* (commited over a period of 10 years) at a highly-respected (exclusive) day-care (preschool) center in Manhattan Beach, CA.

Alcohol plays a role in more than 50% of child abuse cases. Many cases occur due to ignorance of even *most basic post-natal care.* Frustrated parents (many in their teens) have severely beaten infants whose only offense was the crying and fussing that accompanies colic, or teething.

Usually, incidents of abuse *follow a pattern: First,* parent ignores child, withdraws affection. *Second*, parent may verbally berate child, complain child is clumsy, dumb, always under foot, a nuisance, etc. That may lead to *physical neglect;* child may not be properly or regularly fed, dressed inappropriately for weather conditions, lack clean clothing. *Finally, comes physical abuse.*

Nearly half of abuse incidents *could have been prevented* by other adults who realized abuse was probably occurring but chose not to get involved. Because of fear of weaker spouse, or apathy of relatives, friends or neighbors, little or nothing done to protect child. Then, government agencies intervene. Child may be taken from parents—*but, State-operated orphanages and foster homes can be as bad or* worse than child's own home. (Also, some cases reported where State took or tried to take children from parents under guise/charge of abuse because agency did not approve of *religious* training, *Christian* schooling or discipline, etc.)

Child abuse is often the bitter fruit of *humanism*. Those who do not respect The Lord God usually have little or no respect for those made in His image. Humanism does not glorify man as God's handiwork; it *de-humanizes* man, makes it easier to excuse violating the individual either mentally or physically . . . and, young children are *very vulnerable*. God requires nurturing of children (loving care, training, education); false gods call for their exploitation, abuse, and destruction *(Lev. 18:21)*.

Not all child abuse occurs in home or involves physical or sexual violence. Much child abuse *occurs in classrooms of State-controlled schools*. Testimony by some *1,300 parents in seven different* cities during March, 1984, spelled out *"eye-witness accounts of psychological abuse of children in public schools."* Testimony was given at US Dept. of Education Hearings on proposed regulations for Protection of Pupil Rights Amendment (Hatch Amendment) — Section 439 of General Education Code P1232h.

Parents *"related how classroom courses have confused schoolchildren about life, about standards of behavior, about moral choices, about religious loyalties, and about relationships with parents and with peers."*

In her Forward to *"Child Abuse in The Classroom"* (excerpts from the official transcripts of the hearings), *Phyllis Schlafly* states hearings provided documentation of former US Senator S. I. Haya-kawa's warnings that schools have become *vehicles for a "heresy that rejects the idea of education as the acquisition of knowledge and skills"* and instead *"regards the fundamental task in education as therapy."* It is, said Senator Hayakawa, a therapy that seeks to replace *cognitive* education with *effective* (or *manipulative)* education. That, Hayakawa told Senate in 1978, is a *"serious invasion of privacy."*

Commented Mrs. Schlafly, *"These hearings explain how schools have alienated children from their parents, from traditional morality such as the Ten Commandments, and from our American heritage."* *"These hearings explain why we have 23 million adult illiterates who graduated from public schools, and why young people are experiencing high rates of teenage suicide, loneliness, premarital sex and pregnancies."*

It is clear that such heresy in the classrooms of the State-controlled schools can only be classified as *"child abuse"* — *leaving a long trail of wrecked lives and broken families.*

"Sex education" in many if not most State schools is little more than *values manipulation* that encourages a lessening of self-control (abstinence). Such "education" sets stage for subsequent *"child abuse"* of abortion. After US Supreme Court's *Roe v. Wade* decision legalized abortion, *number of abortions doubled in just 4 years* . . . and, in that same period (1972-76), *number of incidents of child abuse soared more than 800%.*

Christian theologian and philosopher Francis Schaeffer commented at the time, *"There has been a dramatic rise of crimes against children since abortion-on-*

demand became legal in the US. We are convinced that this increase is caused in part by the liberalization of abortion laws and the resultant drastic lowering of the value placed on human life and children's lives in particular."

And, professor, author and pro-life crusader, *Dr. Harold O. J. Brown* suggested that legalized abortion may well have caused some parents to reason, *"I didn't have to have him; I could have killed him before he was born. So, if I want to throw him around . . . isn't that my right?*

For a copy of "CHILD ABUSE IN THE CLASS-ROOM," edited by Phyllis Schlafly, write Pere Marquette Press, Alton, Il 62002. Price of indexed 445-page paperback is $4.95.

CONSIDER THE BIBLICAL PRINCIPLES Jacob said of his offspring that they were *"children which God has graciously given Your servant" (Gen. 33:5)*. Children belong to God and are placed in the care of earthly parents as a trust, a stewardship *(Gen. 4:1)*. The Scriptures direct parents to nurture, strengthen, discipline and teach their children—*not* abuse them *(Dt. 6:7; 18-21)*.

In many pagan religions, parents have a life-and-death power over their offspring; in Christianity, the command to honor parents *(Ex. 20:12)* is followed by prohibition of murder *(Ex. 20:13)*. Parents are to be respected *but the authority of the parent is not without limits . . .* they are parents *under God and must obey His law.*

Jesus was indignant with His disciples when they attempted to prevent children from coming to Him

(Mk. 10:14). Children were to be allowed to come and were not to be despised *(Mt. 18:10)*. Those who harm God's little ones will suffer His wrath *(Mt. 18:6 See also Isa. 40:11)*. Unknowingly, faithful disciples render service to Christ by ministering to the needs of little ones *(Mt. 25:35-40)*.

To combat child abuse, preventive measures must be taken and they must begin in the most important unit of society, *the family*. If there is a possibility of abuse in a home, *the involvement of nearby relatives may be crucial*. The relatives must not close their eyes or ears to reality, or hope that the problem will simply "go away." They should *counsel* with the family member, *pray* with and for him or her, offer to *temporarily care for the children* if that will help, and encourage the parent to seek a *Biblical change of heart* and lifestyle through the power of The Holy Spirit. The fruits of The Spirit include patience (forbearance) and temperance (self-control, right self-governance) *(Gal. 5:23)*.

Several decades ago, neighborhoods and communities were strong deterrents to child abuse; *disapproval was clear and swift*. Also, employers would take action against an employee guilty of child abuse. Now, such "closeness" is largely gone and Caesar moves in to fill the void: *Christians should claim that territory for Christ* — not as meddlers or vigilantes but in Christian love and service; it should be part of their witness and their walk for Jesus.

The church should demonstrate its "saltiness" in the areas of child abuse. Each congregation must determine that one of its central functions is to build strong, Christ-centered families—*places of love, learning, Godliness, stability . . . a "fortress" vs. all things harmful from the storms of life.*

Paul commands the mature woman to teach the younger women how to love their children *(Tit. 2:3, 4)*. The mature man should help teach young fathers how to avoid provoking their children to wrath *(Col. 3:21)* and how to raise them in the nurture and admonition of The Lord *(Eph. 6:4)*. God deals mercifully with us because He loves us and he remembers that we are dust *(Ps. 103:14);* parents must know the capacities of their children and not expect more from them than is proper. Discipline is an expression of love and caring *(Pr. 12: 13:24; Heb. 12:6, 7),* and it must never be exercised in wrath or meaness.

God shows special concern *for the fatherless (Ps. 27:10)*. The Hebrew word for "fatherless" indicates that the child may not necessarily be deprived of biological parents but may be destitute, lonely, helpless, and exposed to injury. As God is Father to the fatherless in their affliction *(Ps. 68:5)*, so too must Christ's church reach out to the fatherless in their afflictions *(James 1:27)*. If civil magistrates remove children from their home, the church should be ready to place the children in a *Christian* foster home in which these little ones may be nurtured and brought up in the love and care of God's stewards. Tithes are to go, in part, to the relief of the fatherless *(Isa. 1:17)*.

"Lo," sang the sweet Psalmist, *"children are an heritage of The Lord and the fruit of the womb" (Ps 127:3).*

"Suffer the little children to come unto Me," called Jesus, *"for of such is the kingdom of heaven"* (Mt. 10:14) *"And whoso shall receive one such little child in My name receives Me. But whoso offends one of these little ones which believe in Me, it were better for him that a millstone were hanged about his neck and that he were drowned in the depth of the sea"* (Mt. 18:5, 6).

(Plymouth Rock wishes to credit and thank *Dr. W. David Gamble* who researched, reasoned and wrote this article. Dr. Gamble is a college professor in San Diego, CA, and founder and president of the American Reformation Movement.)

4

COST OF GOVERNMENT

BACKGROUND BRIEFING Christians are no enemies to civil government; it is an institution ordained by The Lord God to insure domestic tranquility *(Rom. 13:1-4)*. We are to support the proper functions of civil government; for this cause we *"pay tribute to whom tribute (tax) is due."* The question, even from Biblical times: *"What is the proper cost of civil government? Just how much is due to Caesar?"*

Today, American workers/taxpayers have reason to wonder if Caesar does not demand more than his just, fair or proper due. *Consider this:* it took 186 years for federal spending to total $100 billion; took next 9 years to reach $200 billion; 4 more years to hit $300 billion, 2 more to reach $400 billion *and only 6 more to zoom past the $750 billion mark!* Today, cost of Federal government is *almost $800* billion ($795.9 billion in fiscal '83). Add *State and local governments* (and special districts — school, etc.) and total annual cost for Uncle Caesar and his nephews and cousins comes to about *$1.2 trillion* (that's one thousand two hundred billion).

Under Reagan administration rate of growth

slowed somewhat but still civil government and its costs continue to increase.

From 1940-80, while total national personal income rose 1,800%, cost of government rose 3,600% (all government, federal, state & local). And, while per capita personal income was increasing 1,000%, per capita cost of government increased 2,000%. Thus, in those 40 years, *cost of civil government increased twice as fast as increase in personal income* and now it's growing at an even faster rate. And, that does not include the tax of inflation which takes about as much as all federal personal income taxes. (During past 10 years cost of government rose at rate three times increase in cost of living.)

Government spending now takes *close to one-half of total US personal incomes.* Cost has been rising *almost twice as fast as Gross National Product* (GNP). In 1940, government took 20% of GNP; by 1980, "take" had expanded to 36%. *Now, more than one-third of all goods and services in US are gobbled up by civil government.*

If govts. were to take their cut from top of your daily earnings, *first three hours would go to Caesar and his cousins. And, those in upper-middle and higher brackets would work well beyond noon to pay their "share" of cost.*

In 1930, 34% of all govt. revenues went to Washington; 66% stayed at state and local govt. level. In 1983, 65% of all govt. funds went to Washington and only 35% stayed with state & local govts. One reason sometimes cited for increase in federal and State costs: increased aid to local govts. However, in past 10 yrs, while federal and state expenditures rose 181%, *local* (own source) *expenditures almost tripled.* Property taxes, about 53%

of all local govt. revenues, *more than doubled.*

(Since 1981, annual spending for *Social Security* has increased more than 45% — $50 billion, not including promised cost-of-living benefits increase. *Dept. of Agriculture's PIK program* (Payments in Kind) has produced *highest govt. expenditures* in history of farm programs — about $20 billion increase, and costs of Medicare and Medicaid have risen 62% — more than $32 billion in just 3 yrs. These and other costs of govt are expected *to continue to increase* as govt more and more takes over areas that *once were a matter of self-reliance* and family and private responsibility. Nation has yet to really learn *there is no such thing as a free lunch.*)

Reagan Administration's budget calls for federal budget of *$925 billion for next fiscal yr.* US Senator *Steve Symms* (R) estimates that means Uncle Sam would be spending *$100 million each and every hour* — and continues Senator Symms, that would be *$15 million an hour faster* than what was spent in 1983 (*plus fact,* it would also *increase federal debt by $15 million an hour*). In two yrs (between 1983 and '85) federal tax collections will *increase by $145 billion* and federal spending by $130 billion. In past 53 yrs, points out Symms, *Congress has increased taxes 193 times* — "but, we have had deficits in all but 8 of those years."

Asked *which level of govt. gives people most for their tax dollar,* only 24% of those polled said federal, a 12-yr low. *Local govts ranked highest* (35%), State govts next (27%).

President Reagan formed *Private Sector Survey on Cost Control* (Grace Commission, so dubbed for

J. Peter Grace, chairman). Commission says *2,478 cuts can be made in federal spending;* details how these can *save $424 billion over three yr period* by just implementing common-sense, good business approaches. $41 billion could be cut from 1984-85 budget, as a starter, without touching Social Security benefits, federal retirement benefits or food stamp program.

Mr. Grace contends vast amounts of taxpayers' money could be saved simply by making federal govt. *more efficient: "federal govt. is worst-run enterprise in America."*

About *one in every 5 non-agricultural jobs in US is in govt.* Grace Commission estimates federal govt. could save about *$48 billion a yr* over next 3 yrs if it provided govt. workers with pay and benefits comparable to those in private sector. Commission asserts *federal payroll costs could be cut by 25%,* says federal employes enjoy much more generous pension, sick leave, vacation and health benefits and greater job security than private sector counterparts.

On subject of pensions: US Senator Edward (Ted) Kennedy's pension kitty from federal govt. now stands at *$1.5 million.* He is one of privileged group of congressmen whose govt. pension trusts total $1 million or more. Others include *Senators John Tower, Robert Dole, Lowell Weicker, and Howard Baker,* and *Representatives John Dingell, Dan Rostenkowski, and 25 others in the House.* will these men give this up to "save" America?

In addition, taxpayers shell out for "dubious" (at least) programs such as *National Endowment of the Arts* (NEA), *National Endowment for the Humanities* (NEH, and *Institute for Museum Services* (IMS)—a total of

$338.5 million in 1984. Are those expenditures conducive to building stronger nation? Are they *legitimate function* of federal govt? *"No way,"* concluded *Heritage Foundation* after studying programs of the three agencies. The NEA, said Heritage, might well be tagged "National Endowment for Pornography" —it has funded *"gross vulgarity, obscenity, viciousness, fierce anti-religion sentiments, contempt for democracy and sheer perversity."*

PERSONAL INCOMES AND GOVERNMENT SPENDING, 1940—1982

	All Govt Spent	Total Pers. Income	Govt Spend. %P.I.	Per Cap. Govt. Spend.	Per Cap. Pers. Income	Gross Ntnl. Prod.	%GNP to Govt. Spend.
	(In billions of $ except for per capita data)						
1940	$ 20.4	$ 78.7	25.9%	$ 155	$ 596	$ 100.0	18.4%
1950	70.3	226.1	31.1	468	1491	286.2	21.3
1960	151.3	398.7	37.9	851	2212	506.0	27.0
1970	332.9	801.5	41.5	1642	3911	982.4	31.7
1980	942.4	1,943.8	48.5	4260	8773	2626.0	34
1982	1,196.9	2,623.2	46.5	5203	11400	3050.0	38

Sources: US Dept. of Commerce, Tax Foundation, GOP Study Committee

CONSIDER THE BIBLICAL PRINCIPLES The form and system of taxation depends largely *upon the form and system of govt. —whether the people worship The Lord God,* or *the State;* whether they put their trust and their obedience in God and His word and way, or Caesar's. *Consider these Biblical principles of taxation,* and how they require a nation of self-reliant, compassionate people who go forth in His name and for His sake.

1. Everyone is to carry his or her *fair share of the cost of govt* (both ecclesiastical and civil). In the Old Testament, there were established two basic forms of taxation: *the head tax* and *the income tax* (the tithe was both a religious and a secular tax).

Every man over age 20 paid the head tax (Ex 30:11-16). The tax was the same for all (1/2 shekel of silver a year). This tax was used for State affairs (courts, military needs, etc.). In addition to this head tax was *the income tax* (the *tithe).*

The *tithe* was not (is not) a free-will gift, it was (it is) a tax required by The Lord God; all are to pay it. *There were two types of tithe.* The "first" or regular tithe — *10% of income, no more no less;* and the *"poor" tithe,* to be paid every other year to help those in need. Together, the tithes came to about 15% of the individual's income. Failure to pay the tithe was (is) to rob God of what is His *(Mal. 3:8-12).*

The "head" tax was paid to the civil authority (the State). The tithe was paid to the local priests (Levites) and used locally. Thus, there was *local authority and representation* regarding the collection and expenditure of the tithe for such functions as education, welfare, and other civic functions. (This principle was adhered to in the early days of this republic; *the county was the basic unit of govt.,* taxes were paid at that level.)

2. *Discriminatory taxation was prohibited (Ex 30:15).* There is to be equality of taxation. *Progressive taxation* (progressive tax rates) *is anti-Biblical.* Each individual (head of household) was to pay the same portion of income to support the govt.

3. *Excessive taxation is theft* (legalized plunder) *and violates both the Sixth and Eighth Commandments.* Excessive taxation destroys capital (the economic "seed"). If this "seed" is confiscated and spent by Caesar, it cannot be invested and employed by God's stewards to "multiply, subdue and have dominion" for The Lord. The purpose of taxation is to raise those revenues necessary to support the proper functions of govt (justice); *it is not to be used for social reform.* Social reform is a part of the work of the church and is to be based on the principles and precepts set forth in God's word.

4. Ideally, there should be *no land or property tax and no estate or inheritance tax.* The earth (land) belongs to The Lord God; to tax the earth is to tax that which belongs to Him *(Ex. 9:29; Ps. 24:1; I Cor. 10:26).* Through the tithe, God makes provision to tax income (i.e. *that which the land produces)* rather than the land itself. The property tax (and the power to tax property) and the inheritance and estate tax threatens the *continuity of the family* (God's basic social unit), *the home and the local community.* (Note how exhorbitant property taxes today are depriving the elderly of their homes and preventing young marrieds from being able to afford real estate.) The property tax opens the door to confiscation, centralization and control and promotes speculation rather than productivity and true wealth.

5. *It is anti-Biblical to tax the receipts* (fruits) *of crime (the sins of gambling, prostitution, sodomy, drug abuse, traffic in liquor, etc.) (Dt. 23:18).* Revenues from such ill-gotten gains are ill-gotten themselves and unac-

ceptable in the eyes of God. By taxing crime, the State legitimizes the immoral and condones both the sin and the sinner.

By failing to follow God's plan and purpose for society, and His system of taxation, we pay the penalty of having to live under an ungodly and oppressive system of taxation. In so doing, we are forced to render in excess to Caesar. Samuel warned of these consequences when the Israelites rejected God and demanded an earthly king (I Sam 8:1-18).

Rev. R. J. Rushdoony writes, *"Without the tithe, a totalitarian State progressively develops to play god over society. With the tithe, the rule of society is restored to God through His ordained law."*

RECOMMENDED READING   *The Institutes of Biblical Law,* R. J. Rushdoony, Craig Press, Nutley NJ; *The World Under God's Law,* Rev. T. Robert Ingram, St. Thomas Press, Houston, TX.

5

CRIMES AGAINST PROPERTY
(PRISON REFORM)

BACKGROUND BRIEFING Every three seconds in US, clock ticks off one more crime against someone's property (theft, robbery, burglary, fraud, embezzlement, etc.). That's about 29,000 each and every day of the yr. And, that does not include capital and other violent crimes such as murder, rape, aggravated assault, kidnapping; about every 35 seconds a crime of that type occurs. *This section deals only with crimes against property. For background and Biblical principles concerning capital crimes, refer to section on Capital Punishment* — in such capital crimes magistrates are not to bear the sword in vain *(Rom. 13:4).*

Number of crimes in US increased greatly during recent yrs. (with slight drop in 1983 — robberies fell 8%, burglaries, 9%). Number of inmates in state and federal prisons now highest in history; more than doubled since 1974 (up 115%): 204,211 in '74, 438,830 in 1984.

In 1983 taxpayers shelled out $10 billion for jails and prisons — an average of $16,000-plus per inmate. In addition to the record number of persons serving prison terms, as of April, 1984, another 210,000 were in jail awaiting trial or doing time for minor infractions. It is estimated *(US News & World Report)* that 1 out of every 350 Americans was behind bars — the world's highest per capita ratio.

Serious overcrowding of virtually all prison facilities now. At present, States are spending or planning to spend about $6 billion on new prisons and jails. (Federal facilities are jammed with 31,000 inmates — 28% over planned capacities.) In New York State prison population is 4,500 inmates *over capacity;* State now spending about $700 million for additional 8,600 beds. In Illinois, number of inmates has *more than doubled in past 10 yrs.* In California, 37,000 inmates are crowded into facilities meant for 26,000 — *and another 2,200 are housed in tents, trailers and barracks.*

Most jails and prisons operate on basis of *retribution rather than restitution.* In most States, *prisons are overcrowded time bombs* (prison riots are frequent). Thus, rising demand for *prison reform,* for an overhauling of the system while protecting the law-abiding citizens, their family and property.

Prisons often termed "correctional institution." More and more they are becoming *centers of violence* — filled with racial tensions, homosexual and ethnic gangs, assaults (even murders), drug trafficking. Human dignity goes by the boards; savagery is often widespread, common-place. In 1983, attacks on prisoners in Texas totalled 541, compared with 171 four yrs ago.

Few prisons are truly "correctional." More often

they are *"schools for crime."* Repeat offenders learn to sharpen their "skills" from older inmates; first-time inmates, many of them young (25% of prisoners are between ages of 18-24), are thrown in with hardened criminals, *emerge hardened themselves.* Thus, they exit determined not to avoid crime but *to avoid getting caught again.*

Taxpayers are forced to pay for convict's housing, clothing, food, educational and medical benefits. (In Chicago, city spends $20,000 a yr to lock up offenders. Inmates are often paid for prison work. Some, such as New York's infamous "Son of Sam" (convicted of multiple murders), received disability benefits via Social Security program.

Approximately 90% of those in jail and/or prison were found guilty of crimes against property—i.e. non violent crimes vs. persons. Average sentence for such crimes range from 3 to 5 years. Dependent upon prison behavior, parole is granted after about 50% of sentence is served (for one reason, to relieve strain on overcrowded facilities). More than 1.3 million Americans are on probation—they are outside of prison as long as they stay out of trouble. And, in many cases, judges are refusing to sentence convicted to prison or jail because of vile conditions in prisons and jails. (An individual convicted and sentenced does not lose basic civil rights—such as personal safety and security in their person.)

What about victims of property (non-violent) crimes? Criminal code is based on retribution (vengeance); *victim is seldom granted restitution.* Generally, victim is forced to seek restitution through civil suit that can be costly in court costs, legal fees and time. On occasion, victim is treated more like a criminal than a claimant.

Movements now afoot to compensate *victims of personal assault* (and, in case of homicide, victim's survivors). Some 30 States have victim "compensation" programs; total budgets involved: about $50 million in taxpayer funds. *Thus, society* (including the victim and his dependents), *not the criminal, makes reparations*.

More States now emphasizing *work programs* (either in prison or through released time). Inmate learns skill and at same time helps reduce taxpayer cost of prison system. Congress approved interstate sale of goods made by inmates, etc. In Kansas, inmates working for steel company paid State $241,000 in room and board over 4-yr period. In Texas, convicts produced some $42.5 million in 1983. Most of funds go to reduce cost of prison system (some inmates allowed to keep small amount of pocket money for personal extras—toiletries, tobacco, etc).

But, none of that money going to make restitution to victim of property crimes (who, actually, helps pay the cost of imprisoning his violator).

Estimated loss suffered by victims of property crime, *more than $6 billion*. Very few plans in process to require felon to make restitution to victims for crimes against individual's property. It is a part of prison reform that cries out for justice—*for the victim*. More and more within justice-prison system feel inmates convicted of crimes against property should be (a) closely screened, and (b) permitted to work on parole with most of the earnings going to reimburse the victim or his estate.

CONSIDER THE BIBLICAL PRINCIPLES 1. Civil prisons (institutions in which persons are held for a lengthy period of time) are *anti-Biblical* except as they apply to satan and his demons (See *I Pet. 3:19; Rev. 20:2, 3*). Satan has succeeded in pawning off on man the punishment God has established for him and his rebellious spirits.

There are no provisions for prisons in God's civil code. The closest thing to a prison in God's order is a temporary holding place ("ward") where bona fide suspects (indicted) are to be held *pending speedy trial and swift punishment* if found to be guilty *(Lev. 24:12; Num. 15:34)*.

2. God's laws for punishment of crimes against property are clear. *The punishment is to fit the crime;* the more grievous the crime, the more severe the punishment (the law of just returns).

The guilty person is to make restitution to the victim: that is part of the penalty-payment God demands of those who break His laws (in the case of the 6th and 8th Commandments). And, mark this: *it is the offender, not society, who is to make restitution.*

God's perfect justice is thus employed: (a) *The guilty person is held accountable* and must really "pay" for his crime (rather than languish in prison, he is to work and earn in money or kind that which is required for reparation of what he stole); (b) *the victim receives the restitution . . .* (the payment goes not to the State but to the offended); (c) *would-be law-breakers get the message in a very positive manner (Dt. 19:20),* and (d) *the citizenry is not compelled to subsidize crime or support the criminal.* Surely the purpose and the workings of God's perfect plan in this is far more humane and equitable (and constructive) than the bankrupt and chaotic system of a humanistic State!

The Biblical laws of restitution (reparations, payment of damages) are set forth in The Scriptures, including:

Restitution is required of the thief (Ex. 22:3). . . . Of one who *wrongfully appropriates* and/or violates another's property *(Ex. 22:5)* . . . of one who *destroys* another's property by arson *(Ex. 22:6)* . . . of one who *loses or damages or destroys* another's property *while it is in his care (Lev. 24:21)* . . . and, of one who *assaults another individual* (thus commiting a crime against a person's "self" — the most basic property of all *(Ex. 21:19).* Generally, restitution is to be required in an amount *not only equal to that which was stolen or lost or destroyed but in a larger amoung sufficient to compensate for loss of time, loss of income, inconvenience, etc.* The punishment of restitution may range *from 100 to 400 percent* of that which was stolen or destroyed, etc.

At its root, crime against property is *a crime vs. God as well as against the person victimized. The retribution for such a crime belongs to God* ("vengeance is Mine"); *the restitution* (part of God's plan of redemption) *is to go to both God and the victim (Lev. 20:46; Num. 5:6-8): that is God's law.* Under the laws of humanism, retribution belongs to the State, restitution is largely ignored, and God and the victim are denied.

God's perfect plan and law provides the perfect solution to man's errors and fall. In the case of property crimes, faithful adherence to His institutes would: (a) Resolve the problems and ease the burden of an ungodly prison system (since 90% of the inmates were found guilty of crimes against property and many of those could be rehabilitated through working to make restitution). (b) Invoke true and complete justice by requiring the guilty to work and earn that which is required for restitution to the victim, and (c) Establish a clear and consistent (and compelling) deterrent for those who might otherwise be tempted to engage in similar criminal acts (and, is that not the finest rehabilitation program — to cause the individual *to repent at the thought* [before the act], *rather than* doing so after the crime?). *Under God's plan and law, there would be fewer criminals and fewer victims and less burden on the taxpayer.*

6

DEBTS & DEFICITS

BACKGROUND BRIEFING In 1791, 3 years after ratification of Constitution, US federal debt was $75 million ($18.50 per capita). Mostly, debt was fiscal hangover from cost of War for Independence. Paying off national debt was top priority to new govt. In his first term, President Washington wrote:

> "I entertain a strong hope that the state of national finances is now sufficiently matured to enable . . . a systematic and effectual arrangement for the regular redemption and discharge of the public debt . . ."

Thomas Jefferson expressed the wish that it were possible to amend the Constitution ". . . . taking away from the Federal government the power of borrowing." Hamilton disagreed: "A national debt, if it is not excessive, will be to us a national blessing."

By 1836, debt virtually paid off: was down to $38,000. From establishment of US Treasury in 1787 until 1983, federal govt. had surpluses in 103 yrs *and deficits in 90*. Budget was in the red *about 32% of the time*. During past 50 yrs, it has been *in deficit 84% of time* and, since 1970, a deficit every yr. Took US about 200 yrs to accumulate first trillion in national debt (hit that mark in 1981). *Projections now estimate US will hit $2 trillion mark by 1986.* Economists warn time is running out; unless mounting deficits are halted, debt-time-bomb could wreck the national economy.

Cost of wars brought splurges: At start of World War I, debt was $3 billion. By 1940, debt was $51 billion and interest on debt was equal to total debt of 1916. By end of World War II, debt was $260 billion ($1,513 per capita).

Today, federal debt is $1.5 trillion (that's one thousand 500 billion). Comes to about $6,000 for every man woman and child in US. In 1983, federal govt. spent $796 billion; took in $600.6 billion — a deficit of $195 billion, about 11% of total Gross National Product (GNP) and more than 100 times the size of the deficit in 1968.

Projected deficits for 1985, *about $200 billion;* $150 billion in 1986, *and maybe $200 +* billions in 1989. All told, deficits in next three yrs could be another $600 billion. If nothing is done to stop fiscal hemmorhage, *per capita federal debt could be as high as $10,000 per capita in 5 years.*

Debt clock keeps ticking away. *Every week, another $3.7 billion; every day, another $528 million* — comes to $22 million an hour, *and that's just* new *red ink. US News & World Report* (5/21/84) predicted that, unless Washington moves to cut deficits, *government debt will jump another $1 trillion by 1990.*

(National Taxpayers Union estimates that total

federal govt. monetary liabilities (outright debt, unfunded obligations—loan guarantees, annuity programs, insurance commitments, etc.) are actually *in excess of $12 trillion . . . about $112,100 per taxpayer.*

(Total current debt in US is *more than $6 trillion:* govt. debt (federal, state and local) is $1.6 billion—up $1.1 billion from 1974 (190%). *Consumer debt stands at $1.8 billion (an increase of 173% since 1974, and business debt* totals $2.6 billion, an increase of 188% during the past decade.)

Just the interest on federal debt comes to $112 billion a yr. That's $2.1 billion a week, about $305 million a day, $13 million each and every hour. Interest costs each man, woman and child in US *about $500 a yr.* Four years ago, 1980, net interest payments on debt were $52.5 billion, came to 2% of GNP, 9.1% of total budget. *Now, interest payments take about 12% of total budget.* And, *Wharton Econometric Forecasting* predicts interest payments *in 1985 will be about $135 billion;* 3.5% of GNP and almost 15% of total federal budget.

Every time the interest rates rise 1%, costs taxpayers another $10 billion for interest on that debt. *In past 5 yrs, we-the-people have shelled out close to $500 billion in interest on the federal debt.*

Are politicians concerned? Some. This yr Congress passed *"Deficit Reduction Act"* as a "down payment" on bringing budget into balance. Boosts federal taxes about $10.6 billion in 1985 and another $16.9 billion in 1986—while cutting expenditures some $4 billion each yr. Critics say Congress birthed a mouse when what is needed is an elephant. Call

Reduction Act a farce (a gimmick so that congressmen can tell constitutents they voted to reduce deficit). Given the way of Congress, they predict new revenues will probably be exceeded only by *new spending* during those yrs. *Rep. Ron Paul* (TX) commented: "My experience in Congress has convinced me that tax increases only compound the deficit problem. Taxes give the politicians more to spend."

(While farmers and other working people struggle to pay debts and swallow inflation, Uncle Sugar gave giant corporations *gift of $12 billion*. Wiped out that amount of taxes owed by such firms as General Electric, Boeing, McDonnell-Douglas, Dow, Du-Pont, etc. Taxes were due on Domestic International Sales Corporations (DISCS) formed in 1971 to receive subsidies for exports. Subsidiaries were to pay taxes on income. But, Congress (at prodding of Senator Robert Dole (KS) "forgave" tax bills.)

Major proposal: The *Balanced Budget — Tax Limitation Amendment.* Designed by Natnl. Tax Limitation Committee, amendment carried in Senate by Orrin Hatch (UT) and Strom Thurmond (SC); in House by Barber Conable (NY) and Ed Jenkins (GA). Has two key provisions: (1) *Total annual federal outlays cannot exceed total receipts,* and (2) *total receipts* (taxes) *shall not increase at rate greater than increase in national income.* Other sections would permit lifting limit (by 3/5 vote) for specific emergencies and would prohibit feds from mandating State programs without providing funds equal to cost of program.

In Senate, *Amendment is out of Judiciary Committee and awaiting vote on floor.* (Two yrs ago, Senate passed it but bill died in House). Now, Amendment remains bottled in House Judiciary under orders from Speaker Tip O'Neill. Supporters seeking discharge petition, are 26 names short of required 218. In Sept, '84, tax limiters presented Speaker O'Neill with *3 million petitions* asking Congress to pass Amendment. (President Reagan supports amendment; Walter Mondale against it.)

Requires 34 States to force Congressional action; Amendment *now only two States short*. Initiative on Montana's Nov. '84 ballot and resolution awaiting action in Michigan legislature (has passed Senate). In California, despite more than enough signatures to put initiative petition on ballot, State Supreme Court bowed to AFL-CIO, NOW, ACLU, and ruled California voters *did not have right* to demand their legislature join others States in call for Constitutional convention on balanced budget amendment.

Opponents claim Amendment not needed; say Congress can produce balanced budget without it. *Proponents of Amendment point to record:* Congress balanced budget only 9 times in past 48 years, only once in past 17 yrs. "Congress," said Senator Peter Wilson (CA) "seems congenitally incapable of disciplining itself." Former director of the federal Office of Management and Budget under Nixon, *Roy Ash,* argues that at best Amendment wouldn't go into effect until 1990 and that might be too late to avert national fiscal crisis.

Opponents say provisions are too stiff, would unduly restrict Congress. Supporters respond that "escape hatches" to deal with emergencies provide enough flexibility. Debate continues — *so do deficits and debt.*

CONSIDER THE BIBLICAL PRINCIPLES The Bible considers debt a form of *slavery. ". . . the borrower is servant to the lender" (Pr. 22:7)*. If we are truly and completely His, we cannot be slaves to any man or men or institution (public or private). Debt permits the past to govern the present and the present to dictate the future. We should not mortgage our future or our children's future; to do so would be to permit others to control that which belongs to The Lord.

God's word recognizes that debt may be necessary in times of acute distress and emergency. However, Scriptures set definite time limits on such debt: *six yrs.* In the seventh (sabbatical) year, debts are to be cleared or forgiven. This is no way excuses the debtor from paying his debts. *"The wicked borroweth and payeth not again: (Ps 37:21)*. Through sabbatical rules, The Lord has established a system to keep individuals from perpetual debt and slavery.

Dr. Gary North, in "An Introduction to Christian Economics," points out that God's written word prohibits both perpetual debt and multiple indebtedness. We are not to make borrowing a habit; we are not to go into debt beyond our ability to pay the debt within prescribed period of time, as we are not to pledge collateral already pledged. *Thus, God's rules protect both debtor and creditor.*

Present debt-economy (a calculated system that favors the creditor) is built on the ungodly concept that the individual (and the nation) need not worry about *perpetual debt* or multiple indebtedness. The system, in fact, encourages debt and caters to the "now" appetite (interest is tax deductible, etc.). Thus, debtor is encouraged to a form of *perpetual economic servitude.*

In *Dt. 28:43, 44,* Moses warned of consequences of debt: *"He shall lend to you and you shall not lend to him; he shall be the head, and you shall be the tail."* Keeping an individual in debt holds him down; a form of economic bondage. The fetters of *inflation* are one device of such bondage; *usury* is another. Part of the material cost of debt is the usury   ted. In many cases, compounded interest exceeds   principal amount borrowed (more than 80% of the $350 billion debt owed by Latin American nations is *for interest* on the principal loaned).

The Bible tells us that we're not to take usury (interest) when we loan to a brother in need. It also tells us that when the collateral is a necessity of life, it must be returned to the debtor when he needs it *(Ex. 22:25-27).* A reasonable charge may be made for the use of money in normal course of business (usually a share of the profits made through the use of the money loaned); the individual is entitled to a fair return on his property *(Luke 19:23; Mt. 25:27).*

The evil of taking (monetary) advantage of a person in distress is clearly prohibited *(Dt. 15* and *Lev. 25* and in Christ's parable of forgiveness, *Mt. 18:27-35).* The evil of those who take advantage of a community (nation) in distress or peril by charging interest on the loans needed to protect or rebuild the nation is also prohibited *(Neh. 5:1-13).*

THUS: Debt (personal and public) should be resisted by the Christians. We must reject debt economy and shun debt, putting our faith in The Lord God, learning self-control and patience. When an emergency or dire circumstance makes debt necessary, it should be on a short-term basis and paid in full by the appointed time. Any thought of perpetual debt is a *no-no*. And, we must work to hold down government deficits and see that govt. debt is paid, because we are commanded by The Lord to provide an inheritance for our children; such inheritance can be destroyed by profligate politicians and irresponsible government.

All that we have is His; it is to be sued for Him. We are not free to serve The Lord when we mortgage ourselves or our property to others, or when the State destroys the value of our earnings and confiscates our property.

The Apostle Paul reminds us of one debt that is *approved* unto The Lord: *"Owe no man anything but to love one another" (Rom 13:8).* Such a debt is always due — *and payable.*

7

EDUCATION

BACKGROUND BRIEFING In 1982-83, expenditures for education in USA (public & private, all levels) totalled *$215 billion* (estimated expenditures for 1983-84, $235 billion). That's about 7% of Gross Natnl Product (GNP), *about 10 times amount spent in 1970, and more than twice that spent in 1979-80*. Since end of World War II, total annual expenditures for education in US have increased from $8.8 billion to $215 billion; are still going up.

In 1982-83, $133 billion spent on K-12 schools. *Cost per student jumped from $294 in 1956 to $2900 in 1982-83.* Even allowing for inflation, that's jump of almost 1,000%. Number of teachers (all levels) increased from 1.2 million in '56 to 3.3 million in 1982-83 (in K-12, instructional staff including administrative personnel now totals 2.4 million). As expenditures and personnel increased, *enrollment in public schools decreased*. Total enrollment, K-12, 1973-74, was 45.4 million; in 1983-84, 39.2 million (a drop in enrollment of 6.2 million.) *But, the costs continue to jump.* Example: In 1963-64, cost of transporting (busing) 37.4 million children was $674 million (about $46.55 per pupil). *In 1980-81* (latest data available) *cost $4.7* billion *to bus 37.7 million pupils* ($219.85 per pupil). Note: In 1950, 27% of Average Daily Attendance (ADA) in K-12 schools were bused; in 1982, more than 55%.

Ominous trend #1: *increasing dependence on Federal and state govts.* for education funds (with money comes control). In 1960, 53% of K-12 revenues came from taxpayers in local school districts. Now, *some 56.6% of all public education funds come from taxpayers via Federal (9.8%) and State (46.8%) processors.* (As of time of this publication, House Committee on Education approved federal expenditures for 1984-85 of *$17.2 billion:* $2.5 billion more than Federal education budget for fiscal 1984.)

Ominous trend #2: *Call for "federal" certification of all teachers.* Recent nationwide surveys by Natnl. Center for Educational Information indicated teacher certification requirements vary from State to State. NCEI urges uniform standards and proficiency tests by national board before any person could be approved for teaching position in any public school in US. *Question:* who will set the standards and "candle all the eggs" thus to control education on national scale?

Ominous trend #3: US Dept. of Education contracting with NEA to develop basic education programs *for nationwide network for school computers.* Thus, again, centralized "programmers" would be in strategic position to force feed local school districts and their students.

Ominous trend #4: proposals recommending

deterioration in State education be solved by concentrating on humanistic philosophers, technologies, and "egalitarianism." Most devoid of basic spiritual values; would establish *two-stream* educational system—one for "elites," one for technicians and workers, etc. *("The Paideia Proposal, An Educational Manifesto,"* by Mortimer J. Adler on behalf of the members of the Paideia Group, is dedicated to the prominent humanists, *"Horace Mann, John Dewey, and Robert Hutchins, who would have been our leaders were they alive today."*

Has increased spending and control raised quality of education? During yrs expenditures for public schools grew by leaps and billions, *test score and achievements ratings dropped drastically.* Public ire mounted as more and more functional illiterates were graduated from govt. school system. College Board's Scholastic Aptitude Tests (the SATs) had steady decline, 1963-1980. Average verbal scores *dropped more than 50 points,* math scores *down about 40 points.* Since 1963-65, when scores peaked, achievement has dropped at rate of approx. 1 month per yr. Average student of '80s assigned about ½ reading and writing required of students a generation ago; takes about 35% less govt and civics (watered down/revised "social studies"), 30% less geography, 20% less math and science (Paul Copperman, as quoted in THE CAPSULE).

A member of the *National Commission on Excellence in Education* (NCEE), Copperman recently up-dated his findings and his concerns: "Each generation of Americans has outstripped its parents in education, in literacy, and in economic attainment. *For the first time in the history of our country, the educational skills of one generation will not surpass, will not equal, will not even approach those of their parents."*

Only 1/4 of students graduated from high school in 1979 functioned at the average level recorded in 1963. Of 2.8 million high school grads in 1984, some 12% classified as "functional illiterates." Another 15% considered "barely" literate. Three out of four businesses and industries find they must re-train such grads before they can employ them. Many students entering college must take remedial course so they can complete freshman yr.

Some States (such as Florida) established *literacy requirements* that must be met before high school diploma awarded. ACLU fought that, said it was discriminatory, but, attorney who argued vs. requirements asked, "if they don't have eighth-grade skills, what are they doing in twelfth grade?"

In one of his earlier reports, educational advisor Copperman observed: "With the passage of the Elementary & Secondary Education Act of 1965, the philosophical and political logjam preventing federal aid to education collapsed . . . each year has seen new federal educational programs . . . the twin historical anomalies of extensive federal involvement in public education and the declining academic achievement are not coincidental . . . *4 years of research . . . have convinced me that the federal government bears significant culpability* (for the decline)."

Concluding its recent report on the state of "public" education in the US, the NCEE commented: *"If an unfriendly foreign power had attempted to impose on America the mediocre education performance that exists today, we might well have viewed it as an act of war."* Hard-nosed educational auditors (reviewing the nation's education system, and the politicians and self-interest pressure groups that have virtually controlled the education during the past several decades) responded: *"It was, indeed, an act of war . . . and the enemy is within . . . it is the humanist establishment that set out to mold US education according to its own design."*

In his latest book, *"NEA: TROJAN HORSE IN AMERICAN EDUCATION,"* Samuel Blumenfeld charges *the NEA heirarchy purposefully set out to viscerate literacy in US.* Why? Because a literate people *will not accept socialistic humanist as the new order.*

It is not just academic bankruptcy that brings anguish and anger to parents; is also *rampant humanism* that works to void traditional values and estrange parents and children, and the *accompanying floodtide of filth, drugs, sex, smut and socialism.* Vandalism, violence, drug abuse, promiscuity, teenage pregnancies and abortions . . . all increased. *Gabler's Educational Research Newsletter* reported 10 most prevalent problems in State school systems in 1982: Rape, robbery, assault, burglary, arson, bombings, murder, suicide, absenteeism and vandalism. As *Dr. W. David Gamble,* American Reformation Movement commented: *When God is barred from the classroom, and morality is thrown out the window,* immorality, *chaos* and calamity enter in.

In past year, some improvement seen in public education. Some local schools struggle against tide of humanism and State bureaucracy, seek to recover excellence. Recent polls indicate that in some areas public beginning to think better of high schools. *US News & World Report* survey of high school student leaders indicated their concerns and suggestions: (1) *raise quality of teachers* (highest priority to improve education, chief complaint re teachers, *failure to make subjects interesting);* (2) *students share blame* by being apathetic about learning, (3) sports and school clubs should be *limited to students with C-or-better average;* (4) 50% rated *alcohol and drug use serious problem* at their school, said peer pressure to try those substances was greatest pressure they faced.

In face of miserable record in educaion during recent decades, *and in contravention of Tenth Amendment to US Constitution* (which reserves responsibility to States and the people thereof), Federal Dept. of Education was established during Carter Administration. Annual budget at start: $14 billion. D.O.E., mainly the spawn of NEA (National Education Assn) whose avowed purpose is to "control education in USA."

In 1980, candidate Ronald Reagan campaigned on promise *to abolish US Dept. of Education.* To date (9/84), nothing has been done along that line; President Reagan has backed away from that commitment. With exception of few stalwart D.O.E. appointees who push to phase out department (thus incurring wrath of Education Secretary Terrell Bell) *it's bureaucracy as usual;* the educational establishment remains in control.

Statistics for this briefing taken from *"Digest,"* National Center for Education Statistics, and *"Estimates of School Statistics: 1983-84,"* National Education Assn.

CONSIDER THE BIBLICAL PRINCIPLES *"Beware, lest any man spoil you through philosophy and vain deceit, after the tradition of men, after the rudiments of the world, and not after Christ"* (Col. 2:8).

Children are "an heritage of The Lord God" *(Ps. 127:3)* entrusted to earthly parents *to be educated in and according to the will and word of God.* Parents are to be "priests unto their families" to "train up the child in the way he should go" *(Pr. 22:6)* both for this time and for eternity. Parents are to care for the child's *soul* as well as the child's *body (I Tim. 5:8),* feeding him or her the milk of the word of God *(I Pet. 2:2) and the bread of life that is Christ (John 6:35).* They are to give the child "meat in due season" *(Lk. 12:42)* through scholarship at home and through the church and school that is true to the word of God. Parents are to teach their children (and see that they are taught) *from the Scriptures*—"precept upon precept, line upon line . . . here a little, there a little" *(Isa. 28:10)* and always in "the nurture and admonition of The Lord" *(Eph. 6:4).* Thus, godly parents are not to turn the care and feeding *(either physical, mental or spiritual)* over to those who would wean them away from God and spoil them with vain deceits or the rudiments of the world.

The parent is to exercise authority over the child in keeping with God's law. Parental authority is not a "right" conveyed by the State, *it is an assignment, a re-*

sponsibility, set forth by God's word (Ex. 20:12; Col. 3:20-24). Those who would deny or interfere with the godly relationship of parent and child will find it "better that a millstone were hanged about his neck" . . . "Woe unto that man by whom offence comes!" (Mt. 18:6, 7).

The true purpose of education — certainly for the godly — is to guide the child so that he may "Study to show yourself approved unto God, a workman that needs not to be ashamed, rightly dividing the word of truth" *(II Tim. 2:15).* And, in the pursuit and attainment of such godly excellence in whatever field or chosen vocation, "to have always a conscience void of offense toward God and toward men" *(Acts 25:16),* to view all things within a Christ-centered world and life perspective . . . *to be, in sum and total, a consistently functioning Christian seeking always to serve The Lord God.*

When the Pilgrims had "builded our houses, provided necessaries for our livelihood, rear'd convenient places for God's worship and settled Civil Governments," they attended to the matter of education so that they could "advance Learning and perpetuate it to Posterity; dreading to leave an illiterate Ministery . . ." Thus, for example, they set forth "the proceedings of Learning" in respect to "the Colledge in Cambridge, in Massachusetts Bay" *(now known as Harvard):*

"Let every student be plainly instructed and earnestly pressed to consider well, the maine end of his life and studies is, to know Jesus Christ which is eternal life John 17:3. and therefore to lay Christ in the bottome,

as the only foundation of all sound knowledge and Learning. And seeing The Lord only giveth wisdome, Let every one seriously set himself to prayer in secret to seek it of Him Prov. 2.3." (New England First Fruits, 1643)

Who will say that Christ Jesus is the foundation and purpose of education in the State schools and colleges of this day? As Rosalie J. Slater has written ("Teaching & Learning America's Christian History") *"It is evident that the de-Christianization of America has received its greatest impetus through the secularization of education."* Godly Christians must not be a part of such a system *(II Cor. 6:14; I Tim. 6:3-5).* If they would be a servant of The Living God, they must provide godly education for their children in the *Christian home,* the *Bible-based church;* and the *Christ-centered church or private school and college.*

The superior academic, fiscal and moral record of Christian education, and the refusal to close The Bible or lower standards, makes the Christian schools the target for the State and ungodly educational heirarchy. With the power of the new Federal Dept. of Education added to the clout of the State machinery and the added impetus of self-interest pressure groups (AFT, NEA, NOW, ACLU, etc.) the assaults on the Christian education will continue and may well increase in frequency and intensity. But, Christian parents who seek to please God — *who know right well that the purpose of education is to train up the child to serve God* — must continue *to maintain and expand a Bible-based literate ministry of education* so that

God is honored and so that His children are prepared for both the here-and-now and the hereafter.

8

EVOLUTION VERSUS CREATION

BACKGROUND BRIEFING State of *Louisiana* law requires public schools *teach scientific evidences for* both *Creation and evolution*. Law is being challenged by ACLU. Case *(Aguillard v. Edwards)* will probably be heard Spring of 1985, in US District Court, New Orleans. (Briefs for summary dismissal have been filed with court. Atlanta atty, *Wendell Bird (Rutherford Institute and Creation Science Legal Defense Fund),* is lead attorney, representing Louisiana (Governor Edwards).

In 1981, *Arkansas* enacted law requiring both Creation and evolution be taught in public schools. Federal district judge ruled law unconstitutional. Also in 1981, *California Superior Court* ruled State must advise school districts that evolution is to be *presented as theory, not fact.* Judge Irving Perluss ruled *religious beliefs must be respected.* All told, *some 16 States* have or have had bills before legislature requiring State schools give *equal time and emphasis* to creation science.

(Major and persistent opponents of creationism: *American Civil Liberties Union* (ACLU) and the *American Humanist Association,* an atheistic organization. *National Academy of Sciences* recently distributed 28-page book urging science teachers *not* to teach creationism in their classrooms. Responding to obvious censorship, *Dr. Richard Bliss,* Institute for Creation Research charged: *"What the anti-creationists are doing to the minds of Americans today is reprehensible in that they are moving to have our children believe what science has proven to be a fantasy."*

Evolution was official dogma of Third Reich, "The German Führer . . . has consciously sought to make the practice of Germany conform to the theory of evolution." (Quote from anthropoligst Arthur Keith.)

(Why take a "creation science" approach rather than Biblical stance? Because Courts have ruled Bible not admissible in public classrooms except as "historical document" or code of ethics void of religious concepts. Thus, if Creation were presented as a Biblical truth, cases would take on additional and difficult legal burden.)

Controversy — *Creation vs. Evolution* — basically centers in three areas: *Constitutional, academic, and scientific.* Here's how battle shapes up:

Constitutional: Evolutionists contend teaching creation in State schools violates First Amendment, argues that would be tantamount to "teaching religion." Creationists respond Constitution demands *"neutrality"* and that is violated by exclusive teaching of theory of evolution, *a basic tenet of religion of humanism.* Creationists also argue such *exclusivity* violates *free exercise rights* of students who believe in creation; violates "establishment" clause of First

Amendment (no State religion); and violates *Fourteenth Amendment* (discrimination on basis of religion). Further, excluding creationism from classroom *violates parental right* to direct child's moral/spiritual beliefs (puts undue burden on both parents and child), and deprives student of *"right to hear"* all relevant educational material (latter point deemed to be a Consitutional right).

Academic: Evolutionists insist requirement to teach creationism violates *academic freedom;* that teacher must be "free" to teach as he or she chooses. Creationists retort, academic freedom means *freedom* (in fact, necessity) *to teach all aspects of a subject;* that it means *freedom to "educate" not indoctrinate,* and that prohibiting or failing to examine creation science is a violation of true academic freedom. Further, they state, "academic freedom" *is not confined to teacher's right to teach but includes student's right to be taught comparative subjects* (freedom to hear, consider, conclude). Thus, a balanced presentation in which creationism and evolution are taught is only way to uphold, practice and preserve academic freedom.

Scientific: Evolutionists argue that creation is a religious myth; that science has proved *that man is a product of bio-chemistry, that life progressed from nothing to one-celled origins to present state through series of biological changes* (over a period of billions of years). Creationists insist that *science proves man was created,* and assert that creation dogma is *supported by far more evidentary fact* than is evolution. *Evolution,* they assert, *is the myth;* it is based on assumptions, conjectures and shifting suppositions. Creationists say evolution is not simply a matter of a missing link but a *chain of missing links*. They point out that Charles Darwin in his *The Origin of Species* warned about unanswered questions and speculations he included in his theory — *800 times* in his book Darwin used such subjective phrases as *"let us assume."*

Further, say creationists, evolution flies in the face of some basic, hard cold facts and laws: (1) the theory of evolution *contradicts the second law of thermodynamics* (without outside interference, all things tend toward the state of greatest disorder). (2) Apollo astronauts found *only 1/8" of dust on moon surface;* if moon and earth had been in existence for billions of years (as evolutionists claim) there should be *at least 100 feet of dust lying on the moon.* (3) *Magnetic field of earth is decaying at a measurable rate;* by reverse projection based on existing date, *it is plain that earth could not have existed in present state for more than 10,000 years.* (4) In Texas riverbed, *fossilized human footprints have been found* alongside *those of dinosaurs* (and both underneath and on top of dinosaur footprints). (5) Earth's population has been increasing through history at *determinable* rate; if man evolved ages ago, as claimed, *population of earth would be many times what it is today.* (6) *Fossil records do not support evolution;* not only is there a "missing link," there are thousands of missing links between supposedly related species. (7) *Evidence of "fossil men" is shaky at best and largely discredited* (many of them "fakes" — Peking man, Piltdown man, etc). (8) *Law of Biogenesis* (living matter comes only from previously living matter).

Here are some points creationists raise vs. evolution: *absence of transitional forms to fill gaps; major theses of evolution have been discredited/discarded* (acquired characteristics, natural selection, large mutation, small mutation, accidental alteration, etc.). Countless experiments dating back to 1780 prove *life does not come from non-life; inanimate does not beget the animate.* Advanced studies in molecular biology show *man's DNA code is totally distinctive* from animals; study of amino acid components attests that *flesh of each species is distinct from that of others*.

As for age of earth, *creationists say earth is "young"*; is proven by extensive research in such fields as *earth spin, comet decay and dust, ocean concentration and sediment, decay of earth's magnetic field, sun shrink, etc.* As for the Great Flood, they assert that fossil finds and stratigraphic records over the face of the globe substantiate the Genesis account.

Writing on the *"big bang"* theory of the earth's origin, and how that might be proof of *Genesis 1:1*, astronomer *Robert Jastrow* concluded with this: *"For the scientist who has lived by his faith in the power of reason, the story ends like a bad dream. He has scaled the mountains of ignorance, he is about to conquer the highest peak; as he pulls himself over the biggest rock, he is greeted by a band of theologians who have been sitting there for centuries."* Praise God!

CONSIDER THE BIBLICAL PRINCIPLES Creation is mentioned *75 times* in passages throughout Old and New Testaments. *Plus Genesis, 23 books* of The Bible allude to God's creative acts. Creation is not some "minor doctrine," *it is the starting point of all Divine revelation,* all other Scriptures build upon creation.

"In the beginning, God created (Hebrew word "bar-rah" means created out of nothing) *the heavens and the earth" (Gen. 1:1; John 1:1, 2).* God created all things and by Him all things exist and consist *(Col. 1:16, 17).* That which is seen was made from that which is not seen (atoms, neutrons, molecules, electrons, etc.) *(Heb. 11:3).* God created plant life (the seed of which is in itself *each after its own kind)* — *God's law of reproduction.* God created animal life (each to reproduce after its own kind) *Gen. 1:11-25).* And, God created man after *His own image, in His own likeness* (His attributes) out of the dust of the earth *(wherein are found all the basic elements)* and He breathed into him the breath of life and man became a living soul *(Gen. 1:26, 27; 2:7).* All flesh is not the same flesh, the flesh of man is *distinct* from that of animal life *(I Cor. 15:39).* And God told man to be fruitful and to multiply (reproduce his own kind; man cannot procreate with animals). For greater detail of God's creative acts, read *Job 38 and 39.*

"And of every living thing of all flesh, two of every sort, shall you bring into the ark, to keep them alive with you; they shall be male and females" (so that after the Great Flood had subsided they might continue to reproduce and multiply — not by evolution but by procreation *(Gen. 6:19).*

In no word, no verse, no book in The Bible is there any evidence of a gradual development of life of any kind. Certain passages show clearly that creation occurred in a short time and that the act of creation involved a miracle *(Ex. 20:11; Ps. 33:6, 9).* (See also *Dt. 32:6; Isa. 43:1; 45:12, 15, 17; Ezra 5:11; Neh. 9:6.)*

These are but a few of the Biblical facts concerning the origin of man and his continuance after the Great Flood. *"Yes let God be true, but every man a liar; as it is written, That you might be justified in the sayings and might overcome when you are judged"* (Rom. 3:4).

Those who attack creationism and fight to keep it out of the public classrooms are most often those same individuals and groups who fight against The Bible. Why the attack on God's written word at the same time that unregenerate man attacks the truth of creation? Because there is power in God's word; thus, man must try to deny the truth of God's word before he can make any headway in attacking/discrediting the facts of creation. But God assures us that all things may pass away *but that His word* (the Truth) *will never pass away.*

RECOMMENED READING: *The Origin and Destiny of Man,* Francis Nigel Lee, Christian Studies Center, Memphis, TN; *The Creation/Evolution Issue,* R. L. Wyson, Enquiry Press, Midland, MI; *The Mystery of Life's Origin: Reassessing Curent Theories,* Foundation for Thought and Ethics, Richardson, TX. *The Genesis Record,* Dr. Henry M. Morris, Institute for Creation Research, El Cajon, CA. For further information and research data on Creation, write Institute for Creation Research, 2100 Greenfield Dr., El Cajon, CA 92021; Creation Social Science & Humanities Society, 1429 N. Holyoke, Wichita, KS 67208.

9

FARMS AND FAMILIES

BACKGROUND BRIEFING Farmers, small landowners, have always been vital to a stable culture. A bulwark of self-government, reliance and independence against reckless, often purposeful, growth of tyranny. Those who produce raw materials (farmers, foresters, fishermen, miners) are originators and producers of new *real* wealth. *Agriculture is the basic industry; the major economic entity, vital to the well-being and stability of the nation.*

American agriculture is world's largest commercial enterprise. Total assets: $1 trillion-plus — equal to 88% of capital assets of all US manufacturing. Produces about 25% of GNP. Employes 3.7 million. *But, millions more directly dependent upon farmers for jobs* (processing, packaging, transportation, sales, etc.). Every farm job lost means *three other jobs lost somewhere down the food/fibre system.*

2.5 million farms occupy half of total US land mass — 1 billion acres (400 million for farming, balance for cattle and livestock grazing, etc.) Carter Administration, as part of its "Global 2000," claimed US was losing agricultural land to urban sprawl at rate of 3 million acres a year. Actually, a US Dept. of Ag's Economic Research Service showed, *US was gaining* — not losing — *cropland.* In 1982, cropland acreage increased from 413-million acre to 421-million acres. *But, in winter of 1983-84, wind erosion did peel off about 3.4 million acres of top soil in 519 counties in the 10 Great Plains states.* That was twice the loss to erosion in 1982.

Average farm size, 429 acres. In 1947, one farmer produced enough food/fibre for 47 persons; *today, one farmer produces enough for 78 persons.* Farm output per man-hour has increased twice as fast as industrial production. Total value of farm commodities in 1980: $136 billion ($69 billion in crops, $67.5 billion in cattle and livestock).

Only 36-cents of retail food dollar goes to farmer/rancher. 87% of those 36-cents goes to cost of production. In past 10 years, farm revenues rose 132% but costs of production rose 153% (wages up 123%, tractors and equipment up 178%, taxes up 68%, etc.). New farm income in 1983 was about $20 billion, down from $30 billion in 1979, and lowest since 1941. *When adjusted for inflation, farmer's income in '82 was less than at any time since 1934.* Profit margins on most crops now about half what they were in 1974. Net income per capita down from $11 in 1950 to $4 in 1983.

Ominous developments in American agriculture! Since 1950, average of 2,000 farms a week have gone out of business. Number of farms in US has declined by 54% since 1945; farm population as % of total US pop is down from 14% in 1950 to 2.7% in 1980 (was a slight upturn in 1982-83 as more families moved to small farms to escape the perils of urban/suburban life).

US Dept. of Ag warns US on verge of having *"few large firms controlling food production."* Dept. fears unique and productive American system of individual/family ownership and operation of farmland is about extinct. *Says in less than 20 years abour 1 million farm families will lose or leave farms.* Then, predicts USDA, just 1% of remaining farm operators *(multinational corporations and conglomerates) will possess half* of nation's farmlands and *control production of at least 1/2 of nation's food/fibre supply.*

In 1969, only 1 in every thousand farms rang up $500,000 sales or more a year. Today, the $500,000 farms number about 1 in every 100. A rise caused by *inflation? Only in small part.* The large farms, encompassing only 8% of all US farmland, turnout more than one-fourth of total value of farm production and *reap 60% of net farm income.*

At same time, purchases of US farmland by *foreign entities* is increasing. As of 1982, some 13 million acres were foreign-owned, an increase of 5 million acres one year. Does that tell the whole story? *Some say, "No."* Warn it is impossible to uncover most foreign ownership because of numbered trust accounts, holdings through US affiliates, and false fronts. Foreign firms also buying other links in US food/fibre chain (processing, marketing, etc.).

Are predictions of farm consolidations and takeovers far-fetched? Worries unfounded? Observers warn, "not necessarily." *Already 7% of largest farmholders control 54% of farmland and about = of all agricultural* sales. Many major corporations into farming in big way (Southern Pacific, Tenneco, Standard Oil of California, etc.). Tenneco, Houston-based oil corp., owns 1 million acres in California. *General Accounting Office (GAO) estimates 50% of US farmland now owned by non-farm operators* — conglomerates, banks, holding companies, etc. Four firms control 83% of all farm equipment manufactured/sold in US. Five multinationals control grain trade. Multinationals have cornered US seed business.

Is bigger better? *Not really.* In fact, bigger can be dangerous. Studies show increased efficiency and productivity comes from improved farm practices, not increased size. Research over period of years indicates highest efficiency can be reached on *400-acre farm.* No real support for argument that megafarms are in public's best interest; cartels and monopolies seldom are. *Size simply creates "superior ability to control market,"* and to stack deck in commodities. Which may explain mega-boast that *"The heart of America's food belt is no longer the Midwest but the trading centers of Chicago and New York."*

Outlook for American Agriculture? *"Catastrophic."* "Farm sector of US . . . teetering on brink of depression reminiscent of the 30s." Debt load and bankruptcies are at a level unseen since that depression. USDA estimates 43% of all farmland is mortgaged. In 1979, 26% of 1-year operating loans held by Farmers Home Administration (FmHA) were delinquent; *in 1982, that figure had soared to 51%. As for all of the FmHA borrowers, in 1984, 41% were behind in payments.*

Cause of crisis? Combination of factors. Poor business practices by some farmers. Greater and more complex demands for business management techniques. Prolonged dependence on government subsidies (which benefit mostly larger operators — 3% of farm operators received 46% of benefits; Southern Pacific conglomerate gets about $3 million a year in farm subsidies). *Excessive debt* load most for land and equipment (farming now a capital intensive industry). Total farm debt soared from $50.5 billion in 1970 to $195 billion in 1983. Increased debt combined with *soaring interest rates (usury)* disastrous for many farmers (rates jumped 24% in 1982, *up a total of 200% since 1977*). Each 1% hike in interest causes 5% loss in net farm income. Such is toll of debt capitalism.

Decreasing margins of profit (margin on most crops dropped 50% since 1974; net income per acre down from $11 in 1950 to $4 in 1982. Also, *govt. farm policies must share blame for crisis:* have virtually killed free market in agriculture. Incidentally, despite vital importance to national well-being, farmers are only about 3% of national vote; that means little clout vs. militant interest groups — check past 10 federal budgets, almost all categories were up except farm support — that went down.

Next, *overproduction and excessive surplusses* depressed prices (good weather and highly competitive markets boosted outputs). (Last year, though, droughts cut crops and farmers harvested less than expected.)

Finally, *"macro-economics."* That includes loss of world markets due to world-wide depression, strength (increased value) of US dollar (which means higher prices to foreign purchases)—agricultural products nation's second-largest export), increased East-West tensions, loss of credit/purchasing powers of under-developed and Third world countries, and unfair trade practices by some European nations.

As more and more family farms go under, question is: *What is govt. doing to halt disastrous tide of bankruptcies and foreclosures?"* US pays $322 million to banks on loans owed by Poland's (communist) government and defers 1982 debt payment for 8 years. Extends $1.6 billion more credit to Brazil. Backs more credit to Mexico. Pours more billions into International Monetary Fund (IMF) and World Bank. Arranges loans and credits for communist bloc nations. Bails our floundering mega-banks . . . *and US taxpayers stand to pick up all or much ot that tab.*

What about the American farmer? Administration wants to curtail emergency loan program, reduce Farmers Home Administration lending by 25% and pay price supports in surplus grain credits. US Controller General charged FmHA *"illegally denies farmers access to emergency disaster loan(s) . . ."* Says farmers in some 500 counties have been improperly denied opportunities for emergency loans to save farms. Thus, more and more farmers are asking, *"How come US bails out foreign nations and international bankers but won't help save the US farmer?"*

Sept. 1984: President Reagan announces *special program* to help farmers unable to pay debts: (1) Farmers Home Admin (FmHA) to *defer for 5 yrs up to 25% of principal and interest* on some farm loans; (2)

$630 million in new govt. loan guarantees available to private banks for additional loans to farmers; (3) FmHA will contract with local banks to handle paperwork and *speed up loan processing*. Des Moines (IA) poll has Reagan 23 points ahead of Walter Mondale — *three times margin in August poll.*

CONSIDER THE BIBLICAL PRINCIPLES In the beginning God created . . . the earth, the seas, the grass, the herbs, the fruit trees (each with its seed within itself), and the fish of the sea and the fowl of the air and the beasts of the earth (each with its seed within itself to reproduce after its own kind) . . . and God created man to be fruitful and to multiply and to replenish and subdue the earth and to have dominion over it *(Gen. 1:1-31)*.

Thus, the earth and the fulness thereof belongs to The Lord God, Creator and Sovereign. And, man is to care for it, to cultivate it, conserve it, and to keep it for The Lord *(Gen. 2:15)*. Man, then, is to be the caretaker, the husband, of God's good earth — not simply to serve self (i.e. survival, comfort, etc.) but, first and foremost, *to serve The Living God*. All that he does, man is to do in a manner and with a purpose that will glorify and honor God *(Col. 3:23)*.

Man is to be fruitful (he is not to waste, misuse or abuse the land or let it stand idle and unproductive). He is to till the soil, farm the land, husband the stock so as to multiply the fruit (crops/stock) it produces. He is not to deplete or ravage the land or deplete the stock. And, he is to *replenish* it, meaning that he is to care for it through those practices and methods that build the soil, that do not cause it to be eroded or sterile or plastic. *The farmer or farm-company failing to care for the land disobeys and dishonors The Creator.*

The family is God's basic social and economic unit. God has established His law to protect the rights, safety and well-being of the individual and his family. Thus, in the apportionment and preservation of the land, Moses was instructed to make sure that *each family was given the right and responsibility of caring for a definite portion of land.* Further, through Moses God set forth certain basic laws to insure that the land would stay with the family *(laws of private property, laws of inheritance),* and that the land would be conserved and cared for so as to provide continuity of sustenance for the family *(laws concerning tilling the soil, letting it lay fallow, keeping it unpolluted, laws of stewardship, etc.).*

Consider some of God's laws regarding His land, its care and use — laws that govern man's stewardship. And, if they seem "far out," perhaps that is a measure of just how far from obedience to God man has strayed.

The farmer is to let his land rest every seventh year. ("Six years you shall sow the field, and six years you shall prune your vineyard and gather in the fruit thereof; but in the seventh year shall be a sabbath of rest unto the land, a sabbath of rest for The Lord. . . ." *(Lev. 25:207; Ex. 23:10,11).* And, to those who asked of The Lord how they would exist during the fallow year, God gave the answer: "(if you obey Me) I will command My blessing upon you in the sixth year and it (the land) shall bring forth fruit for three years" *(Lev. 25:20-22; see also Ex. 16:25-30).*

And, what if man disobeys God, as so many do now?
This: ". . . if you will not hearken unto Me . . . and
if you shall despise My statutes . . . so that you will
not do all My commandments . . . your land shall
be desolate and your cities waste. Then shall the
land enjoy her sabbath . . . even then shall the land
rest and enjoy her sabbaths. As long as it lies
desolate it shall rest; because it did not rest in your
sabbaths, when you dwelt upon it" *(Lev. 26:14-35; see
also II Chron. 36:21).*

Farm land is to remain with the family. It is not to be
sold. "City" land may be sold. If family farmland
must be mortgaged, it is to be released in the Jubilee
year (the 50th year after the week of weeks, or 49th
year) (Lev. 25:8-23).

"Proclaim liberty throughout the land unto
all the inhabitants thereof" (Lev. 25:21).

*There is a deeper meaning to the words on the Liberty
Bell than most people — even most Christians — realize:* our
founding fathers were determined not to be tenants
or bondservants on indentured land. If land is leased/
sold, the price is to be based on its productivity for
that period of years between the date of the lease/sale
and the time it must be released or redeemed (returned) to the family heirs.

*God's laws concerning land prohibit land speculation
(Num. 36:7-9).* Giant land holdings and megafarms
are not in keeping with God's plan or purpose for
His property — "Woe unto them that join house to
house, that lay field to field, till there be no place,
that they may be placed alone in the midst of the

earth" *(Isa. 5:8; see also Jer. 22:17)*. Great proprietor-ships are the scourge of a nation and the enslavers of men.

"And they covet fields, and take them by vio-lence; and houses and take them away: so they op-press a man and his house, even a man and his heri-tage" *(Micah 2:2)*. When the land is held by individ-ual families, worked by the family, and kept as an in-heritance from The Lord God, then men will be free and can direct the affairs of civil government (govt. policies that cause families to lose their land or force them to leave the land are ungodly).

Usury is an abomination before The Lord (Ex. 22:25; Lev. 25:36, 37; Dt. 23:19, 20; Ezek. 22:12-15, etc.). Many of today's farmers are in a position similar to that of the inhabitants of Jerusalem in the days of Nehemiah: "We have mortgaged our land, vine-yards, and houses that we might buy corn . . . There were also that said, We have borrowed money for the king's tribute (tax), and that upon our lands and vineyards . . . neither is it in our power to redeem them; for other men have our lands and vineyards" *(Neh. 5:1-13)*.

Man says God's laws are no longer relevant or binding. ("Where there are religious obstacles to modern economic progress, the religion may have to be taken less seriously or its character altered.") And, who is it that puts its desire and its tactics above the law of God? Not some communist cell or front group; the Committee on Economic Develop-ment (CED) in its "An Adaptive Program for Agri-culture," p. 356, 1962.

BUT, God says, ". . . if you turn away and forsake My commandments . . . and shall go and serve other gods and worship them . . . this house, which is high, shall be an astonishment to every one that passeth by; so that he shall say, Why has The Lord done thus unto this land, and unto this house?" *(II Chron. 7:19-22).*

SUMMARY: The earth is The Lord's and the fulness thereof *(Ps. 24:1).* Agriculture is a Biblical institution ordained by God to care for His earth *(Gen. 2:15; 3:19, 23).* Man is to be God's husbandman, tending the earth to His honor and glory *(Gen. 1:28; Pr. 27:23-27).* God is to be acknowledged and honored through the proper care of His land *(Jer. 5:24).* The fruits of the land will be diminished if sin prevails *(Isa. 5:10; 7:23; Jer. 12:13; Joel 1:10,11).* The first fruits of the land belong to The Lord — whether that be animal, vegetable or mineral *(Pr. 2:9, 10).* The land is to rest, to lie fallow/dormant, every seventh year *(Lev. 25:2);* if God is obeyed in this way, He will bless the land and its product *(Lev. 25:20-21);* if He is not obeyed, He will blight the land *(Lev. 26:32-35).* The land is to remain with the family; and incumbrances on the land are to be released in the Jubilee year *(Lev. 25:8-14).* The products of the land are to be a benefit to all *(Ecc. 5:9).* There is a definite law of charity connected to stewardship of the land *(Dt. 24:19-21; Lev. 19:9, 10; II Chron. 9:6).*

10

GAMBLING & STATE LOTTERIES

BACKGROUND BRIEFING Forty four of these USA have legalized gambling of one form or another. It's estimated that *more than $17 billion a yr* is wagered "legally" (no hard data available on billions wagered *illegally*). 17 States and D of C conduct *"official" lotteries* (AZ, CO, CT, DE, IL, ME, MD, MA, MI, NH, NJ, MU, OH, PA, RI, VT, and WA). Four more considering lotteries this yr: CA, OR, MO and WV.

Lotteries were common in Colonial times, and in 19th Century. Congress and States outlawed them in 1800s after string of scandals. In 20th Century, NH was first state to have state lottery (1964). In 1983, *total yearly take* by just state lotteries was *$5.3 billion* — a nine-fold jump over 1973. About 40% of gross take goes to prize money, 40% is State's skim and balance goes for operating expenses (equipment, administration, agents, commisions, etc.).

In 1982 elections, four states had gaming measures on ballot. MN (64% voted *YES* on parimutuel betting on horse racing), MT (65% VOTED *NO* on expansion of gambling and establishment of state gaming commission), ND (64% voting *AGAINST* outlawing Blackjack card games) and SD (57% voted *NO* to legalizing gambling).

"Big winners" ($15-, $20- and $40-million) grab headlines, promote sale of lottery tickets. But, *odds are against players: picking 4 numbers, 10,000 to 1; 6 numbers, 3.5 million to 1.* Estimated odds on winning Illinois' super Lotto: *7 million to 1.* J. D. Quinn, drctr of NY State Lottery likes to say, *"Chances of winning are less than chances of getting hit by lightning — which is 1 in 1.9 million."*

Estimated *10 million compulsive gamblers in US* (some as young as 14). GAMBLERS ANONYMOUS struggles to help them (96% of those compulsive gamblers interviewed said they began *before* they were 14). Psychiatrist Robert Custer, MD, says *"gambling, like alcohol, is a narcotic."* NJ officials, a State with 350 thousand compulsive gamblers, admit gambling is their *"most neglected health problem."* It is a major cause of *family break-ups (divorce, desertion), child abuse, loss of jobs, debt and loss of property, alcoholism and suicide.*

Proponents of legalized gambling (including State lotteries) promote it as *an easy source of public funds — a "painless"* tax; picture gambling as a source of extra money — and it is . . . *for the gaming industry, crime syndicates and corrupt politicians.* But, *not for the public:* attendant socio-economic ills and civic problems generally result in increased public expenditures that exceed any tax "bonanza."

EXAMPLE: even after NJ legalized gaming (annual revenues, $430 million) State *increased sales taxes* and instituted income tax. *In Nevada,* "gaming empire of the nation," State authorities needed *increase* in property taxes *plus new tax* on hotel/motel rooms to help offset $80 million State *deficit.)*

Promoters of gambling usually boast of *increased employment* and *more business* for State; lead the gullible to believe that winnings are virtually assured. (Odds of winning in Illinois' recent super Lotto, *7 million to one.)*

In addition, they promise splendiferous charities and civic gifts (*have* also *been known to "buy off" churches by contributing to* building funds, etc.).

Opponents counter intro of gambling breeds *decay* and *corruption* that permeates all levels of society. They warn gambling feeds off greed and misery of the weak and seeks to hook the young (*one 17-year old boy piled up $34,000 in gambling debts).* Anti-gambling forces insist *it is immoral for State to encourage/condone/profit from immorality.* They cite statistics that show *gambling brings with it crime* (organized and unorganized) *and vice* (prostitution, assault, robbery, drugs, etc.).

Gambling preys on those who can least afford it. Univ. of Michigan study indicates poor spend greater proportion of income on gambling; thus, says study "govt. receipts from gambling become a regressive tax." (Since Atlantic City [NJ] casinos opened in '78 gamblers have *lost $3.7 billion* — and losses to patrons (not operators) increase yearly. Many of those losers are on *Social Security* or *unemployment compensation;* their dream: to "hit it big." Advertisements by some casinos urged unemployed in New York, Philadelphia etc., to visit Atlantic City while there was "nothing else to do.")

As for higher employment and more business, records indicate employment and revenues may increase for businesses feeding off gambling *but dry up for other enterprises.* And as for economic impact, opponents suggest many of the dollars gambled away would have been spent on tangible items and productive pursuits that could have turned money over and over in market place, thus generating jobs and taxes, etc.

Supporters of legalized gambling argue some people will always gamble, *why not legalize it and let State in on the take?* Opponents counter *availability increases participation and spreads the disease.* Sociologist Edward Devereaux (Cornell Univ) says compulsive gambling has makings of *major socio-economic problem, that it could equal magnitude of drugs and alcohol* "as wagering opportunities become more and more available."

US Dept. of Justice Organized Crime section reports: "The rate of illegal gambling in those states which have some legalized form of gambling was *three times as high* as in those states where there was not a legalized form of gambling."

Atlantic City, NJ, is example of what gambling can to do a city/county. *Gaming casinos are legal, going full-blast there.* City has become *"Las Vegas of the East."* Draws people from as far south as Washington and as far north as Boston. So? Well, Atlantic City now has *third highest welfare rate in USA.* Jobs were scarce in that seaside resort before advent of gambling. With influx of casino workers, how is job market now? *Unemployment is the same as it was before the casinos were opened.*

Local authorities attest to the *high incidence of drug use among casino employees;* also worry as drug culture spreads out *to infect youth.* City has had *"phenomenal" increase in crime* (fastest in State—*more than doubled in 6 yrs*). Downtown churches in Atlantic City report fall-off in attendance (especially at evening services) because many would-be church goers afraid to walk down streets or through parking lots. Few doubt *organized crime* (Mafia) has moved in (Fed. Dept of Justice has opened office there because of persistent spate of federal crimes). *Official corruption* termed more serious than organized crime. *NY Times* describes ties between local/State officials and gambling figures "thicker than blood."

Land values have soared as *speculators* look for quick and sky-rocketing profits. But resultant tax assessments are driving middle and low income residents out of the city. Except for areas around casinos, *city is deteriorating; social problems on increase.* Say residents: greedy operators are insensitive to city's best interests such as need for low-income housing for *displaced elderly who were moved to make way for casinos,* etc. Two redevelopment tracts, *designated for low-income housing,* have been sold to casino operators.

L. M. Clymer resigned as president of *Holiday Inns, Inc.,* because company decided to build and operate hotel-casinos. Mr. Clymer criticized company for ignoring moral principles involved in trafficking in gambling. Said Clymer, the only difference between losing your money in a casino or having a thug rob you is this — *the thug uses a gun.*

(Plymouth Rock gratefully acknowledges the assistance of *Dr. James A. Jeanes,* Executive Vice-President, International Reform Federation, in the preparation of this material. For a more comprehensive detailing of the Gambling Fiasco, write to Dr. Jeanes at *P.O. Box 1208, Merchantville, NJ 08109.)*

CONSIDER THE BIBLICAL PRINCIPLES Gambling is both a fruit and a root of sin; *it springs from sin, it generates* (germinates) *sin.* Consider it first *the result (fruit) of sin.* Gambling is a vice that is spawned by the violation of God's *Tenth Commandment,* "Thou shalt not covet . . ." *(Ex. 20:17).*

Dr. G. Campbell Morgan, renowned Bible scholar, points out that the urge to gamble goes far beyond desire for amusement or entertainment; it involves an *inordinate* (and often uncontrolled) *appetite that is covetousness.* (The Apostle Paul used the terms "lust" and "concupiscence" to describe covetousness *[I Th. 4:5]* and urged Christians to "mortify" such evil in themselves. Covetousness, he wrote, is a form of "idolatry" *[Col. 3:4, 5];* that which a person covets can (will) become his or her "god.")

Covetousness, Matthew Henry commented, is the *very root of evil;* "before the act, the thought: — before the (commission of) sin, the desire.

("Incline my heart unto Your testimonies, and not to covetousness," prayed the Psalmist *[Ps. 119:36].* He warned of the fate of those who covet: "So are the ways of everyone that is greedy of gain; which takes away the life of the owners thereof" *[Ps. 1:19]*. In Proverbs we read, "The desire of the slothful kills him; for his hands refuse to labor. He covets greedily all the day long . . ." *[Pr. 21:25, 26]*. In his letter to the church at Ephesus, Paul cautioned, "For this you know, that no . . . covetous man, who is an idolator, has any inheritance in the kingdom of Christ and of God" *[Eph. 5:5].*)

God's first nine commandments *(Ex. 20:3-16)* forbid certain *overt* sinful acts; the Tenth Commandment forbids (warns against) *internal* sin (sinful thought). As our Savior and our King emphasized *(Mt. 5:27)*, the thought is as sinful as the act itself. *That which invites the sinful act is the basic sin.* In a very real sense, then, *breaking the Tenth Commandment often (usually) results in breaking several more or most of the first nine.*

Consider also this: all men, because of their sinful nature are susceptible to sin *(Rom. 3:23);* and, the wages of sin is death *(Rom. 6:23).* For this reason a loving God sent His only Son to pay the penalty for sin so that whosoever believes on Christ should not die but have eternal life. Thus, sin abounds but grace abounds more abundantly *(Rom. 5:20);* our gracious Heavenly Father has provided the escape from death and the way to life eternal.

Conversely, it is satan, the tempter, who suggests the sin and tempts the sinner (God tempts no man, *James 1:13).* Therefore, may we not conclude (with validity) that the person or agency that condones/promotes/profits from sin is *an instrument of the prince of darkness?* What, then, does that say of the State that "legalizes" and promotes gaming (licenses casinos, slot machines, various games and sports of chance, etc.) and the State that sponsors its own lotteries?

God warned the priests of old *not to accept* the "hire of a whore, or the price of a dog (homosexual), into the house of The Lord thy God" *(Dt. 23:18)* — meaning the tithes or offerings from those who engage in such sins (abominations). Are not the tax receipts on the gains from the sin of gambling (sin-taxes) also an abomination in the sight of God? For, is not the State (the civil authority) to be a minister (servant) of God to the people for good (Rom. 13:1-4). And, when civil authorities encourage gambling *is not the State taking unto itself the role of pimp* — promoting lust and covetousness by encouraging the weak and susceptible to engage in sin for the State's profit?

There is also the matter of acknowledging (honoring) God's total Sovereignty. The individual who gambles deliberately creates uncertainties that would otherwise not exist and are not a part of God's perfect plan and purpose. As Gary North suggests, the person who gambles embraces a *chance-dominated universe,* a cosmos of luck, rather than the universe of order created by The Omniscient and Omnipotent Creator. Such an individual makes his god the god of fortune; he chooses to follow the laws of chance rather than obey the laws of God. Thus, in a very real sense, he puts other gods before God and thereby violates *God's First Commandment* ("Thou shalt have no other God's before me" *(Ex. 20:3).* The gambler-idolator also rejects/disobeys that which Christ, our Savior and our King, emphasized as the *First and Great Commandment* "You shall love the Lord your God with all your heart and with all your soul and with all your mind" *(Mt. 22:37,38).*

Jesus warned, "You cannot serve God and mammon" *(Mt. 6:24).* That which one puts first in life is that which he will serve. Beware, warned Moses, forget not The Lord and His commandments *(Dt. 8:11).*

The person who gambles is *a disobedient steward.* He or she not only fails to use what God has provided to serve Him, but also risks losing those God-given assets through selfish (ungodly) pursuits. Thus, such an individual fails to meet the most *basic requirements of stewardship (Mt. 6:24; 1 Cor. 4:1, 2; Titus 1:7).*

Now, consider gambling (gaming) as the root sin of additional sins:

Gambling is a major cause of neglect of the family and the break-up of the family. Monies that should be spent on food, clothing and housing go for gambling, etc. God's word tells us that the husband is to "cleave to his wife" *(Gen. 2:24; Mt. 19:5),* to provide for her and to love her as he loves himself *(Eph. 5:33). The man who refuses to care for his family is* worse than an infidel *(1 Tim. 5:8). The father is to provide for his children until they* can care for themselves *(2 Cor. 12:14).*

Gambling is often a cause of neglecting/dishonoring parents. This is violation of the Fifth Commandment *(Ex. 20:12)* and a dereliction of filial duty as set forth in The Scriptures *(Mt. 7:11; 15:4; 19:19; Eph. 6:2, 3).*

Gambling has caused many a man to steal, thus leading him to break God's Seventh Commandment *(Ex. 20:15).* It has driven some to murder, thus to violate God's Sixth Commandment *(Ex. 20:13).*

Finally, *gambling often engenders slothfulness and double-mindedness,* leading the individual to neglect his labors and to be caught up in dreams of a "free ride," and the "big win."

God's rule of labor is this: "In the sweat of thy brow shalt thou eat bread" *(Gen. 3:19).* To God's servant, work is no longer a curse but a blessing, it is a way to express love and gratitude to The Lord for all of His many blessings. Each person is to "bear his own burden" *(Gal. 6:5)* and "eat his own bread" *(2 Thes. 3:12)* — meaning, in the modern idiom, "there ain't no such thing as a free lunch." Each individual is to "work with your own hands" *(1 Thes. 4:11, 12)* at whatever calling God has ordained.

Clearly, it is not God's will that man live by the ill-gotten gains of gambling or engage in the sin of covetousness that is the seedbed for additional sins. "Take heed," warned The Master, "and beware of covetousness: for a man's life consists not in the abundance of the things he possesses" *(Luke 12:15)* "For what is a man profited," our Saviour asked, "if he shall gain the whole world . . . and lose his own soul?" *(Mt. 16:26).*

See, Gary North, *The Dominion Covenant: Genesis,* Institute for Christian Economics, pp. 226, 227. Also, H. B. Clark, *Clark's Biblical Law,* Binfords & Mort.

11

HOME SCHOOLS AND CHRISTIAN EDUCATION

BACKGROUND BRIEFING Fastest growing segment of education in US today? *Christian schools.* And, fastest growing segment of Christian education? *Home schooling.* In Los Angeles more than 1,000 home educators convened at workshops and seminars. In Nebraska, a State notoriously anti-Christian-education, 350 gathered for Christian Home School seminars. *So it goes throughout nation.* It's estimated *about 1,000,000* children being taught (tutored) at home: greatest percentage of those are in *Christian* home schools.[1]

Why the exodus from public (State) schools? *Why the swing to Christian education?* It's basic part of "parental revolution" seeking to regain control of their children and strengthen family unit. State-controlled schools one cause of alienation between (Christian) parents and children and breakdown of family. Also parents complain State schools fail in academics, are often plagued by drugs (including alcohol), rife with vandalism, teen-age pregnancy, venereal disease, pornography and promiscuity (lack of discipline).

"Having cast out the Ten Commandments, the public schools now bid the students behave. It is an impossibility . . . teacher and student alike reflect the lawlessness that ever appears in the absence of God's law."[2]

Christian parents concerned about all that—and more. They see an anti-Christian State school system that excludes (denies, belittles) God, contradicts Bible truths, promotes atheism (religion of secular humanism), challenges (works to curtail) authority of godly parents and promotes evolution, situational ethics and rubberized moral values. "Students aware of a teacher's opinion in a classroom, even if obviously wrong, will limit the range of their views and conform their beliefs more to that opinion."[3]

As number of Christian church and home schools accelerates, opposition from govt. education agencies and teacher's union mounts. Why? *Several reasons.* Opponents of Christian education (and those who seek to license/control it) insist they must protect child from "incompetent, neglectful" parents. They argue it's their responsibility because of compulsory education laws. But, some State Supreme Courts have recognized *responsibility is in other hands:* ". . . the responsibility of *parents* not to leave their children in ignorance and in some way make them capable of functioning in society."[4] Further, said Kentucky Supreme Court in 1979: "The State should never use its power to require attendance at tax-supported public schools. Private schools, both church-related and secular, have a right to exist, so long as they rely on private support and meet basic standards of health, safety, and educational effectiveness. . . . Their presence, not their absence, is an evidence of a free society."[5] (*Note:* many States consider home schools private schools.)

Issue is *not* mandatory education. *The issue is* who shall *control education? The parent? Or, State? Or, National Education Assoication* (NEA)?

Opponents of Christian education (whether in home or church) insist they "simply want to ensure a quality education for all citizens." But, retort Christian parents and educators, *Christian school is where the quality education is.* No reports of rape or robbery emanate from Christian schools, no problems with drugs or vandalism, no assaults on teachers. Further, standard achievement test results demonstrate Christian school students (in home and in church) *rank several grade levels above* students in the State schools. Christian parents and educators conclude, issue of "quality education" advanced by the State affords no real grounds for opposition to Christian education. *"If the State were truly interested in ensuring a 'quality education for its citizens,' it would be working to adopt the superior standards and match the achievements of Christian education."*[6]

Why such *strident, persistent* opposition? (1) *Financial*—for school district/apparatus, more students in Christian schools means a lower ADA (average daily attendance) and loss of *state/federal aid* (about $2,000 per student.) And, for teachers and teachers' unions, fewer students in State schools can mean *loss of jobs and political power.* (2) *Control*—rise in Christian education threatens *State's monopoly.* Dr. Anthony Sutton suggests basic purpose of govt.

schools "is not to teach subject matter but to condition children to live as socially integrated citizen units in an organic society . . . (the) absolute State. In this State the individual finds freedom only in obedience to the State."[7]

Those who would outlaw Christian home education assert parents are *not competent to teach*. Test results show parents are *best* teachers of their young. Elaine Rapp contends, "It is not credentials, but the parents' intimate knowledge of the children and their own initiative in accepting and pursuing the sound education of their own children which are important. These provide the real basis for a creative and effective educational program."[8] Reports Meg Johnson, *Home Education Resource Center*, "we often find that certification or a degree in teaching can be a hindrance in some ways. . . . It is a fallacy to imagine that a teacher's certificate would magically make a parent tutor more qualified to educate her own children. The techniques of group management and group discipline, as well as the routines which provide varying forms of 'busy-work' to keep things under control in a classroom simply don't apply at home."[9]

Further, teacher in State classroom has little control over curriculum or texts, or methodology; often simply follows structured teacher's manual. *Parents, by contrast, can select texts, determine curriculum, and use personalized methods* to train their children.

State authorities (and social workers) criticize home education for *"lack of socialization"*—meaning loss of "benefits" from being member of group, not learning how to "function" in society, get along with peers, etc. Parents respond socialization in today's world can be *negative, harmful.* And, many studies show *group learning is not really beneficial,* often stunts individual ingenuity and motivation, and can reduce achievement by lowering it to a common denominator. Further, *what about "peer" group pressure?* A "peer" is one equal in excellence; a companion, *an associate who shares common values and views.* Thus, *proper peer* for Christian young person as he or she is developing in The Lord *is another Christian and other Christian young people.* (More and more Christian homeschoolers are getting together on regular basis for field trips, outings, tours, etc.)

Some Christian parents suggest putting their children in public schools provides an opportunity for them *to witness for Christ.* Witnessing for Christ is important; all of His are commissioned to do so. However, *purpose of school is not to evangelize but to educate;* to train students to grow in that mind which was in Christ Jesus. Further, placing immature young Christians in *harm's way* (negative environments and ungodly pressures) may force them to take stand that even an adult Christian might find difficult. To do that to child would be counter to Christ's teachings *(Mt. 18:6, 7).*

Finally, Christian education challenges (meets head-on) *religion of humanism* that has gained control of most if not all of State education systems. Secular humanists cannot allow that. For humanists, *education is key to victory in battle for minds of young people* — and thus, key to their design of the future.

"I am convinced that the battle for humankind's future must be waged and won in the public school classroom by teachers who correctly perceive their roles as the *proselytizers of a new faith: a religion of humanity* that recognizes and respects the spark of what the theologians call divinity in every human being. These teachers must embody the same selfless dedication as the most rabid fundamentalist preachers, for they will be minister of another sort, *utilizing a classroom instead of a pulpit to convey humanist values in whatever subject they teach,* regardless of the educational level—preschool, day care of large state university. (Emphasis added)

"The classroom must and will become an arena of conflict between the old and the new— the rotting corpse of Christianity . . . and the new faith of humanism, resplendent in its promise of a world in which the never-realized Christian ideal of 'love thy neighbor' will finally be achieved." (John Dunphy, "A New Religion for a New Age," *The Humanist,* Jan/Feb, 1983, p. 25)

Dr. W. David Gamble of *American Reformation Movement* emphasizes: "Mr. Dunphy is correct when he states that the classroom has become an arena of conflict between Christianity and secular humanism. Both religions place a premium on education. . . . *Any Christian school which does not challenge and rebuke humanistic education is not truly Christian.*"[10] Dr. Cornelius Van Til wrote, "If you say you are involved in the struggle between Christ and Satan in the area of family and in the church, but not in the school, you are deceiving yourself. . . . You cannot expect to train intelligent, well-informed soldiers of the cross of Christ unless the Christ is held up before men as the Lord of culture as well as the Lord of religion. It is the nature of the conflict between Christ and Satan to be all-comprehensive."[11]

CONSIDER THE BIBLICAL PRINCIPLES   Children do *not* belong to the State. *They belong to God* and by Him are *entrusted to parents for care and training in His word and way.* "Lo, children are an heritage of The Lord: and the fruit of the womb is His reward" (Ps. 127:3). "And he lifted up his eyes, and saw the women and the children; and said, Who are those with thee? And he said, The children which God has graciously given me" *(Gen. 33:5).* See also *Dt. 7:13; 28:4; Ps. 24:1; Ezek. 16:20, 21; Isa. 8:18.*

GOD gives parents, not Caesar, *responsibility for educating child* (wisdom and training). "And, ye fathers, provoke not your children to wrath: but bring them up in the nurture and admonition of The Lord" *(Eph. 6:4).* "Train up a child in the way he should go: and when he is old, he will not depart from it" *(Pr. 22:6). "And these words which I command you this day, shall be in your heart: And you shall teach them diligently unto your children, and shall talk of them when you sit in your house and when you walk by the way, and when you lie down, and when you rise up? (Dt. 6:6-9).* "Now I say, That the heir, as long as he is a child, differs nothing from a servant, though he be lord of all; But is under tutors and governors until the time appointed of the father" *(Gal. 4:1, 2).* See also *Dt. 11:18-21; Pr. 4:1-27; 23:12, 13; Titus 1:6; Heb. 12:9-11.*

GOD has set the home, not the school, *as the basic center of learning; the church and the school are but extensions of the home and parents.* "Therefore shall you lay up these words in your heart and in your soul, and bind them for a sign upon your hand, that they may be frontlets between your eyes. And you shall teach them to your children, speaking of them when you sit in your house . . . and you shall write them upon the door posts of your house and upon your gates . . ." *(Dt. 11:18-21).* See also *Gen. 18:19; Ex. 10:2; Dt. 4:9; Pr. 31:26-28; Isa. 38:19; Joel 1:3; I Tim. 3:5.*

TRUE knowledge (wisdom) *comes from God through His word and not from the ways or wiles of the world.* "The fear of The Lord is the beginning of wisdom: a good understanding have all they that do His commandments . . ." *(Ps. 111:10). "Casting down imaginations, and every high thing that exalts itself against the knowledge of God, and bringing into captivity every thought to the obedience of Christ" (II Cor. 10:5).* "If any of you lack wisdom, let him ask of God, that gives to all men liberally and upbraids not; and it shall be given unto him" *(James 1:5).* "In Whom are hid all the treasures of wisdom and knowledge" *(Col. 2:3).* See also *Dt. 7:12-16; Ps. 90:12; Pr. 21:30; Isa. 55:8-9.*

GOD'S word is measure of all things, the scale on which His people are to weigh all issues of life; He is the foundation of true education. "To the law and to the testimony: if they speak not according to this word, it is because there is no light in them" (Isa. 8:20).

"Man shall not live by bread alone, but by every word that proceeds out of the mouth of God" *(Dt. 8:3; Mt. 4:4).* ". . . yea, let God be true, but every man a liar; as it is written, 'That you might be justified in your sayings, and might overcome when you are judged' " *(Rom. 3:4).* "Beware, lest any man spoil you through philosophy and vain deceit, after the tradition of men, after the rudiments of the world and not after Christ" *(Col. 2:8)* See also *Dt. 11:1; Php. 4:8.*

THE purpose of education is to train the child to be a faithful servant of God, to seek to be holy even as He is holy; and to be equipt (competent) to fulfill God's cultural mandate and Great Commission (Gen. 1:26-28; Mt. 28:18-20). *The goal is not to gain degrees or fame but to promulgate the faith.* "And herein do I exercise myself, to have always a conscience void of offense toward God, and toward men" *(Acts 24:16).* "Let this mind be in you, which was also in Christ Jesus" *(Php. 2:5).* "They are not of the world, even as I am not of the world. Sanctify them through your truth, Your word is truth" *(John 17:16, 17).* "And they that shall be of You shall build the old waste places: You shall raise up the foundations of many generations . . ." *(Isa. 58:12).* See also *Ps. 1:1-3; 78:1-7; Titus 2:11-15.*

ACADEMIC freedom is not license to study evil or the ways of evil. "Cease, my son, to hear the instruction that causeth to err from the words of knowledge" *(Pr. 19:27).* ". . . yet I would have you wise unto that which is good and simple (innocent) concerning (as to what is) evil" *(Rom. 16:19).* "Beloved, believe (trust) not every spirit, but try (prove) the spirits whether they are of God: because many false prophets are gone out into the world" *(I John 4:1).*

CHRISTIANS are not to have the ungodly as peers; parents must protect their children from the pressures of worldly peers. (No parent may render unto the world/ Caesar that which belongs to Christ!) "Be ye not unequally yoked together with unbelievers: for what fellowship has righteousness with unrighteousness? and what communion has light with darkness" *(II Cor. 6:14-18).* "My son, if sinners entice thee, consent not" *(Pr. 1:10-19).* "He that walketh with wise men shall be wise: but a companion of fools shall be destroyed" *(Pr. 13:20).* "And be not conformed to this world but be transformed by the renewing of your mind, that you may prove what is that good and acceptable, and perfect will of God' *(Rom. 12:2).* "Let no man despise (look down upon) your youth; but be and example of the believers, in word, in conversation (lifestyle), in charity, in spirit, in faith, in purity" *(I Tim. 4:12).*

(For list and order form for cassettes of seminar and workshop speakers at 1984 Los Angeles County Christian Home Educators write: CASSETTE MINISTRIES, P.O. Box 158, Yucaipa, CA 92399.)

RECOMMENDED READING: HOME EDUCATION AND CONSTITUTIONAL LIBERTIES, John W. Whitehead and Wendell R. Bird, $4.95, Crossway Books.

Notes

1. *The Freedom Report,* as quoted in Christians for Freedom of Education in Wisconsin, p. 2, April, 1984.

2. Rev. Louis De Boer, *Resistance VI — Public Schools,* The Pilgrim, June 1974.

3. R. Berenda, *The Influence of the Group on the Judgments of Children,* as cited by Dave Haigler and Bill Ambler in Home School Defense Manual, p. II-27, 1982.

4. Court cases cited in *The Home Study Journal,* Christian Liberty Academy, p. 3, 1982.

5. *Ibid.,* p 4.

6. *The C.L.A.S.S. Review,* #4, Christian Liberty Academy Satellite Schools, p. 4., 1984.

7. Dr. Wm. David Gamble, *The Conflict in Education: Christianity vs Secular Humanism,* On Teaching, American Reformation Movement, April, 1984.

8. *The Parent as Tutor,* Home Education Resource Center, Winter Bulletin #14, 1984.

9. *Op. cit.*

10. Dr. Wm. David Gamble, *Op. cit.*

11. As quoted by Dr. Wm. David Gamble, *Op. cit.*

12

HUMANISM

"By the year 2000 we will — I hope — raise our children to believe in human potential, not God." So said Gloria Steinem, militant feminist and editor of *Ms.* magazine. *". . . any child who believes in God is mentally ill,"* wrote Paul Brandwein in *The Social Sciences.* Brandwein boasted that national "mental health programs" are being developed to help children who believe in God to have healthier, more balanced attitudes.

". . . the Bible is not merely another book, an outmoded and archaic book . . . it has been and remains an incredibly dangerous book," asserts educator John Dunphy.

What is all this? *Humanism. The root and fruit of humanism.*

And, what is humanism?

James Curry, 1969 president of American Humanist Association, said, "Humanism is a polite term for atheism . . . Humanism . . . relieves mankind from the necessity either to believe in God or to look to Him as the fundamental source of all good."

Mr. Curry was echoing, in essence, the words of

another humanist and signer of the first *Humanist Manifesto* (1933), John Dewey:

> "There is no God, and there is no soul. Hence, there are no needs for the props of traditional religion. With dogma and creed excluded then immutable truth is also dead and buried. There is no room for fixed law or permanent moral absolutes."

Humanism, adds Mr. Dunphy, is "*. . . a new faith: a religion of humanism.*" It holds that tradition theism is "*. . . a unproven and outmoded faith*" and that "*Salvationism, based on mere affirmation, still appears as harmful* (as it ever was), *diverting people with false hopes of heaven hereafter. . . .*"

Is Mr. Dunphy correct? Is "humanism" a religion? *It is,* decreed the US Supreme Court in 1961 *(Torcaso v. Watkins)* and in 1964 *(U.S. v. Seeger).*

Some, including many Christians, discount the existence of humanism; think it is simply a figment, a fantasy concocted by religious zealots. But, *humanism is real, indeed.* It has a specific dogma and definite goals. Consider some of its basic tenets. They are set forth in *Humanist Manifesto I* (1933) and *Humanist Manifesto II* (1973). Weigh the humanists by their own words. Did not our Lord and Master warn, "For by your words you shall be justified, and by your words you shall be condemned" *(Mt. 12:37).*

- *Humanism denies the existence of God.*

  "As non-theists, we begin with humans not God, nature not deity." ". . . we can discover no divine purpose or providence for the human species. While there is much we do not know, humans are responsible for what we are or will become. No deity will save us; we must save ourselves." *(HM II)*

• *Humanism holds that man creates his own God.* (God, insist the humanists, is a product of man's imagination).

"The cultivation of moral devotion and creative imagination is an expression of genuine "spiritual" experience and aspirations. We believe, however, that traditional dogmatic or authoritarian religions that place revelation, God, ritual or creed above human needs and experience do a disservice to the human species. Any account of nature should pass the tests of scientific evidence; in our judgment, the dogmas and myths of traditional religion do not do so." *(HM II)*

• *Humanism denies The Creator, and his creation.*

"Religious humanists regard the universe as self-existing and not created." "Second, Humanism believes that man is a part of nature and that he has emerged as the result of a continuous process." *(HM I)* "Rather, science affirms that the human species is an emergence from natural evolutionary forces . . ." *(HM II)*

• *Humanism denies the existence of man's soul.*

"Modern science discredits such historic concepts as . . . the 'separable soul.' " "As far as we know, the total personality is a function of the biological organism transacting in a social and cultural context." *(HM II)*

"There is no credible evidence that life survives the death of the body. We continue to exist in our progeny and in the way that our lives have influenced others in our culture." *(HM II)*

• *Humanism denies the hope of Salvation and ridicules the fear of judgment.*

"Promises of immortal Salvation or fear of eternal damnation are both illusory and harmful." "Too often, traditional faiths encourage dependence rather than independence, obedience rather than affirmation, fear rather than courage." *(HM II)*

• *Humanism holds there are no absolutes, no set right or wrong.*

"We affirm that moral values derive their source from human experience. Ethics is *autonomous* and *situational,* needing no theological or ideological sanction. Ethics stems from human needs and interest." *(HM II)*

Humanist Manifesto I and II are *endorsed by National Education Association* (NEA). And, as Peter Frogley of Light Education Ministries has written, "the proponents of humanism have become the driving force behind education." In an interview with the *Boston Herald* in 1982, humanist Charles F. Potter commented that "Education is thus a most powerful ally of Humanism and *every American public school is a school of Humanism.*" (Emphasis added)

How deeply do the roots penetrate into the State-controlled, taxpayer-funded school system? What is being propagated in those classrooms? Inspect a few of its evil fruits:

1. *God is denied in the classroom,* separated from State, State schools and (during school hours) the State's students. God's written word is also barred except as a quaint historical manuscript or a refernce to an outmoded set of ethics.

2. *The increasingly discredited theory of evolution is found in most State school textbooks; is taught in classrooms of most State schools.* Efforts to obtain at least "equal time" for Creationism have been consistently denied (and usually ruled against in courtrooms). Humanists protest consideration of Creation, say it is a religious myth. Yet, assert Christians, evolution is humanistic theory of humanism which has been decreed a religion.

3. *The Ten Commandments are removed from public school and barred from classrooms.* ". . . we reject those features of traditional religious morality that deny humans a full appreciation of their own potentialities. . . ." *(HM II) The new-world words are situational ethics and flexible moral values* (concept that there are no absolute rules, whatever seems right, whatever "feels good" as long as you don't interfere with others). Within that framework, a *pluralism* that decrees all viewpoints equal and all modes of expression acceptable—the profane as well as the noble, the perverted as well the pure.

4. *Self-authority and the autonomy of man* (apart from God) *expounded.* "Reason and intelligence are the most effective instruments that humankind possess. There is no substitute: neither faith nor passion suffices in itself." "Although science can account for the causes of behavior, the possibilitites of individual freedom of choice exist in human life and should be increased." *(HM II)* Thus, we beget the "ME" generation—juvenile anarchy, self-centeredness, self-indulgence, self-gratification. Editorialized THE HUMANIST magazine (1976): "Nothing tha is part of contemporary life is taboo." (Including gu ters and garbage.)

5. *Sexual permissiveness not only tolerated but promoted.* "In the area of sexuality, we believe that intolerant attitudes, often cultivated by orthodox religions and puritanical cultures, unduly repress sexual conduct." "The many varities of sexual exploration should not in themselves be considered 'evil.' " ". . . individuals should be permitted to express their sexual proclivities and pursue their lifestyles as they desire." "Moral education for children and adults is an important way of developing awareness and sexual maturity." *(HM II)*

6. *Opposition to free individual enterprise and promotion of collectivism* (socialism-communism). "The humanists are firmly convinced that existing acquisitive and profit-motivated society has shown itself to be inadequate and that a radical change in methods, controls and motives must be instituted. A socialized and cooperative economic order must be established to the end that the equitable distribution

of the means of life be possible. The goal of humanism is a free and universal society in which people *voluntarily* and intelligently cooperate . . . Humanists *demand* a shared life in a shared world." *(HM I)* (Emphasis added) "World proverty must cease. Hence extreme disproportions in wealth income and economic growth should be reduced on a worldwide basis (through an international authority)." *(HM II)*

7. *One-world government and "global citizenship" instead of patriotism and national sovereignty.* "We deplore the division of humankind on nationalistic grounds. We have reached a turning point in human history where the best option is to transcend the limits of national sovereignty and move toward the building of a world community in which all sectors of the human family can participate. Thus, we look to the development of a system of world law and a world order based upon transnational federal government." *(HM II)* "What more daring a goal for humankind than for each person to become in ideal as well as practice, a citizen of a world community." *(HM II)* Of such is the gospel of humanism. And, this, also: —*Proabortion* (". . . the right to abortion . . . should be recognized")

- *Pro-gay rights* (". . . [we do not] wish to prohibit by law or social sanction sexual behaviour between consenting adults . . . a civilized society should be a tolerant one")
- *Pro-ERA* (". . . equal rights for both women and men to fulfill their unique careers and potentialities as they see fit, free of in-

vidious discrimination") and

- *Pro-guaranteed annual minimum wage for all.*

Thus, the battle rages: God's Word vs. the "reasonings" of man. The humanists know that, if Christians do not: *"I am convinced that the battle for humankind's future must be waged and won in the public school classroom by teachers who correctly perceive their roles as the* proselytizers of a new faith: *a religion of humanity . . .* These teachers must embody the same selfless dedication as the most rabid fundamentalist preachers . .

". . . for they will be ministers of another sor *utilizing a classroom inste*   *f a pulpit to convey humanist values in whatever subject th* *y teach . . ."* (John Dunphy, "A New Religion for a New Age," The Humanist, Jan/Feb, 1983)

RECOMMENDED READING: For a more comprehensive analysis of Humanist Manifesto I and II, see *A Critical Review of Humanist Manifestor I & II,* Homer Duncan, MC International Publications, 2451 34th Street, Lubbock, TX 79411-1689, 38 pages, $1.00; *The Battle for the Mind,* Tim LaHaye, Fleming H. Revell, 247 pages, $4.95; *Humanism in Textbooks; Secular Religion in the Classroom,* The Mel Gablers, P.O. Box 7518, Longview, TX 75607 (Ask for T-588, send contribution to cover cost of printing and postage.)

CONSIDER THE BIBLICAL PRINCIPLES The Lord God — not man — is Sovereign. God, alone is the Creator — not man, not biochemistry. He is the source of all power. *"And He is before all things, and by Him all things consist" (Col. 1:17).*

The earth, and the heavens, and the seas—and man—did not evolve, they were created. By The Lord God. "In the beginning, God created the heaven and the earth" *(Gen. 1:1).* "And God said, Let the earth bring forth the living creature after his kind·. . . And God said, let us make man in our image, after our likeness . . ." *(Gen. 1:24, 26).* "All things were made by Him; and without Him was not any thing made that was made" *(John 1:3).*

Humanism is not new to this world. It made its entrance in the Garden of Eden. It slithered in, subtle and beautiful to behold—and evil.

"And the serpent said to the woman, you shall surely not die: For God knows that in the day you eat thereof (of the tree of the knowledge of good and evil), then your eyes shall be opened, and you shall be as gods, knowing good and evil" *(Gen. 3:4, 5).*

"You shall be as gods!" And Eve fell, and Adam—and man has been falling for that snare and delusion ever since.

Humanism calls for the worship of the creature rather than The Creator. God's word makes it clear: those who do so are liars. "Who changed the truth of God into a lie, and worshipped and served the creature more than The Creator, who is blessed forever" *(Rom. 1:25).*

Humanists reject God's word and God's truth. They are corrupt, doers of abominable works. "Behold, you walk every one after the imagination of his evil heart, that they may not hearken unto Me" *(Jer. 16:12).* "The fool has said in his heart, There is no God. They are cor-

GOD'S WORD *(Christian creed)*	**MAN'S WAY** *(Humanism's dogma)*
God's truth is absolute *(John 17:17)*	Man seeks his own (relative) truth *(John 18:38)*
The wisdom of God *(I Cor. 1:18-25)*	The wisdom of men *(Jer. 9:23, 24)*
God's thoughts *(Isa. 55:8, 9)*	Man's reasoning *(Mt. 16:22, 23)*
Steadfastness *(Gal. 5:1)*	Compromise *(II Chron. 19:2)*
Assurance/Positive *(II Pet. 1:19-21)*	Doubts/Uncertainties *(Luke 24:19-27)*
Revelational Ethics *(Mt. 4:4; Ps. 119:11)*	Situational Ethics *(Mt. 22:23-29)*
The will of God *(Acts 24:16)*	Philosophy of men *(Col. 2:8)*
Christ-centered *(Php. 2:5)*	Man-centered *(Judges 21:25)*

(Based on a tract by Rapids Christian Press, Wisconsin Rapids, WI)

rupt, they have done abominable works" *(Ps. 14:1)*. "The hand of our God is upon all them for good that seek Him; but His power and His wrath is against all them that forsake Him" *(Ezra 8:22)*. "There is none that understands, there is none that seek after God. They are all gone out of the way, they are together become unprofitable; there is none that does good, no, not one" *(Rom. 3:11-12)*.

The humanists put their gods before God; they create a false religion. "Thou shalt have no other Gods before Me" *(Ex. 20:3)*. "But there were false prophets also among the people, even as there shall be false

teachers among you, who privily shall bring in dam-
nable heresies, even denying The Lord" *(II Pet. 2:1)*.

*The humanist holds that man is autonomous, that man
is the means and measure of all things.* He puts himself,
and human reason and intelligence above God; he
relies on man's intellect and reasoning rather than
God's word; God warns us to turn away from such
ungodly individuals. "For men shall be lovers of
their own selves, covetous, boasters, proud, blas-
phemers, disobedient to parents, unthankful, unholy, without natural affection, trucebreakers, false
accusers, incontinent, fierce, despisers of those that
are good. Traitors, heady, high-minded, lovers of
pleasures more than lovers of God; having a form of
godliness, but denying the power thereof: from such
turn away" *(II Tim. 3:2-5)*.

*Humanism seeks to please man (self and society), rather
than God.* Thus, they cannot please God. "For do I
now persuade men, or God? or do I seek to please
men? for if I yet pleased men, I should not be the
servant of Christ" *(Gal. 1:10)*.

Thus, there lies the heart and the heat of the battle for the minds and souls of our children — and the
fate of our nation. Dr. Robert Simonds has marked
some of the battle zones:

> *The right to life* (for the pre-born and the elderly)
> vs. Abortion on demand and euthanasia. *Heter-
> osexuality* (husband and wife and family) vs.
> Sodomy. *Morality, chastity and fidelity* vs. sexual
> license and promiscuity. *Christian virtues and
> health* vs. licientiousness and VD and Aids and

herpes. *Christian faith and creation* vs. religion of atheism and evolution. *Parental rights and responsibilities as ordained by The Lord God* vs. State's rights and child rights above the parent's.

For the Christian, the follower of Christ, there is no alternative: *"The Word of God has been revealed in Personal and in written form — in Christ, that is, and in Scripture. As Christ is the Complete Personal Word of God, valid in all times and places, Scripture is the absolute written Word of God, applicable in all times and places."* Professor Neal Frey, Chairman of History and Social-Science Dept., Christian Heritage College, El Cajon, CA.

"But as for me, and my house, we will serve The Lord" (Joshua 24:15b).

13

INFLATION

BACKGROUND BRIEFING Inflation is *"the artful plundering of the people"* through debauchery and manipulation of the nation's money (medium of exchange). It is accomplished by governments (printing presses/fiat money) or usurers (fractional reserves and interest rates). Prophets of ancient Israel warned against such deceit and robbery. They decreed that value of money be determined *not* by number of units in circulation but by actual weight of precious metal (gold or silver) in each unit of money (coin). In 808 B.C., Amos took higher powers (civil authorities) to task for *"making the ephah small and the shekel great and falsifying the balance by deceit (Amos 8:5)*

Ancient Roman Caesars, when they had reached explosive level of taxation and feared revolt of the people, resorted to inflation (a subtle and insidious form of taxation) by *adding baser metals to coins* — and also *shaving gold coins* and using shavings to mint more coins.

In 1690, to meet payroll for soldiers, Massachusetts legislature issued *paper money* (against expectation of revenues from taxes). Solders lost out (had to accept discounts in order to use the money); but, govt. got off hook, was relieved of its debt and avoided revolt by soldiers. That prompted Bay Colony govt. to issue *a sea of paper money* to cover *all* of its governmental expenses. P   money drove gold and silver out . . . finally   hasing power of fiat *dropped to 1/8th of its face   lue.* It was only after Spanish milled coins were imported to serve as currency that economy recovered. (Otto Scott, *"Paper Money in Colonial America,"* Chalcedon Report, 6/84).

Continental Congress issued fiat (paper money) to help pay for American War for Independence. Without backing, currency became worthless (thus, the expression "Not worth a Continental"). France went through a reign of paper (fiat) money (1789-1796). It was the pits: Even church property was confiscated as "backing" for accelerating issues of fake money. Before final financial ruin and spiritual depravity took over, cost of a barrel of flour had soared from 45-cents to $45.00. Finally, there was no bread at any price ("Let them eat cake!").

In Germany, in 1920s, printing presses went wild turning out "money." Some *300 paper mills* and *2,000 printing houses* went at it day and night. At the end, *the big red balloon exploded;* a loaf of bread cost 1.25 trillion marks and people were using wheelbarrows to carry their wages (paper "money") to market to buy food.

In 1947, President Harry Truman warned Congress, *"We already have an alarming degree of inflation and, even more alarming, it is getting worse."* When Mr.

Truman spoke those words, the 100-cents of purchasing power of 1940 dollar had already shrunk to 63-cents. The inexorable ratio (law) between increase in money in circulation and decrease in value of monetary unit had set in: *the gangrene of inflation was spreading.*

As Neil McCaffrey put it, "With inflation alone, people must earn about *ten times* what their fathers earned in 1935 to stay even. And with inflation plus taxes, they have to earn about *thirteen times* more to keep up."

In August, 1984, *American Institute of Economic Research* calculated that, during 12-year period *1971-1983,* inflation embezzled about *$3.3 trillion in lost purchasing power from savings accounts, insurance policies, pensions,* etc. That $3.3 trillion (implicit tax of inflation) was equal to all (explicit) federal income taxes paid during those same 12 years. (Which means that *Americans paid twice as much for government than politicians let on:* They paid *once* in direct taxation and *once* in indirect taxation of inflation.)

Today we are told that purchasing power of dollar is about *33-cents.* That is about one-third of the story. That 33-cents is figured on an arbitrary price index set at 100 in *1967.* But, in 1967, the 100-cents of purchasing power of 1939 dollars had already shriveled to less than 50-cents. *So, figure it this way:* compared to 1939 dollar in your pocket is worth about 14-cents.

Why the sliding scales and rubber yardsticks for *Consumer Price Index* (CPI)—1939, 1967, 1977, etc.? Well, when purchasing power of monetary unit (dollar) declines to an "indefensible" level and voters get restless, base year for the index is changed to make it appear dollar is worth more than it is. Why? Because it is easier to *"falsify the balance by deceit"* than it is to engage in discipline necessary to halt inflation and restore integrity and value of money.

"And I heard a voice in the midst of the four beasts say, A measure of wheat for a penny . . ." (Rev. 6:6). That's about a dry quart of wheat for a day's wages.

[The following table portrays the erosion of the US dollar in terms of purchasing power. It makes clear the real cause of inflation: *the increase in fiat (paper) money by government and/or the central bank* (Federal Reserve money changers). Note: From 1980 through 1983, US had the *greatest increase in money supply ever* — up $28 billion 1980-1981; up $36 billion, '81-'82, and up $42 billion, '82-'83. All told an increase of *$107 billion* (24%) *in those three years.*]

U.S. MONEY SUPPLY, FEDERAL SPENDING & DEBT, AND YOUR DOLLAR

	Money Supply[1]	Fed. Spend.	Fed. Debt	GNP	Purch. Power of $2	
	----------------(in billions of dollars)----------------				1940	1967
1940	$ 66.0	$ 9.1	$ 42.9	$ 100.0	100	—
1960	141.9	92.2	290.9	506.5	47	—
1965	169.5	118.4	323.1	691.1	44	—
1967	185.1	158.3	382.6		42	100
1970	216.5	196.9	544.1	992.7	36	87
1975	291.0	326.1	914.3	1,549.2	25	61
1980	414.5	580.3	1,146.9	2,633.1	17	39
1982	478.5	728.4	1,146.9	3,050.2	15	35
1983-84	552.7 (9/15/84)	796.0	(*)1,500.0	(e)3,067.7	13	33

(*) US In May, 1984, US Senate voted to raise debt ceiling to *$1,697 billion;* US House voted to boost debt ceiling to *$1,837 billion in 1985.*

(1) currency in circ + demand deposts, etc.

(2) Based on 1940 &1967 indices as noted

Sources: US Dept of Commerce, BLS; Economic Report of The President, 1984.

CONSIDER THE BIBLICAL PRINCIPLES *Inflation violates Biblical principles and precepts; it breaks God's laws,* including thievery, covetousness, and deceit. It takes advantage of the elderly, threatens the stability of the home and robs the laborer of his fair wage and the investor of his fair return. It discourages thrift, inhibits self-control, invites irresponsibility, weakens the tithe, and goes against God's ordained purpose for civil government (to be minister of justice — protect citizens and their property).

"You shall not steal," says The Lord *(Ex. 20:15).* Inflation steals. It is a thief; a sneak thief. By reducing the values of the medium of exchange, it robs the productive of their wealth. It plunders property which is to be used to serve The Lord (in fact, it takes "first fruits" that belong to The Lord) and it erodes or destroys that which should be handed down by the family from one generation to the next . . . thus endangering the survival of the family unit.

"You shall not steal, neither deal falsely, neither lie to one another" (Lev. 19:11). Inflation is a deceit, a hidden tax. Through it, government deals falsely with the people; it leaves the person's money in his pocket while destroying its value. Biblical law demands honesty in all things including weights and measures and it demands it from the ruler (the governors) just as it demands it from the citizen (the governed). The prophet Amos warned against debauching the monetary unit. Isaiah condemned the adulteration of silver with dross *(Isa. 1:22).* Ezekiel prophesied to the Israelites concerning the consequences of debasing money *(Ezek. 22:18-22),* so did Isaiah *(Isa. 1:25).*

Jesus drove the money changers from the temple, not only because they were desecrating The Lord's house but also because they were cheating the people (*"you have made it a den of thieves"*) (*Mt. 21:13*). And, again, did not our Savior and our King tell us to give *full measure, tramped down and running over;* inflation does just the opposite — it gives short measure, siphoned off and depleted.

"You shall not covet," said The Lord (*Ex. 20:17; Luke 12:15*). Inflation is fruit and the seed of covetousness. It plays upon greed and appetite, it springs from greed and appetite. It proceeds from *"the carnal mind"* (which) *is at enmity against God"* (*Rom. 8:7*).

"The laborer is worthy of his hire," (*Luke 10:7; I Tim. 5:18*). Inflation, by depreciating value of the monetary unit, forces the working man to work more but earn less; it robs the worker and the producer of the fruit of his labor and sneaks it off to government, bankers, and non-producers (thus, it *"muzzles the ox that treads out the corn"* so that he is deprived of a fair portion of that which he produces. It is difficult for the employer to pay the employee *"that which is just and equal"* (*Col. 4:1*) when the value of the medium of exchange is manipulated and adulterated.

Those who are in higher office (public officials) are to be "ministers of God" to the people for good. When those higher powers violate the integrity of the public medium of exchange (or, when they permit or assist others in such manipulation), they destroy the property of the people; thus, they are not servants of the people or ministers of The Lord God. They seek, in fact, to be their own gods building their own temples.

The greatest sin (and cost) of inflation is not economic but *spiritual:* it is the sin of the wicked heart that denies God, and refuses to obey his laws, and robs those who are created in the image of The Living God.

14

JUSTICE AND THE COURTS

BACKGROUND BRIEFING Concern over *power grabs by federal courts* is increasing. Within that system is growing tendency to abrogate powers reserved to other b˙ nches of govt. — *and to the States, and to the people.* ". . . (the courts) are reaching into areas once considered the preserve of legislators, administrators and the family." *Example:* US Supreme Court in Roe v. Wade (re abortions) took unto itself power to decide which innocents should live and which should die. *Example:* US federal judge arbitrarily took over Boston schools and virtually controlled them for years until he was satisfied schools complied with his plan for desegregation. *Example:* US federal judge in Louisiana overruled elected State judge who tried to uphold right of parent and child to choose school on basis of residence.

Such power, now increasingly exercised by federal courts, was never intended by framers of Constitution. To prevent accumulation of power by federal courts, framers added *Article III,* which reads in part:

"In all cases affecting Ambassadors, other public ministers, and Counsuls, and those in which a State shall be party, the supreme Court shall have original Jurisdiction. *In all other cases* before mentioned, the supreme Court shall have *appellate* Jurisdiction both as to Law and Fact, *with such exceptions and under such regulations as the Congress shall make."* (Emphasis added)

Checks and balances are essential to the maintenance of justice. Thus, Congress reserved the right *to restrict and, if need be, eliminate* the power of the Supreme Court to hear cases other than those few situations allowed under its original jurisdiction. In Federalist Paper No. 18, Alexander Hamilton wrote that the Court *"has been carefully restricted to those causes which are manifestly proper for the cognizance of national judicature; that in the partition of this authority; a very small portion of the original jurisdiction has been preserved to the Supreme Court, and the rest to subordinate tribunals. . . ."*

In the past, Supreme Court has recognized Congress' authority over its power to decide issues. In *Wiscart v. D'Auchy,* Court held that "The Constitution distributing the judicial power of the United States, vests in the Supreme Court an original as well as appelate jurisdiction. . . . Here, then, is the ground *and the only ground* on which we can sustain an appeal. If Congress has provided no rule to regulate our proceedings, we cannot exercise our appellate jurisdiction; *and if the rule is provided, we cannot depart from it."*

It is the Congress, not the Court, that is the supreme law of the land. And, in plain language, the Constitutional place and role concerning the courts is laid out: *Congress is to bridle the federal courts in their exercise of power.*

Taking note of the importance of checks and balances, James Madison nevertheless wrote that *"in republican government, the legislative authority necessarily predominates"*—since it is the closest to the people and theoretically is most responsive to their will. Clearly, then, it is up to the elected representatives in Congress to regulate and control the courts.

Today, however, Congress backs away from its responsibility in this regard. Generally, Congress will not even vote on a bill if its members think the Supreme Court might rule the proposed legislation unconstitutional. Thus, *it is the Court that bridles Congress!* And, thus the all-important system of checks and balances is jeopardized.

The answer, in the American Constitutional system, *is for the Congress to step forward.* In this way, the courts can be prevented from becoming the engines of tyranny.

(Plymouth Rock expresses appreciation for the valuable assistance of John W. Whitehead, Esq., in the preparation of this section. Mr. Whitehead is a Constitutional Atty., and president of the Rutherford Institute.)

CONSIDER THE BIBLICAL PRINCIPLES   In His infinite wisdom and justice, The Lord God gave man the pattern for right civil government: *the theocratic republic.* It was this form of civil govt. He ordained for the Hebrews; it was this form of civil govt. that was, in large measure, the matrix for the American republic, as established by our founding fathers.

In the Hebrew Republic, as in ours, there were

three branches of govt: the executive, the legislative, and the judicial (see Isa. 33:22). As was the case when our nation was founded, God was acknowledged as Supreme Sovereign; His laws were law, spiritual and civil; they were the fundamental basis for laws and statutes enacted. *Each of the 12 tribes was sovereign in its own right* (as were the original 13 States). The 12 tribes were a *union (one nation) under God;* there was unity in God and in matters of national import; yet, no tribe could trespass on the sovereignty of another.

Within this structure, and at each level, The Lord God commanded there be established *a system of checks and balances* (since He above all others was aware of the sinful nature of man). The authority of the *judges* was checked by the *senate* (comprising the leaders (princes) of the tribes. The power of the senatorial council was checked by the ·'   of the judicial, and *the power of the people.* And,   hole was under the restraint and constraint of the *Dwine Constitution* (Covenant) established by the Lord God and accepted by the people at Mount Sinai *(Ex. 20. See also Dt. 5:3, 27).*

When God permitted the people to have earthly kings *(I Sam. 8)* the kings were required to "write him a copy of this law in a book and read therein all the days of his life" *(Dt. 17:18, 19).*

Consider, now, the *judicial system* (justice) as God ordained it in that first republic—and note the similarities to that which was part of this American republic.

Through Moses, God established *a system of superior and inferior and circuit courts (Ex. 18:21; I Sam.*

7:15), with a supreme court to hear matters of dispute between the tribes and such matters of national importance that might come before it. God also set forth the requirements (attributes) of those who should be *elected judges (Ex. 18:21, 22)*.

Under God's perfect plan, the courts were *readily available to every man* without going far to obtain justice, and without waiting long to secure it (fair and speedy trail):

"Judges and officers shalt thou make thee in all thy gates, which The Lord thy God giveth thee, throughout the tribes; and they shall judge the people with just judgment" *(Dt. 16:18)*.

As a protection against hasty decisions, the individual had *the right to appeal* his case—in some instances all the way to the highest court in the land *(Dt. 7:8, 9)*.

All justice was to be based on righteous judgements *(Dt. 25:1; Ps. 82)*. The corruption of justice is an abomination to The Lord *(Pr. 17:15)* and perverted justice is not justice but is against God's will *(Isa. 59:14)*. Justice is to be meted out equally, and even-handedly. No man is above the law, no man is below the law *(Dt. 1:16, 17; John 7:24)*.

In God's eyes, *justice is synonymous with righteousness;* where there is no righteousness, there is no justice. When man disobeys God, when he denies God and refuses God's laws, he spurns justice and encourages sin. Man without God can only produce sinful (unGodly) laws *(Hab. 1:4)*. Thus, as Rev. R. J. Rushdoony has written, "To restore justice, *we must* restore God to His rightful place in our personal and national lives."

Further, *we must restore God's laws* as the law of the land and determine that those who are entrusted with the powers of the judicial system are men who adjudicate the laws faithfully in obedience to the word of God. Those who are to judge must judge righteously, according to His word, without fear or favor . . . faithfully, and with a perfect heart *(II Chron. 19:6-9).*

RECOMMENDED READING: *Law and Liberty,* R. J. Rushdoony, 1977, Thoburn Press, Tyler, TX; *The Hebrew Republic,* E. C. Wine, American Presbyterian Press, Wrightstown, NJ.

15

KEEPING THE LORD'S DAY(S)

BACKGROUND BRIEFING In recent years, bills to change national election days from Tuesday to Sunday come before committees of US Congress. To date, none have passed either House. However, attempts to switch federal elections to Sunday will likely continue. Three former presidents have supported legislation (Nixon, Ford and Carter). Legislators in several states are considering introduction of similar legislation. That such an ungodly proposal advances prompts consideration of the issue and Biblical principles involved. Making secular election day out of Sabbath would truly rob The Lord God and *render unto the State (Caesar) that which God has expressly commanded be kept whole and His.*

Proponents argue Sunday elections for federal office (congress, president) *would insure larger voter turnout.* Cite higher turnouts in countries where elections are held on Sunday (Europe, Latin America), compare those voter turnouts with declining number of citizens in USA who bother to vote. (Only 63% of registered voters cast ballots in the 1960 presidential elections; 55.4% in 1972; 56.5 in 1976, *only 53% in*

1980. Ronald Reagan was elected president by *about 23%* of all citizens of voting age. Turnout is even lower for congressional elections.)

Opponents dismiss idea that day of week has anything to do with low election turnout; say decline in turnout is *evidence of voter apathy;* that low participation is not due to any inconvenience (of elections held on weekday) but to *loss of confidence/lack of trust* in politicians and political parties (as reflected in public opinion polls "campaign promises are seldom kept," "party-control of Congress changes but nothing really changes in Washington," "why bother to vote, it doesn't mean anything," etc.).

More importantly, stress religious leaders, *Sunday elections would repudiate America's Christian heritage.* As Pastor Joseph C. Morecraft, III, has written: "From our very beginning we have respected the sanctity of The Lord's Day which God's law has placed on that day. These bills are a blatant, audacious disregard for Christian morality. It would mean the uprooting of an established Christian moral order in this country, and the replacing of it with a moral order that is rooted in pragmatism and in the findings and preferences of human experience. . . . The United States will not exempt itself, cannot exempt itself, from the judgment of God if it disregards the day which God has declared is His to be kept holy throughout all time."

"The enactment of a Sunday election law will strike a further blow at the work of the churches. Such intrusions always create unusual absenteeism from the churches and their schools. What the churches are seeking to do for our nation is not only important, it is essential, it is needed as never before. . . . we do not need less teaching of spiritual values, but more." (Dr. Samuel A. Jeanes, "Whose Side Are The Politicians Really ON?")

Dr. Jeanes points out that Sunday-elections would have effect of *reducing number of days each year* in which churches reach largest audience with Biblical principles, and would diminish number of days on which major portion of dedicated gifts are received *to finance evangelism, education, and missions.*

"There is one aspect of America's Christian heritage that most of us today are unaware of. *The English 'pilgrim' exiles who left the Netherlands for the New World in 1620 came here so that they could have the freedom to keep The Lord's day holy as the law of God demands."* They were the first to attack the riotous manner in which the English celebrated certain religious festivals. "In 1618, James I of England made life difficult for the Puritans by his 'Book of Sports' in which he encouraged Sunday athletics and Sunday dancing. It was also his wish that 'the bishop of the diocese take the like straight order with all the Puritans either constraining them to conform themselves or leave the country.' " (*Morecraft*, "A New Assault on The Sabbath"). "The human reasons for leaving Leyden (Netherlands) . . . were many and forcible. . . . (the Pilgrims) were pained by the open

profanation of the Sabbath day prevalent among the
Dutch. So rife was this evil that even the Dutch
ministers deplored their inability to keep their people
away from Sunday sports and labour . . ." ("Pilgrim
Fathers in New England," *John Brown, D. D.,*
Revell, 1895.)

Pilgrims and Puritans and most early American
Christians were *Scripturists.* For them, The Bible was
truly the book of life; God's laws were the laws by
which they governed themselves and their public
(civil) affairs. It was much the same in the Virginia
Company's Jamestown where the penalty for neglect
of the Sabbath was severe. God's Fourth Commandment was obeyed; the Christian sabbath was
"remembered" *(Ex. 20:8)* — it was kept holy.
"Sunday," wrote Alexis de Tocqueville, "is rigorously
observed (in America) . . . Public opinion, much
stronger than the law, obliges everyone to show himself at church and abstain from all diversions." Sabbath laws were commonplace in early America;
many remained on books far into 19th Century.

Keeping the Christian sabbath (Sunday) is recognized in the Constitution of the United States, *Article 1, Section 7 (2): "If any bill shall not be returned by the
president within ten days (Sunday excepted) after it shall
have been presented to him, the same shall be a law, in like
manner as if he had signed it. . . ."*

In *Connecticut,* legislature passed law tht
employer could *not* force employes to work on the
Sabbath, holding that to do so would be to violate
the individual's freedom of worship. *State Supreme
Court decreed law was unconstitutional,* held that it pro-

vided preferential treatment on the basis of religon. US Dept. of Justice now seeking to reverse the State court's decision.

Akin to move toward Sunday elections is call for *repeal of laws that prohibit business-as-usual on Christian sabbath.* Seven-day-week entreprenuers invoke "free enterprise." Opponents of desecrating Sabbath endorse free enterprise but insist it is not a hunting license to wipe out traditional moral standards. Void of Christian ethic free enterprise is humanistic, ultimately equates with law of jungle. (It was, for example, unbridled and irresponsible "free enterprise" that fostered child labor; it was Christian ethic that impelled men to push for child-labor laws to end such abuse.)

The foundation for our social structures," writes Dave Haigler in *Dominion Forum,* "must be the law of God, especially as we see it summarized in the Ten Commandments. Embodied in the Fourth Commandment is a recognition of men's need for a day of rest and worship. It is a merciful provision, with special notice given to the needs of men who labor in service to others."

In sum, this: *"Choose you this day whom you will serve."* God? or, mammon? Where your treasure is, there will your heart—and your laws—be also.

CONSIDER THE BIBLICAL PRINCIPLES God's word instructs us to "remember" the Lord's Day "to keep it holy" *(Ex. 20:8-10).* Christians have two reasons to keep the Sabbath: 1) because God The Creator and Sovereign commanded and, 2), as a memorial of the resurrection of Him who died and rose again that we might have life (in essence, *"this do in remembrance of Me"*).

Whereas The Lord God instructed the Hebrews to keep the Sabbath because He blessed it and hallowed it *(Ex. 20:10)* and because God told them to keep it as a memorial to their deliverance from bondage in Egypt, we who are under the New Covenant are to keep The Lord's Day for expanded reasons. Consider this under the definition of "sabbath" in Webster's *1828 "American Dictionary of The English Language"*:

"SABBATH, n. 1. The day which God appointed to be observed by the Jews as a day of rest from all secular labor or employments, and to be kept holy and consecrated to His service and worship. This was originally the seventh day of the week, the day on which God rested from the work of creation; and this day is still observed by the Jews and some Christians as the sabbath. But the Christian church very early began and still continues to observe the first day of the week in commemoration of the resurrection of Christ on that day, by which the work of redemption was completed. Hence it is often called *The Lord's Day.* The heathen nations in the north of Europe dedicated this day to the sun, and hence their Christian descendants continue to call the day *Sunday.* But, in the United States, Christians have to a great extent discarded the heathen name and adopted the Jewish name sabbath."

(*Note:* While the pagans referred to Sun-day as the day of the sun, "Sun" is the inspired Hebrew name referring to The Messiah — the light of the world *(Malachi 4:2)*. Saturday was known as the day of Satur (Hebrew, "Stur"), a variation of the name, satan.)

Some suggest that Christians did not observe the Sunday sabbath until Constantine and the Roman Catholic church. Historical records indicate otherwise. In 140 A.D., 182 years before Constantine, Justin, the Martyr, clearly reported that the first day of the week (Sunday) was observed as the Christian sabbath: "On Sunday we held our joint meetings, for the first day of that on which having removed darkness and made the world, Jesus rose from the dead." (*Apology for The Christians,*" Vol. 2, p. 98).

The Lord's day speaks of resurrection, of redemption, of restoration. It is a reminder of the reaffirmation of the cancellation of sin-debt through the power of the precious Blood of The Lamb. The essence of the Christian sabbath is *true rest* — resting in the blessed assurance of salvation through the indescribable love of The Triune God. Sunday, then should be a day of rest and restoration for the Believer; a day of peace apart and away from the turmoil and trial of the world. *"Thou shalt not work"* (Ex. 20:10; Dt. 5:14). Works of mercy (healing, caring) and public safety (police, fire, heat, light and communications, etc.) and faith (preaching/teaching) must continue (*Josh. 6:1-5; Mt. 12:5, 11; John 5:5-23*).

The Lord's day, then, is to be a day of rest, or

restoration. Man needs rest, he must have rest to live. Yet, without Christ Jesus as his Savior there is no true rest, no real life.

The Lord's day is also to be kept holy (hallowed) —a day which is used to honor The Lord by studying His word-truth and proclaiming it, a day when knowledge is acquired and stored that it may be applied in all days *(Heb. 10:25)*. True, every day is His day and every day should be a holy day in that we live in Him and for Him; yet, in a very real sense, Christ is The Lord of The Lord's day; the Sabbath was made for Him (the true and perfect Word made flesh) and for His own, His redeemd *(Mark 2:27, 28)* . . . thus, it stands as a visible witness to the principle of regeneration that comes only through Him.

In a very real and definite way, keeping The Lord's day, recognizing it as holy, involves a root principle of self-and civil government: *the principle of God's sovereignty.* If we permit self, or State, to pre-empt The Lord's day we permit (sanction) usurpation of God's sovereignty and disobey His commandments; we put man's law (civil, economic, and social) above God's law. And, of transcendent importance, if we reject the Christian Sabbath, if we fail to keep it holy, we not only dishonor God, we reject the all-embracing truth of Christ's redemptive work by refusing to keep it in remembrance of Him and His love.

Honoring of The Lord's day—the Christian sabbath—does not mean simply an outward "show" of godliness *(II Tim. 3:5)*. Such a shallow, irreverent charade is to mock The Lord God and God will not be mocked. The keeping of His holy day is to be a deep, honest, total (wholesome) pouring forth of our love for Him, a manifestation of our delight in obedience to the word of God. (". . . not only they who profanely break, but they who keep it heavily and wearily, who find it rather a burden than a delight, may justly suspect that the love of God is not in them." Richard Leighton, "Whole Works," as cited by Roderick Campbell in *Israel and The New Covenant,* Pres. & Reformed Pub. Co., 1954).

Freedom from seven-days-a-week labor (slavery) was one of the reasons for the exodus *(Neh. 9:13, 14);* thus, the sabbath was a day of liberation and symbolized liberation just as the Christian sabbath symbolizes liberation (freedom from/victory over death) through Christ, our Liberator, our Redeemer.

Unnecessary work (buying and selling) should be prohibited *(Neh. -13:15-22).* Such prohibition is a mark of the nation that honors and obeys The Lord God. Given the state of the nation in this day, such prohibition is unlikely. However, it is not only possible but essential for Believers to refuse to desecrate The Lord's day — *as did His people of old. Thus, we set an example and make clear our testimony for The Lord* (Neh. 10:31).

Keeping The Lord's day, recognizing it as holy, involves one of the root principles of self and civil government in Christ: *the principle of God's sovereignty.* If we permit self, or State, to pre-empt The Lord's day, if we allow it to be rendered unto Caesar, we permit (sanction) usurpation of God's sovereignty; we allow man's laws (civil, social, economic) to be put above God's law. Thus, to break the 4th Commandment is also to break the 1st Commandment *(Ex. 20:3)*. Failure to keep The Lord's day holy is a form of robbery, of denying His property, and His authority. The nation that fails to keep His day, will it not pay for its sin just as Israel was required to pay for its refusal to keep (observe) a sabbath for God's earth *(II Chron. 36:21)*?

In his book, *Church & State in the United States,* Philip Schaff wrote (1888): *"Destroy our churches, close our Sunday-schools, abolish The Lord's Day, and our republic will become an empty shell, and our people would tend to heathenism and barbarism."* Did Schaff have a vision of this day in which we live and see The Lord's day ignored and dishonored? Perhaps, but in essence he was simply echoing the warning found in *Isaiah 58:13-14:*

> "If you turn away your foot from (i.e. turn away from keeping) the sabbath, from doing your pleasure on My holy day; and call the sabbath a delight, the holy of The Lord, honorable; and shall honor Him, not doing your own ways, nor finding your own pleasure, nor speaking your own words: Then shall you delight yourself in The Lord, and I will cause you to ride upon the high places of the earth and feed you with the heritage of Jacob your father: for the Mouth of The Lord has spoken it."

Thus, it would seem clear: in our desire and our Christ-centered word to restore America, it is vital that we who are His keep His day, keep it holy, keep it unto Him. And, if we will not how can we expect others to do so? If we will not honor The Lord's day, what does that do to our witness? God's word makes it crystal clear: *He honors those who honor Him.*

(Plymouth Rock acknowledges the following source materials that were invaluable in the preparation of this section: *The Necessity of Public Recognition of the Christian Sabbath,* Dr. Francis Nigel Lee; *Day of Rest Threatened,* David Haigler, Dominion Forum; *A New Assault on The Sabbath,* Joseph C. Morecraft, III, *The Institutes of Biblical Law,* R. J. Rushdoony.)

16

LOVE, MARRIAGE AND THE FAMILY

BACKGROUND BRIEFING Are traditional values of marriage and family kaput? Dead, or dying? Are they no longer important? Many women liberationists say so. Dr. Margaret Mead once predicted God's institutions of marraige and family were on the way out. The thrice divorced "high priestess" of anthropology declared *"In the past, a man and a woman could be married 30 years and still have something to say to each other. But this is not the way life is today. And, it's reasonable that married individuals should have recurrent choices in their marriage."*[1] Psychiatrist David Cooper denounced family as a *"secret suicide pact,"* "an ideological conditioning device in any exploitative society."[2] Meaning, apparently, that in an open society there would be no families.

Traditionaly, "family" has meant husband and wife (or father and mother and their children). Noah Webster's *1828 American Dictionary of The English Language* defined "family" as "1. . . . a household, including parents, children and servants . . . 2. Those who descend from one common progenitor (forefather) . . . Thus, Israelites were a branch of the family of

Abraham." *Webster's New Collegiate Dictionary* (1981) defines family as "a group of individuals living under one roof and usually under one head (household) . . . 5: the basic unit in society having as its nucleus two or more adults living together and cooperating in the care and rearing of their own or adopted children."

As Dr. Joel Nederhood observed, "family" today is often defined in *evolutionistic* terms: there is something, some unit, called "a family" but term does not always refer to traditional standards; often embraces/promotes open-ended *"social relationships."*[3] The "traditional" family has in many cases become the "extended" family encompassing homosexual "marriages," unwed partners, group relations and mate-swapping.

In Communist China, State's planned parenthood rules permit one child per urban couple, two for rural families. Since son is seen as worker and provider for aged parents, female babies — generally less wanted — are abandoned or disposed of. Reports from inside Red China reveal harrowing testimony of gynecologists who admit: "Our work is midwifery and murder. Just before child's head appears we must give lethal injection on its head. If a woman has a first child we act as midwives. If she has a second, we must kill it. This is our work and the orders which we have to carry out." (Inside Mainland China, July 1984)

Is family-control unique to Communist China? Michigan Alliance of Families (MAF) raised fears a proposal in that State could contain seeds of similarity. MAF reports State plan called for establishment of

K-12 "genetic education," regional "genetic clinics" and "genetic disease control" centers to prevent birth of handicapped, retarded or "defective" infants. Plan also called for health education curriculum including classroom discussion of all "types" of "families"—lesbian, homosexual, communal, etc. Thus, warned MAF, traditional (Biblical) concept of family would be just one type of family. (For further information on Michigan plan, write MAF, P O Box 241, Flushing, MI 48433.)

In Washington State, juvenile courts were authorized to take child from home if "conflict" between parents and child could not be resolved by "counselling." Parents could be summoned for (a) forbidding child to attend movies, (b) spanking disobedient child, (c) instructing child in religious faith, (d) sending child to Christian school. (*In Sweden,* similar laws. There, in 1982, State took 12,000 children from parents under *Youth Care Act.* Young marrieds largest group seeking to leave that nation to avoid such State intrusion and control.) Thus, parental authority is pre-empted by State and thus family structure is invaded and weakened. One of top priority goals of socialists in subverting a nation is destruction of the family as the basic unit.

How goes the family in these United States?

From 1970-75, the number of unmarried couples *more than doubled.* Today in USA 1.5 million unmarried couples are living together as "families."[4] Number of *single-parent* families in USA has *doubled* since 1970. In 1981, 21% of 31.5 million families with children were headed by single parent (90% of them women).

Families headed by *unwed mothers* increased from 234,000 in 1970 to more than 1 million in 1981 (up 350%). Number of families *headed by divorced women* rose from 956,000 in 1970 to almost 2.7 million in 1981.[5] It is estimated that 45% of the babies born in 1976 will be living with a single parent before they reach age 18. According to Dr. Harold Voth, formerly of the Menninger Clinic, by yr 2000, one-half of young Americans will not have grown up in traditional families. Emphasized Dr. Voth, strong families build strong nations. He warned *Equal Rights Amendment* (ERA) would propel us into "gender free" society. "Differences between men and women will be erased and the heterosexual bond will be weakened. *A weak nation never lasts long.*"[6]

In 1900, for every 1,000 population in US there were 9.3 marriages and only .7 divorces. Rates held fairly firm, increasing to 12 marriages and 2 divorces per 1,000 population in 1940. After dip during '60s (to 8.5/1,000) marriage rate increased slightly in 1970s. For 1982, Census Bureau counted 2.49 million marriages (10.8 per 1,000 population).[7]

Is USA godly nation? *Not when it comes to divorce.* In past 50 yrs, number of divorces in US *has soared 700%.*[8] Today, US has *highest* divorce rate in world: Italy has lowest. In 1982 in USA, one divorce for every two marriages; a total of 1.2 million divorces (5 divorces every 1,000 persons in nation).[9] *When both husband and wife are faithful Christians* (one in Christ) *surveys indicate likelihood of divorce is only 1 in 1525.*[10]

With weakening of family, comes other tragedies. *Teen age pregnancy* rate in USA one of highest in Western world; 40% of teen age mothers are 17 or younger.[11] One out of every 3 babies born in the city of New York in 1983 was born out of wedlock. More than one-fourth of those births were to women 19 or younger.[12]

Reagan Administration, in support of parental rights and responsibilities, said federally-funded family planning clinics must advise parents when teenage daughters given birth control prescriptions (including advice about abortion). Some 60 groups banded together to fight regulation; charged it was invasion of child's privacy. Supporters insisted parents have right to know about child's activities in such areas, and right to know about prescriptions that might affect child's health and future. *Courts disagreed; outlawed regulations.*

Premarital sex rates for women *more than doubled, 1930-71,* then rose to new high in 1976. During 1935-49, 12% of women who were first married between ages 14 to 29, had already birthed a child out of wedlock or were pregnant when married; by 1965-79, that figure doubled to 24%. Today, almost 30% of women under 30 who marry for first time are pregnant at the altar.[13] Sociologists O'Connell & Rogers suggest increasing numbers of births out of wedlock "reflect societal views and a lessening of the social stigma attached to bearing a child outside of marriage."[14]

But, check abortion statistics. Despite drop in 1983, still running about *1.5 million each year!* And, this: *76.9% of abortions performed on unwed mothers* — and *64.7% on women under 25* yrs of age.[15]

1965-75 witnessed most recent and perhaps most drastic *sexual revolution*. What brought it on? Some blame drugs, the "Pill," rejection of traditions, destablizing impact of Viet Nam. Others say, *"No, those were not causes, those were effects."* They cite these forces: *humanism in State education,* pervasive and pernicious effects of *debt economy and inflation, and "liberalism"* of '50s and '60s.

Education: After WWII, humanists increasingly dominated public school system. Produced hedonistic, narcissistic *"ME" generation seeking self-gratification.* Dr. Joel Nederhood contends educational "techniques used are designed and intended to alienate children from their parents both as loving authority figures and as teachers of traditional value systems. . . . Children are taught that parents who disagree with humanistic ideas are *old-fashioned* . . . (and are) taught *self-gratification; amorality and non-responsibility."* "It should be obvious to all of us that the current viewpoints regarding human sexuality *do not* strengthen the family . . . *disregard of Biblical teaching concerning the sacredness of marriage* . . . (viewing) high school students as people with rights of their own as far as sexual expression is concerned. They are *expected* to be sexually active . . . *sex is* (taught as) *a plaything."*[16] Sex education is generally devoid of moral values, concentrates on method and contraception, including abortion. (See "Sex Education and Values Manipulation")

". . . perhaps the most deadly assault on the family ever mounted was *the compulsory school attendance scheme.* Here the school was raised as a center of the public order which displaced the family. . . . Today the school-centered order is being forced with a militancy and evil intent that cannot but raise alarm." Rev. T. Robert Ingram, D.D.[17]

Government: In addition to State laws and regulations, Federal government intrudes. "Year Of The Child" brought further efforts to transfer parental rights to (a) child and/or (b) public agencies. US House of Representatives, in 1983, voted to form "Select Committee on Children, Youth and Families." Already 13 House Committees on children and youth.

Economics: Socio-economists have tied weakened family and rise in juvenile delinquency to spiral of inflation. Government binge of debt-and-deficits, mounting inflation and taxation, and swings into recession, forced many women out of home into laborforce to make ends meet. *Since 1950, number of mothers working outside home has tripled.* Only 12 percent of households have breadwinning father and fulltime home-maker mother. 26.3 million married couples (62% of all marrieds) have two incomes (i.e. both husband and wife are wage earners).[18]

Some *33 million children* in US have mothers who work full time. In 1983, 33% of mothers with babies *under 7 months* were employed outside the home and some 5 million children *under age of 5* were in some type of child care program.[19] Expected that by yr 2000, some 80% of married women will work outside home.[20]

Balancing demands of home and career a growing dilemma for mothers working outside home.

Biblical role of wife and mother often takes second place. Thus, home and family weakened. Congressman Jack Kemp (NY) wrote, in eyes of the liberals *"Washington is both father and mother to American family."*[21] Insists best thing to do to help families in economic (and thus social) area is to curb inflation and reduce taxes so parents can increase income and more mothers can stay home to care for children. Many mothers look to "cottage" industries (doing various types of work at home) to supplement incomes while staying home with children. Labor unions oppose that, say it violates labor laws and is "front" for sweatshop operations.

Liberalism: Sexual revolt and permissiveness spawned (encouraged) by rising liberal tide during '60s. Leftward swings were evident in most areas of national fabric during those years. Now, flotsam and jetsam of that period is cast up on nation's social and economic beaches. *People are reassessing,* says Ann Clurman of pollsters Yankelovich, Skelly & White. *"They are moving away from extremes."*[22] Daniel Yankelovich sees turn away from sexual adventurism as "part of a larger phenomenon of society going through a sober, responsible phase."

CONSIDER THE BIBLICAL PRINCIPLES   Both marriage and family were ordained by The Lord God. "And The Lord God said, It is not good that the man should be alone; I will make him a help meet for him." "And the rib which The Lord God had taken from man, made He a woman, and brought her unto the man. And Adam said, This is now bone of my bones, and flesh of my flesh: she shall be called Woman, because she was taken out of Man. Therefore shall a man leave his father and his mother, and shall cleave unto his wife: and they shall be one flesh" *(Gen. 2:18, -22-24)*. "What therefore God has joined together, let not man put asunder: *(Mark 10:9)*. Christ performed His first miracle at a wedding in Cana of Galilee *(John 2:3)*. His presence at the wedding indicated His blessing and His approval.

Marriage is a life-long covenant. "For the woman who hath a husband is bound by the law to her husband so long as he lives; but if the husband be dead, she is loosed from the law of her husband" *(Rom. 7:3; see also Malachi 2:14-15; Eph. 5:31)*. The one-flesh relationship of husband and wife is sacred; it typifies the unified and everlasting relationship between Christ and His church *(Eph. 5:24-32)*.

Marriage is the only moral sexual outlet. Pre-marital or extra marital sex is *unholy and forbidden by The Lord*. "Nevertheless, to avoid fornication, let every man have his own wife, and let every woman have her own husband. Let the husband render unto the wife due benevolence (her due): and likewise also the wife unto the husband." "Defraud (deprive) not one the other, except it be with consent for a time, that you may give yourselves to fasting and prayer; and come together again, that Satan tempt you not for your incontinence" *(1 Cor. 7:2, 3, 5)*. (Note: fornication includes every manner of sexual sin.)

God's word clearly states that husband is to be the head of the house. But, He is not to abuse this station (that the wife is subordinate does not mean she is inferior for she is equal in God's sight). "But I would have you know that the head of every man is Christ; and the head of the woman is the man; and the head of Christ is God" *(1 Cor. 11:3)*. "Wives, submit yourselves unto your own husbands, as unto The Lord. For the husband is the head of the wife, even as Christ is the head of the church; and He is the Savior of the body. Therefore as the church is subject unto Christ, so let the wives be to their own husbands in every thing. Husbands, love your wives, even as Christ also loved the church and gave Himself for it . . . So ought men to love their wives as their own bodies" *(Eph. 5:22-28; see also Gen. 3:16; 1 Peter 3:1-9)*.

As head of the household, God places definite responsibilities on the husband. Too many men fail in these and thus force the wife to fill a role which is assigned to her spouse. "But if any provide not for his own, and specially for those of his own house, he hath denied the faith, and is worse than an infidel" *(I Tim. 5:8)*. "And, ye fathers, provoke not your children to wrath: but bring them up in the nurture and admonition of The Lord" *(Eph. 6:4; see also I Cor. 14:34, 35)*.

The Christian woman's goal, in light of God's Word, is to prepare for a Christian marriage, to be a strong and loving Christian wife and mother and in all things a living witness to the love and power of Jesus Christ. "That they may teach (train) the young women to be sober (responsible), to love their husbands, to love their children, To be discreet, chaste, keepers at home, good, obedient to their own husbands, that the word of God be not blasphemed" *(Titus 2:4, 5: see also I Tim. 5:14)*.

God's word makes it very clear that children are given, by Him, to parents, not to the State; that *children are to be trained by the parents,* not the State *(Gen. 28:3; 33:5; Pr. 22:6; 4:1-5)* — "hear, ye children, the instruction of a father, and attend to know understanding"). In The Bible, the word, "father" does not mean the State.

God desires that His own (Christian parents) have several children; His command that we are to be fruitful and multiply has not been rescinded (Gen. 1:28). "Lo, children are an heritage of The Lord: and the fruit of the womb is His reward. As arrows are in the hand of a mighty man; so are children of your youth" *(Ps. 127:3-5).*

God counsels children to discipline their children; the parent who truly loves and cherishes the children God has given will correct them and guide them, and help them gain wisdom in The Lord *(Pr. 13:24; 23:13; 29:15).* True and godly love includes leading the child in the path of The Lord and protecting him or her from those who would separate them from Jesus Christ. In God's family unit, the proper exercise of parental authority is an act of love; such authority is not to be turned over to, or usurped by the State: the father is to govern the home.

Children who obey their parents are pleasing to The Lord *(Col. 3:20). Children are to honor their parents, to obey them, and to provide for them.* "Children, obey your parents in The Lord, for this is right. Honor your father and your mother; which is the first commandment with promise; That it may be well with you, and you may live long on the earth" *(Eph. 6:1-3;*

see also *I Tim. 5:4*).

As Abraham, Isaac and other Old Testament servants of God sought to please Him by choosing their mate from God's own people, so *Christians are to marry Christians. We are not to be unequally yoked in marriage with unbelievers (II Cor. 6:14-18; I John 1:7;* see also *Ps. 1:1; Amos 3:3; I Cor. 5:33). Further, one looks in vain to find "dating" in the Scriptures! Dating is yoking, unequal yoking is disobedience to God (Heb. 6:4-6).* Marriage with the guidance of parents is God-ordained *(Dt. 7:3; Jer. 29:6; Gen. 38:6,* etc.). *Christians should seek and rely on God's direction,* not physical attraction, *in choosing mate. I Cor. 7:36-38,* indicates parents' approval should be obtained before children marry. The blessing of parents is vital to the well-being and destiny of a child and his children. *(re Jacob and Esau).* A marriage will never really be what it could and should be without the enthusiastic blessing of parents involved.

NOTE: Plymouth Rock Foundation recognizes, with gratitude, the invaluable assistance of PASTOR RONALD E. WILLIAMS of *Hephzibah House,* a Christ-Centered ministry for troubled girls, 508 School St., Winona Lake, IN 46590.

RECOMMENDED READING: *Growing Up God's Way,* John A. Stormer, Liberty Bell Press, Florissant, MO 63062, *The Christian Home As It is In The Sphere of Nature and The Church,* Rev. S. Phillips (1859), pp. 4-51, *Teaching and Learning America's Christian History,* Foundation for American Christian Education, San Francisco CA 94132.

Notes

1. As quoted in St. Louis (MO) *Globe Democrat*, 7/9/84.
2. *Time*, 4/9/84, p. 75.
3. *Education For The Family*, The Back To God Hour, 9/26/82.
4. Natnl. Center for Health Statistics, Public Health Service.
5. *Idem.*
6. *Natnl Right To Life News*, 8/78.
7. Natnl Center For Health Statistics.
8. *Idem.*
9. *Idem.*
10. *Growing Up God's Way*, John A. Stormer, Liberty Bell Press, p. 164.
11. Stat. Abstract, US Bureau Labor Statistics.
12. UPI, Manchester (NH) *Union-Leader*, 4/26/84.
13. *Idem.*
14. *Parade Magazine*, 6/24/85. p. 21.
15. Natnl Center for Health Statistics.
16. Dr. Joel Nederhood, *op. cit.*, pp. 10, 11.
17. "Erosion of The Family," *The Christian News Encyclopedia*, p. 931.
18. "Woman Power," *Parade Magazine*, 5/27/84, p. 16.
19. "She's Come A Long Way," *USN&WR*. 8/6/84. p. 48.
20. Dr. Harold Voth, *op. cit., National Right To Life News*.
21. *Washington Post Natnl Weekly Edition*, 8/20/84, p. 29.
22. *Time*, 4/9/84. p. 76.

17

MAKING COVENANTS WITH GOD'S ENEMIES

BACKGROUND BRIEFING *Ninety-five percent* of technology used by Soviet military-industrial complex came from the West—especially the United States. That's the claim made by *Anthony Sutton*. The basis for his assertion? Detailed documentation based on extensive research (3-vol. *Western Technology and Soviet Economic Development*) And, an Asst. Secy of Defense estimates 150 Soviet weapons systems (including SS-20 missiles now threatening Western Europe) incorporate US-developed technology.

Asks author *Steven V. Cole,* "When the history of this century is written, will the United States be seen as a nation that sold its enemies the means with which to destroy it?"

August 31, 1983: Soviet interceptor plane shot down unarmed *Korean Air Lines Flight #007.* Murdered: 269 innocent victims including *US Congressman Larry McDonald.* (Experts subsequently testified before Congress *plane was downed by Soviet missile* closely modelled on US Sidewinder missile and utilizing parts and technology developed in USA. Sidewinder is highly advanced item in US arsenal.)

Says Joel Skousen, *"I believe American corporations who contributed to the missile technology that killed these people should feel the anger of the American people . . . There never will be a better time to raise the issue of 'technological treason' . . ."* (*At White House,* after shoot-down of Flight 007, top aides decided not to cancel okay of sale of pipeline equipment to Soviets. *Might lose votes in Peoria,* home of Caterpillar, maker of that equipment. Licensing restrictions were lifted at request of president of Caterpillar so that firm could resume sales to USSR.)

Reported *Don Bell:* Even while US Marines were being killed in Beirut by Soviet/Syrian-backed Druze, *US Secy of Ag John Block* and US agribusinessmen and farm equipment mfgrs. were *in Moscow selling combines, reapers and other farm machinery . . .* and making plans *to finance and construct factories in USSR* for manufacture of other farm equipment, etc.

President Reagan assails Soviet Union as "focus of evil" in modern world; insists he "has significantly slowed the transfer of valuable free world technology to the Soviet Union." *Commerce Dept data reveal increase in all types of trade with Soviets*—plus continued bailouts on loan defaults, etc. Columnist *William Safire* reports Reagan Administration *opened "floodgates" of trade.* Wrote Safire: *"it's not merely 'business as usual' (with USSR) but more business than ever."*

In 1981, US exports to Communist bloc nations

totalled $6.5 billion. US exports to Soviets *under Carter, $2.2 billion/yr; under Ford, $1.9 billion/yr; under Nixon, $442 million/yr. Under Reagan, exports have averaged $2.5 billion/yr* (not including $10 billion grain deal signed Aug. '83). In past 2½ yrs, US Export-Import Bank authorized *$620 million in new credits to Soviet bloc;* that's an increase of 45% over the last two years of Carter Admin. More than $100 billion has been loaned to communist nations by West. Warns Congressman Ron Paul (TX), much of that money can be used indirectly to finance revolution in the Caribbean and Central America. The Communist nations now owe US banks more than *$70 billion* (should debtors default, taxpayers pick up tab). Congress recently voted *$8.4 billion more for International Monetary Fund* (IMF), *did not restrict* use of that money to non-Communist govts.

In Nov., '83, Congress approved $25 billion foreign aid bill — *after deleting language to prevent any funds going to Communist nations.* That was two months after confirmed reports that Soviet troops had *slaughtered 105 Afghani women and children* by trapping them in an underground irrigation channel and set them on fire.

USA's Ex-Imp Bank also okayed *$100 million in new credits (and promised more aid and hi-tech sales) to Communist China.* In addition, Washington okayed *import of $800 million of textiles from Red China* even as US textile industry struggles vs. foeign imports and tries to recover from recession.

Leonid Brezhnev, late pres of USSR, explained détente to the Warsaw pact nations: *"We need their*

(US and Western world) *credits, their technology and their agriculture."* Why? Because said Brezhnev, *"we are going to continue massive military programs and by the middle 80's we will be in a position to return to a much more aggressive foreign policy designed to gain the upper hand . . ."*

Richard Nixon, in his latest book, *Real Peace,* points out that following the Russian revolution (1918) Western corporations rushed to do business with USSR. *Wrote Nixon:* "That first round of economic cooperation in the 1920s did not bring the West and the Soviets closer together. It did help turn the Soviet Union into a much stronger adversary. . . . *by trading with an aggressive, expansionist power you are fueling a fire that could eventually consume you."* (Italics added for emphasis).

And, consider *Smoot-Hawley Tariff Act* of 1930. It *prohibits importation of products from any country if products manufactured by slave labor.* US Customs Commissioner *William von Rabb* recently tagged at least 36 different Soviet imports made by forced labor. von Raab asked *SecState George Shultz* to ban importation. (Committee for Defense of Human Rights in Soviet Union claims *at least 1,200,000* prisoners serving long-terms in USSR slave labor camps.) To date, Shultz has *failed* to act on von Raab's recommendation.

Proponents of trade with USSR say it's key part of *building/promoting détente.* "Rubblehappy" businessmen engage in a propaganda campaign to legitimize US-USSR trade, reported Washington weekly, *Human Events.* Group attacks any sactions against the enemy.

In 1981, Brezhnev boasted: *"We are achieving with détente what our predecessors have been unable to achieve using the mailed fist."* V. I. Lenin put the matter in (Soviet) focus:

> *"The capitalists of the world and their govts, in pursuit of . . . the Soviet market, will close their eyes to the higher reality and thus will turn into deaf-mute blindmen. They will extend credits, which will strengthen . . . the Communist party . . . and, giving us the materials and technology we lack, they will restore our military industry, indispensable for our future victorious attack on our suppliers. In other words, they will labor for the preparations for their own suicide."*

CORPORATIONS DOING BUSINESS WITH THE USSR

Listed here are some of the major American firms that have sold or helped sell vital technological equipment or have had science and technology transfer contracts with the Soviet Union.

ALLEN-BRADLEY (machine tools), ARMCO STEEL, BECHTEL (construction), BOEING, BORG-WARNER (machine tools), CHASE MANHATTAN BANK (loans and financial arrangements), CLARK EQUIPMENT (machine tools), CONTROL DATA (advanced computers), DOW CHEMICAL, EL PASO NATURAL GAS (gas technology), EXXON, GENERAL DYNAMICS (aeronautical technology), GENERAL ELECTRIC, GULF OIL [James E. Lee, Chairman of Board, claims a personal relationship with God: "I turn to His Word every day for guidance and inner strength .`.`." *Gulf,* along with TEXACO, MOBIL AND CITIES SERVICE, is *major proponent of US trade with Marxist Angola,* a "Communist surrogate"], HEWLETT PACKARD, HONEYWELL (computers), TEXRON, UNION CARBIDE, XEROX (electronics).

For a more complete list of corporations doing business with Soviet bloc nations, write to Joel Skousen, Conservative National Committee, 450 Maple Ave., Suite 310, Vienna, VA 22180.

Those pushing trade with Soviets argue "if we don't sell it to them, someone else will" and insist such trade bolsters US economy/employment. Business with devil is thus rationalized (see *Mt. 16:26*). The fruits of such rationale, according to Lenin? *"The bourgeoise* (citizens of free societies) *will sell us rope; and then we will let the bourgeoise hang itself."*

Sale of sensitive *hi-tech* equipment is especially *treacherous*. US is often *only* source; thus, to sell such unique and advanced equipment or know-how to Soviets is, as Skousen puts it, *"technological treason."*

Consider sales to Soviets of *just four types of hi-tech items*. These enabled USSR to develop both first-strike capabilities and advanced nuclear defense management system:

- Entire Soviet defense management system designed by and utilizes *American-made computers (IBM 370 and Control Data Corp's Cyber 73/76)*
- Latest generation of Soviet ICBM missiles could not operate without their *US-designed micro-chips and integrated systems* that insure reliability and pinpoint accuracy.
- *Centalign-B micro-precision ball-bearings* from US enabled USSR to perfect inertial guidance and separation systems for its multi-warheaded ICBM/MIRVs *(Bryant Chucking Grinding Co,)*
- State of the art *anti-submarine equipment* give Soviets capabilities that exceed those of the US *(Geospace Corp)*.

Advocates of trade with Moscow cry, *"free trade."* *Joel Skousen,* of Conservative Natnl. Committee, retorts: *"The right to defend oneself against an enemy of our freedom is a higher principle than the right of free trade."* Skousen urges: *stop trading with USSR and refuse to trade with any allied nation that trades with Soviets.* He emphasizes that in trade with Communists there can be *"no distinction between non-military and strategic items;"* concludes US corporations doing business with Soviets "(are) *clearly aiding an enemy of* (our) *freedoms."*

Recently Soviets boasted their latest-generation ICBMs are so accurate one travelled thousands miles and hit its target—*a small wooden peg.* How do they do it? Experts say purloined US technology. And, proliferation of *chemical and biological terror weapons by USSR?* US continues to export vital chemical and biological agents and gene-splicing data to Soviet-bloc nations *(Reader's Digest,* Sept., '84, pp. 54-58).

Soft trade with USSR policies are promoted by Secretaries *Shultz* (State), *Regan* (Treasury) and *Baldridge* (Commerce). And, Mr. Reagan continues to okay *sales of sophisticated oil and gas tools and technology.* Soviets badly need oil drilling and pumping eqpt., corrosion-resistant metallurgy, seismic and acoustical devices, etc., to develop oil fields and transmission lines to (a) replenish dwindling supplies and (b) forestall severe economic crises.

Former Asst. SecCommerce, *Lawrence Brady,* urged Reagan switch export control of such sensitive items from "liberal" State Dept. to tougher Dept. of Defense. Brady argued switch was justified (necessitated) on security grounds (*seismic* devices can be used to detect *submarines,* corrosion resistant metals can be used for *naval weapons,* etc.). State Dept. still in control; hard-liner Brady resigned to run for Congress (and has been replaced by a liberal, pro-McGovern Democrat).

Said *US Senator William Armstrong* (CO) in April, 1982: "The great irony for Americans who will be asked to tighten their belts in order to pay *($1.6 trillion)* for our defense needs is that much of the additional money . . . is required *to offset Soviet weapons that probably could not have been built without our assistance.* . . . In the last 10 years alone, the US and other Western nations have sold to the Soviet Union and its satellites more than $50 billion worth of sophisticated technical equipment *the Communists could not produce themselves.*"

CONSIDER THE BIBLICAL PRINCIPLES The followers of Jesus Christ are *in this world* to be His servants and His vice-regents *in the here and now.* We are to be effective in His work, thus we must be aware of and seek to exert a Godly influence on social, economic and (geo)political affairs and policies. And, because we are His and because He is our King, *we must give pre-eminence to Him and to His word* in all things and above all powers and must seek to influence elected officials to do the same.

What does God demand of His people in regard to those nations that are His enemies? What does He command regarding those that have set themselves against The Living God as a matter of their national policy? *This:*

"Should you help the ungodly, and love them that hate The Lord? Therefore is wrath upon you from before The Lord" *(II Chron. 19:2).*

"Surely You will slay the wicked, O God: depart from me therefore, you bloody men. For they speak against You wickedly, and Your enemies take Your name in vain. Do I not hate them, O Lord, that hate You? And am I not grieved with those that rise up against You? I hate them with a perfect hatred: I count them my enemies" *(Ps. 139:19-22).*

Those who are His are not to do business with or make covenants with God's enemies. Further, *God's people as a nation must not make or condone covenants with His enemies. . . .* for if we do, His wrath shall be upon us. To be yoked with the forces of evil *in any manner* is to disobey God. Such alliances and/or agreements deny His Supreme Sovereignty, place trust in the pacts and treaties of fallen men and place such alliances ahead of covenants with The King of Kings and His assured fruits of obedience. (Do not those who make agreements with the Soviet Union in essence put the Communist Manifesto on a par with, or even *above,* the *Christian Manifesto [Ps. 2, Acts 4:24-31]?*)

God's word would seem to make it very clear: His people are not to be yoked with or trust in those who compromise with God's enemies *(Ex. 23:32; Deut. 7:2; II Cor. 6:14).* To do so it to make "a covenant with death and with hell" *(Isa. 28:15).*

"I have hated them that regard lying vanities: but I trust in The Lord: *(Ps. 31:6)*. "It is better to trust in The Lord than to put confidence in man. It is better to trust in The Lord than to put confidence in princes (ungodly rulers/leaders)" *(Ps. 118:8, 9)*. "So are the paths of all that forget God; and the hypocrite's hope shall perish: whose hope shall be cut off, and whose trust shall be a spider's web" *(Job 8:13, 14)*.

Consider Ahab (I Kings 20-21). Ahab, king of Israel, was threatened by Benhadad, king of Syria, who demanded tribute. The elders and people of Israel urged Ahab not to give into Benhadad *because he had mocked The Lord God*. Ahab resisted Benhadad and, despite the superior size and power of Syrian forces and that of 32 kings who sided with Benhadad, *God gave Ahab and the tiny army of Israel a mighty victory.* Why? So that "ye shall know that I am The Lord" *(I Kings 20:28)*.

But: following victory, Ahab covenanted with Benhadad *(I Kings 20:34)*. Without so much as chastising Benhadad for his blasphemy against The Lord God, Ahab feted him, set him free, and allowed him to return to his own land rather than destroy him and his forces as The Lord God had commanded *(I Kings 20:42)*.

Our nation and its leaders would do well to take note: for disobeying God, and for making covenant with God's enemy, Ahab was eventually killed in battle and the Israelites were taken into captivity *(I Kings 20:42)*.

Consider, also, Hezekiah, a man who had walked with The Lord and had been mightily blessed. In victory and vanity, *Hezekiah entertained God's enemies and showed them his treasured possessions — including his armory (II Kings 20:12-17).* Thus said The Lord, "Behold, the days come, that all that is in your house, and all that which your fathers have laid in store unto this day, shall be carried into Babylon; nothing shall be left . . ."

Or, hearken to the case of *Asa, king of Judah. As* made covenant with the king of Syria, an idolator *who loved not The Lord.* Because of that, God condemned Asa and his people to a time of wars *(II Chron. 16:3-9).*

Who, today, is numbered among God's enemies? What political system denies God, and persecutes His people? *Surely — the USSR, The Soviet Union, Marxism, the Communist party,* as distinguished from the Russian people — *must be considered one of God's arch enemies.*

"The struggle agains the Gospel and Christian legend must be conducted ruthlessly and with all the means at the disposal of Communism." (Radio Leningrad, August 27, 1950).

Heed the words of V. I. Lenin: "ATHEISM IS A NATURAL AND INSEPARABLE PART OF MARXISM, OF THE THEORY AND PRACTICE OF SOCIALISM." And, these words of *Josef Stalin:* "WE HAVE DEPOSED THE CZARS OF THE EARTH; *WE SHALL NOW DETHRONE THE LORD OF HEAVEN."*

Is not the official Communist position plain? *The*

State is god. The One True God must bow to the Kremlin-god. Communism is *anti-Christ.*

> *"We hate Christians and Christianity. Even the best of them must be considered our worst enemies. Christian love is an obstacle to the development of the revolution. Down with love of one's neighbor! What we want is hate. . . . Only then can we conquer the universe."* (Lunarcharsky, Russian Commissioner of Education, quoted in US Congressional Record, Vol. 77, pp. 1539-1540)

Communism is one of the most virulent, most militant anti-Christian systems in the world today. It *denies God;* it *mocks God;* it *persecutes His people:*
In the USSR, *from 1918 to 1977, some 250,000 clergy were liquidated, 88,000 religious buildings were destroyed, $4 billion in church funds confiscated.* As early as 1975, TIME magazine reported that *"Though the plight of Soviet Jews and intellectuals is far better publicized in the West, Baptists have suffered every bit as much. At least 700 have been jailed and one civil rights leader reports that Baptists have comprised more than 1/3 of known political prisoners during the past two decades."*

COMMUNISM'S BLOODY RECORD

"And another, a red horse, went out; and to him who sat on it, it was granted to take peace from the earth, and that men should slay one another: and a great sword was given him" *(Rev. 6:4).* Consider the cost of Communism's red ride across the world:

Between *21-32 million* slaughtered as Communism was established in the USSR. *15,000 Poles* exterminated in the Warsaw uprising in 1944. In 1956 *Hungarian Revolt,* more than 15,000 were killed. In three years following Communist take over of *Czechoslovakia,*

152,000 Czechs were executed or sent to slave-labor camps and many died there. In *Lithuania, 1.2 million* were liquidated or deported during the first 15 yrs of Communist rule. *In China, more than 64 million* have lost their lives under Communism. In *Vietnam,* Communists killed 700,000 persons from 1953-59. In *Cambodia, between 1.2 and 2.5 million persons were murdered* in just two yrs of Communist mandated genocide. All told, between 150 and 200 million persons have been liquidated since that red horseman started its sweep across the earth . . . *"and a great sword was given him . . ."*

Since Marxists/Communists are avowed enemies of God, are they not also the enemies of God's people? How, then, can a nation whose President and Congress *proclaim 1983 "The Year of the Bible"* and acknowledge *"The Bible as 'the rock on which are republic rests' "*—how can such a nation permit its Chief Executives, its public officials, its business elite and its megabankers to make covenants that yoke the USA with its avowed enemy?

May we not see *a parallel between those who do business with the Soviets today and the money-changers and usurers in the time of Nehemiah?* Are they not similar to those who sought to profit from the citizens of Jerusalem who worked and sacrificed to rebuild the city's walls/defenses *(Neh. 5)*? And, did not Nehemiah find it necessary to "set a great assembly against" such men. Did he not realize, then,—and should we not realize, now,—that (as Micah wrote) "a man's enemies are the men of his own house" *(Neh. 7:6)*.

Because we have permitted such entites within our nation to trade with God's (and our) enemies, and because some have sought a false measure of security in such trade, have we not *"made lies our refuge and under falsehood"* hid ourselves *(Isa. 28:15)?* Thus warns The Lord: *"Shall not My Soul be avenged on such a nation as this?"* *(Jer. 5:9, 29).*

Rev. Joseph C. Morecraft, Chalcedon Presbyterian Church, Atlanta, GA, emphasizes that *Romans 13:3-4* "clearly indicates that the maintenance of a strong and effective defense program, sufficient to protect the citizenry from any lawless enemy, is essential to godly rule. *To do otherwise—to allow the nation's families to stand in a vulnerable position—is irresponsible and immoral."* A nation cannot be strong, it cannot effectively protect its people, when it does business with and makes covenants with God's enemies.

The apostle Paul points out *(Rom. 13)* that the State is given the power of the sword to be "a minister of God, an avenger who brings wrath upon the one who practices evil." Warns Rev. Morecraft: "A nation that sheaths that sword because of partiality . . . that sheaths it because of humanistic sentimentality . . . stands condemned by Almighty God." And, a nation that knowlingly undermines its own defenses (blunts its sword) by making and permitting covenants with God's enemy—*that nation will be held answerable by God just as surely as were Ahab,* and Asa, and Hezekiah . . . *and their people.*

> "Woe unto them that call evil good . . . that put darkness for light . . . Which justify the wicked for reward . . . Therefore as the fire devours the stubble, and the flame consumes the chaff, so their root shall be as rotteness, and their blossom shall go up as dust; because they

have cast away the law of the Lord of Hosts, and despised the word of the Holy One of Israel" *(Isa. 5:20-24).*

How then should God's people — those who would obey Him and serve Him — *seek true security?* With whom shall we make covenant for godly peace and safety?

"Now know I that The Lord saves His anointed; He will hear him from His holy heaven with a saving strength of His right hand. Some trust in chariots, and some in horses: but we will remember (rely on) the name of The Lord Our God" *(Ps. 20:6, 7).* "But if you shall indeed obey his voice, and do all that I speak; then I will be an enemy unto your enemies, and an adversary unto your adversaries" *(Ex. 23:20-22).*

REFERENCE SOURCES AND RECOMMENDED READING: *Conservative Digest,* Oct, 1983, pp. 19-33; *Don Bell Reports,* Nov. 4 and 11, 1983; *Globescan,* Oct 24, 1983, pp. 1, 2; Nov. 7, 1983, p. 10; Richard Nixon, *Real Peace,* Little Brown & Co., NY, 1983; *Afghanistan Informer,* Afghan Youth Council in America, Washington DC; Miles M. Costick, *The Economics of Détente and US-Soviet Grain Trade,* The Heritage Foundation, Washington, DC; *Congressman Ron Paul Reports.* "National Suicide," Nov. 23, 1983; *US News & World Report,* Nov. 28, 1983, p. 23; Joseph Finder, *Red Carpet,* Conservative Book Club; *Washington Inquirer,* Sept. 23, 1983; *Christian News Encyclopedia,* pp. 1619-1635; Jack Anderson and Dale Van Atta, "Poison and Plague: Russia's Secret Terror Weapons," *Reader's Digest,* Sept. 1984, pp. 54-58.

18

MILITARY CONSCRIPTION AND DRAFTING WOMEN

BACKGROUND BRIEFING Massachusetts and Virginia resorted to military conscription in 1777 during American War for Independence. *Other colonies rejected compulsory service, raised troops via local militia.* US Constitution provides for military conscription *via State militia* (ART I, Sec 8, xvi). Constitution also *limits draftees to domestic service to (1) uphold laws of the Republic, (2) put down insurrection, and (3) repel invasion* (ART I, Sec 8, xv).

Both North and South used military conscription (draft) during war between States. In North, loopholes and public resistance held draftee total to 47,000 (98 federal draft "registrars" were killed in anti-draft riots.) In 1917, President Woodrow Wilson, backed by US Supreme Court, was *first to send draftees into battle on foreign soil.*

First peacetime draft enacted in 1940 and extended in 1941, then continued through World War II. In 1946, Congress extended draft to 1947; then let it lapse.

Second peacetime draft come in 1948. Selective Service System put on skeleton basis and then expanded for Korean and Vietnam. *Draft was then allowed to expire in 1972.*

President Jimmy Carter called for *registration for draft* on Jan. 23, 1980. All men reaching age of 18 now must register with Selective Service. *President Carter's draft registration order included women* (see below). He stated pre-draft registration would (1) serve notice on USSR that US was prepared to halt further Soviet expansion and (2) would cut lead time for Selective Services process in event of emergency mobilization.

Reagan administration *continued* pre-draft registration; co   *have held young men receiving Federal funds for education must register for draft or lose loan or grant.*

Opponents charged registration was a ploy, a sop to calm mounting public concern over executive ineptitude. Some saw it as *first step toward easing nation into third peacetime draft;* argued what was needed was not gimmicks or draft but backbone and consistency in defense and foreign policies. As for speeding up mobilization if and when needed, opposition contended studies had shown first inductees could be delivered to training centers within 25 days of call; that regular military, national guards and reserve could hold the fort for that period, and that armed service could not digest a greater influx any more rapidly.

Advocates of peacetime draft contended all-volunteer forces not working; said services could not meet quotas for required standing forces. Opponents responded better to take funds from the $7 billion

to battle is from The Lord God and not from the would-be gods of this world, or the fruit of ungodly ambition of evil design. We must earnestly seek His will in prayer and meditation and be guided by His word, written and revealed.

God's word makes it clear, also, that *only defensive wars may be justified* in His sight. We are not to aggress or molest the rights of others. Defending ourselves against injurious attack is a far different matter than rendering evil, or even rendering evil for evil.

We could not suppose that God would shed His divine providence on those who seek to defend His gift of liberty (as The Bible demonstrates that He has done and will do) if defensive war were inconsistent with His will or His law. Liberty is a trust committed to us by The Lord God; we are accountable for its use and are duty-bound to protect and preserve it.

If, however, the call to battle is clearly from men or forces of ungodly intent, if it is calculated (even covertly) to serve unrighteous cause (manipulated by agents foreign or domestic) then Godly Christians must search their hearts and take their stand: *There is another King, One Jesus!* Because we are His and know that we are accountable to Him, we must obey God rather than man *(Acts 5:29).* We must seek always to please Him rather than men *(Gal. 1:10).*

The Prophet Samuel foretold of unholy conscription when he urged the people of Israel not to reject God for an earthly king ("like all other nations"). *"They have not rejected you,"* God said to Samuel, *"they have rejected Me. Hearken unto them . . . (but) show them the manner of the king that shall reign over them"* (I Sam.

8:5-9). Thus, included in Samuel's warning was this: (1) *anti-Biblical military conscription* (outlawed under God's reign) would be enforced (for the king's purposes); (2) *compulsory labor forces* would also be enforced, and (3) conscription would include *both young men and young women* — and God will not hear their cries because they chose to worship and obey the god-state (Moloch) rather than The One True and Triune God *(I Sam. 8:11-18)*.

Therefore, we must weigh compulsory military conscription — and the potential drafting of young women — *on the scales of God's word* and measure our decisions on these matters *according to His perfect will and perfect laws.*

19

MONEY, MORALITY AND GOLD

BACKGROUND BRIEFING Over the yrs., sound money advocates have pushed for a return to *gold standard* and a disciplined currency. Opponents labelled gold a "barbarous" metal; tagged pro-gold spokesmen "gold bugs" and kooks. Now, as nation's fiscal turkeys come home to roost, money backed by intrinsic metals (gold, silver) looks more attractive. Rep. Jack Kemp (NY) says *"choice between two systems (gold vs. fiat money) is most crucial of our generation."*

Advocates of gold standard contend it would (1) force *monetary/fiscal discipline on govt and banks,* (2) *restore domistic confidence* in dollar, (3) stabilize purchasing power of dollar, (4) *lower interest rates* (and reduce cost of servicing private and public debt), (5) renew incentives to *save and invest,* (6) hasten solid *economic recovery,* and (7) regain *citizen's control over govt. spending and debt.*

Opponents say gold (or intrinsic metal) standard *unrealistic and unworkable;* argue there is too much "money" (paper dollars) outstanding, that it would be too difficult to switch. Vermont Royster, *Wall Street Journal* columnist, writes: "The problem with gold standard is not what so many allege, that is, that 'it won't work.' Quite the opposite. *It works very well indeed,* forcing a monetary discipline upon kings, dictators, parliaments and people." And, one might add, bankers, politicians, and bureaucrats; it would pull the plug on the money machine.

Proponents of gold standard say value US Treasury puts on US gold stock is unrealistic and at odds with open market price (about $350 and ounce, 9/24/84). As for any "run" on the metal if gold standard were reinstituted, they insist that once public knew for sure dollar was *backed by gold,* people would rely on "good as gold" paper receipts (gold notes). As for price (value) of gold, free market should set that; money, after all, is simply a commodity.

Opponents contend there is no need for gold or silver standard, that "monetary management" is a science now, can *"fine tune"* the system, *curb inflation,* and allow for economic growth. Gold standard advocates point to miserable record of "managed" fiat money, say it has been tried, and found disastrous. Look at US record:

1690 — Mass. Bay Colony issued non-convertible (irredeemable) currency; by 1714, purchasing power of paper money *dropped 70%*. *1775* — Continental Congress issued unbacked paper money; four yrs later, value of those dollars was worth 1/1,000th of purchasing power of gold (thus, *"not worth a Continental"*). *1862* — US issues irredeemable paper money, consumer prices *more than doubled in three yrs*.

1934—FDR decreed foreigners could redeem dollars for gold but US citizens could not; *inflation jumped to 7% a yr, unemployment ranged from 14% to 25%* until start of World War II. And, say "gold bugs," look what happened when Nixon completely uncoupled dollar from gold— *purchasing power of dollar dropped and price of gold went up.*

Gold advocates contrast that sorry record with yrs when US was on gold standard. *After war between States,* US returned to gold standard and prices returned to pre-war levels. Over next 25 yrs, *inflation averaged about 1% a yr.* Period from *1879-1914 was era of "classic gold standard"*—"unprecedented economic growth, productivity, and innovation." And, when gold convertibility was restored in 1944, tax rates were cut by 1946, real GNP expanded, inflation dropped from WWII high of 20% to 0, and federal budget was balanced in five of the seven yrs between 1945-'52. Also, as Malcom A. Forbes, Jr., noted, the boom period of 1950-60 occured under so-called Gold Exchange Standard. Forbes points out that longest recession/depression cycles took place while US was off gold standard and that while gold standard was in effect, such down cycles were much shorter.

"Conventional" economists ("monetarists" such as Milton Friedman and also Keynesians such as Yale Univ's. James Tobin) strongly *oppose gold standard.* Dr. Friedman insists "we are on a path toward monetary discipline" already. Not so, counter pro-gold spokesmen: *growth of big govt. has not been halted,* only slowed—and already politicians are caving into militant special interest groups that "demand" their "rights." *Lewis Lehrman,* one of few pro-gold members of US Gold Commission appointed by Pres. Reagan, asserts *irredeemable currency always accompanied by deficits, inflation and high interest rates.* Unbacked money, says Lehrman, is "handmaiden of war, protectionism and big govt" (no nation ever went to war without debasing its currency). Rep. Kemp argues return to gold standard is vital to success of Reaganomics, says program will not work without redeemable currency.

For all its merits, *gold standard is not a panacea.* Economist *Henry Hazlitt* warns, gold *"is not important as an isolated gadget but only as an integral part of a whole economic system* . . . govts (must) respect private property, economize in spending, balance their budgets, keep their promises, and refuse to connive in overexpansion of money or credit."

Unless govt. is prepared to return to such a system, and prove that by its deeds, continues Hazlitt, it would be pointless to force it to on a real gold bases . . . "it would be off again in a few months. And, as in the past, the gold standard itself, rather than the abuses it destroyed, would get the popular blame."

F.Y.I.

SEPT. '84—Federal debt $1.5 trillion. Add state and local govt. and *debt. total exceeds $1.8 trillion.* In 1983, federal govt. spent $796 billion; up $68 billion over '82, up $139 billion over '81. Estimated that about *$200 billion of 1985 federal budget* will be deficit. Cost of servicing fed debt (interest) now *about 13% of total budget* . . . that's *$112 billion* and that's more than all US govts spent in 1955.

Since 1940, total govt. spending *(fed, state & local)* has zoomed from $20.4 billion to $1.8 trillion a yr. Biggest jumps came after Nixon *unhooked dollar from gold.* In 10 yrs, 1974-1984, federal spending rose from $267 billion to $796 billion and federal debt soared from $486 billion to $1.8 trillion. Rep. Ron Paul (TX) says here is grim story of 10 yrs of a dollar backed only by "politicians' promises": money supply up 186%; prime rate up 271%; Dow Jones, down 57%; bond mkt, down 61%; consumer prices, up 173%. *And, chew on this: American Institute of Economic Research* figures that from 1971-'83, *inflation embezzled about $3.3 trillion* (in lost purchasing power) *from savings accounts, insurance policies, annuities, pensions,* etc. That $3.3 trillion was equal to the total federal income taxes paid during those 12 yrs.

Between 1980-83, *most dramatic ever increase in money supply* — $28 billion in '80-'81; $36 billion in '81-'82, and $42 billion in '82-'82. That's an *increase of $107 billion* (24%) in three yrs.

Under President Reagan, rate of federal spending has slowed *but still going up.* Social Security (FICA) tax hike and TEFRA (Tax Equity and Fiscal Responsibility Act of 1982) have put fed's take higher than ever. *(TEFRA is largest tax increase in peacetime US history* — $218 billion over 5 yrs.) *National Journal* says: "No category of taxpayer will have significantly lower taxes in 1984 than in 1977." yet, many in Congress ignore building tax revolt and push for more spending . . . and tax reform (read that, tax increase). Investors not convinced federal spending or deficits will be reduced, see *higher interest rates and down-turn in economy coming in Spring of 1985* . . . every increase of 1% in unemployment means a $25 billion loss in federal revenues, increased federal spending—and increased deficits.

CONSIDER THE BIBLICAL PRINCIPLES In His holy and unchanging word, God established definite principles concerning money (the medium of exchange for goods and services). He sets forth weights and measures so that money will be an honest and dependable commodity *(Ezek. 45:9-12).*

Before coins were struck (and long before paper currency was used as a "warehouse receipt" for specie), various weights and measures of precious metals were accepted as media of exchange. *Gold and silver were used as the money of God's established govt.* (Hebrew Republic) *(2 Kings 12:13).* When coins were ˮ uck (gold and silver), the purchasing power of the coin was based upon definite weights of the metal used. True weight was essential because it insured that the metal was pure (fine gold, etc.) and that the coin had not been filed down or clipped. The names and denominations of the coins have changed but the principle remains the same: *whatever is used for money* (medium of exchange) *must be honest, must be of full value, must not be adulterated, and must be on constant and continuing* (fixed and permanent) *value.*

> *"A just weight and balance are The Lord's: all weights of the bag are His work"* (Pr. 16:11).

God warns us against deceit and dishonesty in money matters. *"Divers weights and divers measures, both of them are alike an abomination to The Lord"* Pr. 20:10.

> *"You shall do no unrighteousness in judgment, in meteyard, in weight of measure. Just balances, just weights, a just ephah* (bushel) *a just hin* (liquid measure), *shall you have"* (Lev. 19:35, 36). *"You shall not steal, neither deal falsely, neither lie to one another." "You shall not defraud your neighbor, neither rob him"* (Lev. 19:11, 13); see also Luke 6:38). *"You shall not have in your bag divers weights . . .*

*You shall not have in your house divers measures . . .
But you shall have a perfect and just weight, a perfect
and just measure shall you have*" (Dt. 25:13-15).

As the Apostle Paul wrote to the Christians of
Rome, we "*must provide things honest in the sight of all
men*" (Rom. 12:17; see also II Cor. 8:21). And, we
who are His are warned "*that no man go beyond and defraud his brother in any manner: because The Lord is the
avenger of all such, as we also have forewarned you and testified*" (I Thes. 4:6). "*In any manner . . .*": Surely that
applies just as much to money matters as it does to
every area of life here-and-now.

Is fraudulent money (money that is dishonest in
weight and measure or value) included in such sins
as *thievery, fraud and deceit? Yes!* One of the sins for
which God took Israel to task—one of the sins for
which He may well take or be taking this nation to
task—is *the adulteration of money* ("*your silver is become
dross* (Isa. 1:22-23).) And, as for those who instigate
and those who condone such fraud, they are called
"*companions of thieves.*"

Consider the following Scripture; view it in
terms of the manipulation of our nation's monetary
system, in terms of what that does to the working
man and woman, to the elderly, to the young—view
it in terms of the violence done to them and to their
property:

"Are there yet the treasures of wickedness in the
house of the wicked, and the scant measure
that is abominable? Shall I count them pure
with the wicked balances, and with the bag of

deceitful weights? For the rich men thereof (those who have profited from such deception and fraud) are full of violence, and the inhabitants thereof (those who insist that weights are honest and the scales are true) have spoken lies and their tongue is deceitful in the mouth" (Micah 6:10-12).

Nations share in the sins of their rulers; the people are culpable of the crimes committed in their name. Consider "the constitution" of God's Ten Commandments:

There at Mount Sinai, to whom did The Lord God Almighty speak? Did He speak not only to the people of Israel as individuals but also to the Israelites *as a nation assembled? (Ex. 20:1, 2)* God desired that His commandments (and those laws and statutes that followed) were to be obeyed not only by each person but also by the nation, as a corporate body over which He was King. *(What is a civil government but the sum total of the self-government of its individual citizens or subjects?* People do, indeed, get the type of civil government they resemble — that is, the type of civil government their self-government produces.)

Consider, then, God's Eighth Commandment" *"You shall not steal."* That applies both to the individual, and to the nation. And, money that is dishonest, money that is rigged and of false weight or measure, money that loses its value between the time it is earned (or invested) and the time it is spent (or withdrawn) is money that steals. Thus, such evils as "legal tender" laws (which engender counterfeit money), unbacked paper money, currency debasement — those break the Eighth Commandment. They are un-Biblical; they are an abomination.

Consider, also, God's Tenth Commandment: *"You shall not covet . . . "* Adulterated money is *covetous* because it springs from a desire for that which belongs to another; the fact that such theft may be surreptitious or "legalized" cannot hide the evil desire and design: *covetousness is the seed of thievery, and thievery is the fruit of dishonest money.*

Money is not only a medium of exchange, it is one of the measurements of a nation's *morality: A moral people will demand a moral money system;* only an immoral people will condone, accept, encourage, an immoral currency. Why? Because it temporarily releases them from self-discipline; it allows them to cater to their appetites and baser desires . . . while putting off the full reckoning until a later date. *Money and morality go hand in hand;* as a people's morality declines, so goes the worth of its money.

"God shortens the life of the nation that condones short-changing and defrauding by fraudulent money, scales or other measures." (R. J. Rushdoony, *Institutes of Biblical Law,* p. 472).

Christians must not shy away from, or be oblivious to, fiscal affairs and economic disciplines. Those matters are very much a part of life here-and-now, and very much a part of being obedient to God's laws, and principles and precepts as set forth in His word. Calling for a return to and a maintenance of honest money is very much a part of *our responsibility* under the dominion charter and of *our work* for the reconstruction of the Biblical foundations of our nation.

Finally, some caveats: Godly Christians must surely realize that gold and silver are not the be-all, end-all answer to our fiscal problems; they are simply *instruments* to help secure monetary discipline; a means of *enforcing obedience to God's laws* of honest weights and measures. If it were not for man's fallen nature, such external disciplines would not be needed.

And, we must not — *must not* — make of silver or gold or any metal or gem an idol or a graven image. *"You shall not make with Me gods of silver, neither shall you make unto you gods of gold"* (Ex. 20:23). How grievous a sin that would be! Soon after The Lord God had delivered the Israelites from Egyptian bondage, and while Moses and Joshua were still on the Mount with God (Ex. 32) recall what took place. After Aaron (the high priest!) had made of the people's gold earrings a molten calf, what did the people proclaim? *"These be our gods, O Israel, which have brought you out of the land of Egypt."*

How great was God's wrath? So great that He would have destroyed the people if it had not been for Moses' intercession.

Let the wrath of God at Mount Sinai be a warning. *There are to be no other gods before him.* Honest weight and honest measures, to be sure. Redeemable currency to deal honestly and to preserve and multiply that which God has given, yes. But, only as monetary discipline to control the depraved nature of men.

Not as an idol. Not as a god. *But, as a commodity to serve The Lord!*

RECOMMENDED READING: *Inflation: Fiat Money in France,* Andrew Dickson White, Foundation for Economic Education, Irvington, NY, *An Introduction to Christian Economics,* Gary North, The Craig Press, Nutley NJ; *What You Should Know About Inflation,* and *Economics in One Lesson,* Henry Hazlitt, Van Nostrand, New York, NY; *Money and Man,* Elgin Groseclose, University of Oklahoma Press, Norman, OK.

20

NATIONAL DEFENSE

BACKGROUND BRIEFING In 1972, US signed strategic arms limitation treaty (SALT I) with USSR Hailed by some as "dawn of global peace." Others warned USSR could use SALT to "gain a potentially disastrous military advantage." Who was correct? Ex-SecDefense, *Melvin Laird,* said worst US fears "are rapidly becoming reality." Laird stated, *"It is incontrovertible that the Soviet Union has repeatedly and flagrantly and indeed contemptuously violated the* (Salt I) *treaty"* to gain *"decisive military superiority"* and has *dishonored their most fundamental agreements with the US."*[1] Former SecState, Henry Kissinger, architect of SALT I, admitted treaty did not slow down USSR's drive for military supremacy but in fact accelerated it.

Carter Administration sought to make "SALT II" centerpiece of its US defense and foreign policy, claiming US and USSR have "equivalency" in terms of overall components. Those opposing SALT II argued "equivalency" comparisons were meaningless, that USSR was even then ahead of US in vital areas of power — and that SALT II would give them further opportunity to surpass US in other areas. Further, said SALT opponents, US lacks positive information on Soviet missile production and deployment and verification virtually impossible under terms of treaty. Reagan Administration opposed SALT II, proposed *Strategic Arms Reduction Talks* (START). Soviets walked out of meetings on that agreement. Many USSR-watchers, including military and diplomatic defectors from Soviet Union and Iron Curtain countries, warn *"first strike on USA"* remains a keystone of Soviet's master plan.

Recent report by *General Advisory Committee on Arms Control and Disarmament* details 17 major Soviet arms control violations during 25-yr period, 1958-1983. Report makes it evident that violations have come in *"areas of offensive strategic weapons, the kind that could be used for what Soviet military literature calls the "crushing nuclear first strike."*[2] In Fall, 1984, issue of *Foreign Policy* journal, *Dr. Colin Gray,* eminent strategic weapons expert and member of President's advisory committee, wrote that conclusions of serious Soviet cheating *"has been reached by two very careful studies. . . ."* And, added Dr. Gray, "On compliance questions, the Administration has acted as if it were chairing an academic seminar discussion . . . *Indeed, like its predecessors, the Reagan Administration has no policy on what to do about Soviet treaty violations.* Thus, American behavior . . . suggests that Soviet cheating is condoned."[3]

Decline of US defensive capabilities did not start with SALT I. Came thru *"unilateral internal* (US) *decisions" during the 1960s.* Expenditures to defend nation (including assistance to allies in NATO, etc.)

dropped from *49% of budget* (1960) to *23.6%* in 1980. Such decisions cancelled, delayed or reduced to virtual impotence vital defense programs. (For example: In mid-'60s US froze number of strategic weapons in hopes Soviets would follow suit. *But, USSR did not.* Soviets still outspend US 3 to 1 on strategic nuclear weapons. In past six yrs, Soviets have deployed 800 new ICBMs — *US has not deployed a single new ICBM for 13 yrs.* In past 14 yrs Soviets have deployed 60 nuclear-powered submarines with nuclear missile launching capabilities; *US has deployed 3.* Soviets have deployed 230 new strategic bombers in past 10 yrs; *US has not deployed one new bomber in past 15 yrs.*[4] In 1983, while US built 750 tanks, Soviets built 3,000; while US built 600 fighter aircraft, Soviets built 1,300.[5]

As a result, military experts feared US could not meet a Russian global challenge, Some suggested US might have difficulty defending its own shores. Reagan Administration has made strengthened defenses major program. Has fought for increased Dept. of Defense budgets, increased number of ships in US fleet including nuclear powered missile-carrying Trident subs (with more under construction), increased tactical aircraft, tanks, anti-aircraft weapons, intial production of MX defense missiles, deployed short-and-long range ICBM missiles, resumed construction of long-range B-1 bomber to replace 30-yr-old B-52s. Defense spending slated for fiscal 1985, $292.9 billion, just under 30% of total federal budget.[6]

Public opinion polls indicate that vast majority of

voters (in high 80%s) want US to be strong; majority opposes any treaty that would not be subject to practical verification of nuclear weapons, and some-70% would oppose any treaty that would prohibit anti-missile defenses of US cities and industrial centers (as did Salt II).

"HIGH FRONTIER"

In general, US defense programs have been based on idea of "Mutual Assured Destruction" (MAD)—*a perpetual balance of terror between the world's two super-powers.* MAD hope is balance of terror would make it unlikely that USSR would attack US because massive retaliation would result in both nations being virtually (if not completely) destroyed in nuclear war. In such quandry are those who (1) call for *"Freeze"* to hold destructive might at existing levels and invite Soviets to do some (2) those who insist nuclear arsenals be increased to forestall USSR attack. At foundation of this MAD thinking is *supposition that nuclear weapons* (long-range ballistic missiles) *are the "ultimate" weapons;* that they will dominate military affairs from now on; that there is no real strategic defense and only strategic offense offers any hope. (USSR way ahead of US in civil defense, has many "hardened" sites [underground shelters, etc.]).

But, there may be another way. As US Senator William Armstrong (CO) writes in the Foreword to *We Must Defend America: A Strategy for National Survival:* "Our advantages in space technology *can provide a non-nuclear shield against the long-range nuclear missiles which MAD considers the 'ultimate weapons.'* "

Thus, "High Frontier" called "Star Wars" by some. A comprehensive new US strategy that addresses national security . . . at a cost to taxpayer below all other available alternatives to meet possible Soviet threat.

Keystone of High Frontier strategy is *three-tiered* defense (the first two tiers in outer space) that can provide 96%

assurance of safety for all targets of Soviet long-range missiles.

- (1) A spaceborne defense system capable of destroying at least 50% of a Soviet long-range missile salvo vs. the US in the early minutes of trajectory (when missiles have been fired and are reaching orbital altitude).

- (2) A second layer of spaceborne defense capable of inflicting further significant loses (a second 50%) on missiles that may have escaped the first spaceborne shield.

- (3) An on-site defense of individual US missile silos to insure the survival and launching of those missiles.

The initial High Frontier system (*Global Ballistic Missile defense*—GMBD) would involve up to *432 satellites 300 miles out in space. Satellites positioned and rocket-armed so as to intercept Soviet missiles that might be fired against US.* (For a more detailed analysis of the High Frontier program, see *We Must Defend America: A New Strategy for National Survival*, Lt. General Daniel O. Graham, Conservative Press, P.O. Box 1430, Falls Church, VA 22041.)

General Daniel Graham, USA, Ret., project director of High Frontier, estimates that most of three-tiered project *could be completed by 1988,* and all of it by 1993. He states basic space technology for program already exists. Program's major critics are Pentagon bureaucrats, those wedded to the Mutual Assured Destruction concept who see offensive weapons as *only* solution, and those who argue that project is not feasible or that it would escalate global insecurity by putting weapons in space. President Reagan has authorized basic research and development on the High Frontier program.

Jane's, the authoritative military publisher in Great Britain, believes *Soviet Union is far ahead of US in application of space technology* (says US is well in advance in space technology *but "USSR more energetic in applying" our technology.* The magazine, *Spaceflight Directory,* believes USSR could have "star-wars" weapons (high energy lasers) *in orbit in five years* (1989). Reg Turnbull, Jane's editor said American spaced-based lasers eventually *could make current Soviet nuclear weapons obsolete, "creating another decade during which the West could feel safe against the possibility of surprise nuclear attack."*[7]

Despite Reagan Administration's staunch position on increasing defense spending and beefing up armed services, *in other areas of national defense* (economic and geopolitical) *Administration seems schizoid;* blatantly contradicts itself. EXAMPLE: *Soviets facing serious grain shortage* that strains its troubled economy and could cause civil unrest. Experts feel that crunch, *if left on its own,* could force Soviets to spend more *on domestic problems* and *reduce military spending.* But, President Reagan announced (Sept., 1984) USSR may buy *another 10 million metric tons of corn and/or wheat from US*—about double the amount previously authorized. *EXAMPLE:* Despite widespread acknowledgment that USSR lags far behind US in *high tech* and needs such equipment for military advances as well as industrial development, *US Dept of Commerce cancelled restrictions on export of strategic high tech items*—also blocked efforts by Dept of Defense to have say in deciding what types of strategic goods could be sold to USSR.[8]

And, consider this: *US State Dept. wants to give tens of thousands of square miles of petroleum-rich seabed and five strategically located islands to USSR.* (Covert move involves area of Bering Sea called *Navarin Basin* and five islands discovered after 1867 treaty with Russia.) *Howard Phillips,* Conservative Caucus, reports State Dept. in *secret negotiations* to abandon US claim to islands and release them to USSR.[9]

GENOCIDE TREATY: SUICIDE FOR U.S.?

In speech before B'nai B'rith on 9/6/84, President Reagan called for US Senate to *ratify UN Genocide Convention.* Mr. Reagan stated he wanted treaty ratified by Oct. 4, 1984. Senate Foreign Relations

Committee voted 17-0—*Senator Jesse Helms* (NC) voting, "Present."[10]

Genocide treaty was adopted by UN on Dec. 9, 1948. President Truman submitted treaty to US Senate for ratification in 1949. Presidents Eisenhower, Kennedy, Johnson and Nixon also sought ratification during their Administrations. *US Senate has consistently refused;* maintained it was against the best interest and security of the nation (Stalwarts such as Senators Sam Ervin, John Bricker, Robert Taft, William Knowland, Harry Byrd and Barry Goldwater have led fight down through the years.) Thus, treaty has sat in Senate for 35 yrs. *Now Reagan Administration pushes to have it ratified.*

Those who have fought, and now fight, ratification warn it is *extremely dangerous.* American courts have held that treaty signed and ratified by Senate becomes part of supreme law of land and (where there is a conflict) overrides all federal and state laws including the Constitution and its Bill of Rights. (Secretary of State under Pres. Eisenhower, John Foster Dulles, once stated, *"Under our Constitution, treaties become the supreme law of the land. They are indeed more supreme than ordinary laws, for Congressional laws are invalid if they do not conform to the Constitution, whereas treaty laws can override the Constitution. Treaties . . . can cut right across the rights given the people by the constitutional Bill of Rights."*[11]

Primary impetus for treaty came from world reaction to Nazis' slaughter of Jews during World War II. (*Communists have committed infinitely more genocidal murders than Nazis; continue to do so—yet are "exempt" from treaty's provisions.* Soviets refused to ratify treaty until reference to actions against "political groups" was struck from document. Thus, treaty exempts genocide of "political groups" and USSR claims those they have liquidated were in "political groups," that threatened Soviet State.

Treaty goes far beyond genocide (murder to exterminate), which all moral people oppose. It encompasses such *twilight zones as attempting* (by act or statement) *to cause "mental harm" to a member of a minority group,* etc. Thus, a nation that commits mass murder—against "political groups"—is exempted but someone who allegedly causes "mental anguish" is subject to the full force and effect of the treaty.

Genocide Treaty applies not only to governments and governmental agencies *but also to individual citizens.* Thus, opponents warn, even on the basis of spiteful, spurious charges (made for propaganda purposes, etc.) a US citizen could be hauled up before *international penal body*—and, if citizen were in this nation, *US Government would be bound to grant extradition so that citizen could be tried by international court.*

Then, too, no guarantee and strong possibility that any "international court" *would be stacked against US and its citizens*—as most UN committees and agencies are now. (Opponents of ratification point to recent (5/10/84) decree of International Court of Justice—The World Court—against US. Court demanded US "cease and refrain" from restricting or blocking access to Nicauraguan ports by ships carrying arms and ammunitions to Sandinista forces spreading communism in Central America.

Supporters of treaty say US refusal to ratify it has been "a source of embarrassment" in international circles. Ratification of the treaty, they argue would give other nations a "better opinion" of US. Opponents retort, junking the Constitution and its Bill of Rights and making American citizens prey for international courts is a high price to pay for avoiding some "embarrassment" and cowtowing to "world opinion."

In 1952, fearing that US might ratify Genocide Convention, *American Bar Assn.* adopted resolution calling for a Constitutional Amendment stating *"A provision of a treaty which conflicts with any provision of this Constitution shall not be of any force and effect."*[12] Senator Helms has tried to have such reservations appended to any ratification action by US Senate. Reagan administration insists they are not needed.

CONSIDER THE BIBLICAL PRINCIPLES God's people are forbidden to make deals (pacts, alliances, treaties) with ungodly men or nations or groups. Those who do enter into such treaties will be *"trodden down by them"* (Isa. 28:15-18).

We are to be on guard against (a) external enemies who might attack and (b) internal enemies (false prophets and ungodly forces) who would seduce God's people with cries of *"Peace, when there is no peace" (Ezek. 13:10).* We are to shun godless negotiators who are "like foxes of the desert" with their shams and illusions that would cause us to lower our defenses *(Ezek. 13:4). "How can one enter into a strong man's house, and spoil his goods, except he first bind the strong man? And then will he spoil his goods" (Mt. 12:29).*

Those who make alliance with the ungodly build walls with "untempered mortar"—walls that will not stand because they are not based upon God's word but are based on agreements with God's enemies *(Ezek. 13:10, 11).* Our defenses are to be based on *"the tried stone, a precious cornerstone, a sure foundation" (Isa. 28:16, 17)* which is The Word of God, Christ Jesus.

Christians are to be for peace; we are to pray for peace and work for peace; we are not to be belligerent or offensive. We are told to love our personal enemies, to pray for them, and to work for their salvation *(Mt. 5:44).* But, God's word does not tell us to love His enemies! Like David, we are to hate God's enemies with a "perfect hatred" *(Ps 139:19-24)*—that is, a hatred that stems from our love of The Lord God,—and hate to see him defied. And, the Apostle Paul warns us against being *unequally yoked* with forces of darkness. He urges us to *hold ourselves separate* from such ungodly entities and agencies *(II Cor. 6:14-18; Eph. 5:6, 7, 17).* If we make peace with God's enemies, do we not make an enemy of God? *(Mt. 12:30).* When we supply God's enemies (those who deny Him and mock Him) we are their accomplices; thus we sin against God! (And all those who hate God love death.)

In Psalm 120, David cries out: *"My soul has dwelt long with him that hates peace. I am for peace, but when I speak they are for war."*

We have no right to molest others but God places upon us the responsibility to protect our family and neighbors and the helpless *(I Tim. 5:8; Mt. 19:19; James 1:27)*. If defense becomes vital *(Rom. 12:18)*, then we must be sure of our ability to defend ourselves successfully *(Lk. 14:31)* and to have as our goal the total suppression of evil *(Num. 21:14)*. To adopt the mentality to live and let evil live is to go against God's will. And, if it comes to battle, we must pray and thank The Lord, as did David and God's other warriors, for showing us how to wage such a war victoriously *(II Sam. 22:35);* being His "battle axes and weapons" *(Jer. 51:20)* and going "into the gaps and make up the hedges" for Him *(Ezek. 13:5)*.

God's work through Nehemiah gives a perspective on such pacts as SALT I and II, etc. Jerusalem was desolate, virtually defenseless and surrounded by enemies; the walls, towers and gates were down. Did God use Nehemiah to make a pact with the Horomites, the Ammonites and the Arabs? *No.* He used Nehemiah to *rebuild the city's defenses.* Note the sequence of events:

(1) *Nehemiah prayed* that God would help Jerusalem, *he confessed its sins, he asked God to cleanse the hearts of the people* and to *have mercy* on them *(Neh. 1:5-10)*.

(2) *God moved through king Artaxerxes* to send Nehemiah to Jerusalem (and to give him "letters of

credit" for needed supplies and materials) *(Neh. 2:1-8).*

(3) *Nehemiah inspected the defenses and assessed what was needed to protect the city (Neh. 2:13-15).*

(4) *Giving God all the glory,* he inspired the people to "have a mind to work" rebuilding the walls *(Neh. 2:17-20).*

(5) *Through prayer, Nehemiah overcame* ridicule, blandishments, deceit, threats and greed.

(6) *He put men on guard both night and day,* and established an *early warning sytem* in case of attack *(Neh. 4:8, 9).*

(7) *Nehemiah armed the people,* putting half on guard at the walls and half at work rebuilding the walls (and the builders kept their swords and spears at their sides while they worked) *(Neh. 4:13-23).* Thus *with God's guidance and protection,* the wall was rebuilt in 52 days and God's enemies were astounded *"for they perceived that this work was wrought by God"(Neh. 6:16).*

(8) *Nehemiah established a Godly government, kept watchmen on the walls, and secured Jerusalem's defenses against future attacks (Neh. 7:1-4).*

In *Kings 11:2,* God warns His people against those nations that are against Him: *"Go you not unto them, nor let them come into you, for surely they will turn your hearts after their gods."* In the marginal comments on this verse, The Geneva Bible observes: "How it is a thing that greatly offendeth God that such as fear Him and profess His religion, should join in amity with the wicked." *Psalm 125:3* tells us that the rod of the wicked shall not rest upon the lot of the righteous. How then can we strive to be righteous in His sight if we dare to supply the makings of the rod to the unrighteous?

Our God is a mighty God; He is the Living God. None is as mighty as He. He makes the sun and He makes it stand still; He forms the rain and makes it drop, or hold. *Is not The God of all equal to all times, even these?* And, if we are His and seek to be on His side, shall He not deliver us? What, then? Shall we have intercourse with those who mock Him? Shall we do business with those who persecute His own? Are we not to live by the word of God *(Dt. 8:3).* How shall we, who are his, *"declare His glory among the nations and His wonderful works among all people"* if we enter into league with those who deny Him, who disdain His word, and oppress His children?

What, then, shall we do? (1) Strive to walk in His ways; seek to obey His will in all things, (2) Be separate from the world and one with Him and His — for those who would be friends with this world (system) are enemies to God *(James 4:4),* (3) refuse to aid or abet or join with those (individuals, groups or nations) that are God's enemies, and (4) call upon The Lord for He will deliver us and we shall glorify His name *(Ps. 50:15).*

"But if you shall indeed obey his voice, and do all that I speak, then I will be an enemy unto your enemies, and an adversary unto your adversaries" (Ex. 23:20-22).

Notes

1. *Reader's Digest,* December 1977.
2. "Why Is White House Folding On Crucial Issues?" *Human Events,* 9/29/94, p. 1.
3. *Idem.*
4. Letter, American Security Council, September, 1984.
5. Letter, Major General John K. Singlaub, USA Ret., Council for Inter-American Security, October 1984.
6. UPI, Washington, *Manchester* (NH) *Union-Leader,* 9/29/84, p. 1.
7. UPI, London, *Keene* (NH) *Sentinel,* 9/26/84, p. 17.
8. "Why Is White House Folding on Crucial Issues?" *Human Events,* 9/29/84.
9. Howard Phillips as quoted in *Don Bell Report,* 9/4/84.
10. UPI, Washington, *Manchester* (NH) *Union-Leader,* 9/24 p. 2.
11. "Genocide Treaty A Threat To Your Liberty," *Howard Phillips Issues and Strategy Bulletin,* 9/17/84, pp. 1, 2.
12. "The Genocide Convention: Still A Bad Treaty," *Human Events,* 9/22/84, pp. 1, 12.

21

RELIGIOUS LIBERTY

BACKGROUND BRIEFING What is state of *religious liberty* (freedom to worship/First Amendment) in US today? Consider actions, trends and developments at Federal and State levels.

First, the good news: Congress passed *Church Audit Procedures Act* (CAP) authored by US Senator Charles Grassley (IA) and Rep. Mickey Edwards (OK). *Hailed as significant victory for religious liberty.*

New law requires Internal Revenue Service to adhere to specific rules before being able to examine financial records of church. If IRS fails to comply with law, court *summons served on church can be dismissed.* Further, law puts statute of limitation on such examinations at three years (in past IRS has waited far longer than that before demanding to see church records). New requirements will not impede IRS probes of fraudulent or criminal tax evasions (many by "paper churches" that in some cases use Lord's name "in vain" to avoid taxes). At same time, law intended to curb IRS abuses of legitimate churches. Heavy-handed demands often resulted in violation religious liberty and tradition of *"innocent until proven guilty";*

also caused heavy legal fees for congregations and harrassment of pastors and church boards, etc.

"Equal Access" law passed. Protects rights of 16 million students in 18,000 secondary public schools to meet for religious purposes after hours. Prior to enactment, school authorities generally refused Christian student groups permission to meet "on campus." Has been hailed as "strongest statement for religious freedom" by any Congress in this century.

US Circuit Court of Appeals ruled Nebraska officials violated rights of church members and visiting pastors at *Faith Baptist Church,* Louisville, NE. Acting with approval of State judge, at 6 am on Oct. 18, 1982, 15 carloads of sheriff's deputies and police raided church during prayer vigil; forcibly removed 85 laymen and visiting pastors from sanctuary, and padlocked church. *Court ruled State had no business* interferring with worship service or worshippers, held that authorities were in violation of First Amendment. State may appeal. Church members and visiting pastors intend to pursue the case; *suing State and arresting officers for $66 million in civil damages.*

Also in Nebraska, State seems to have softened stern anti-Christian school attitude that caused 7-yr church-state battle. *New State law* gives some lee-way to Christian education and would allow church schools to avoid teacher certification requirements. However, some Christian education leaders fear new law contains seeds of peril. Are watching to see how State will administer new provisions.

(NOTE: Although Pastor Everett Sileven was released from jail, he may be forced to return to complete 5 months sentence if State Supreme Court refuses his appeal. In meantime, out on $10,000 bond put up by churches and pastors from across nation.)

In Texas, *Appeals Court upheld right of Corpus Christi Baptist Church* (Pastor Lester Roloff, now deceased) *to operate center for troubled teenagers free from undue control and interference by State Dept. of Human Resources.* Center has outstanding record of rehabilitation for "socially terminal" children through program based on Biblical principles.

In Maine, *US District Court ruled in favor of Maine Assn. of Christian Schools.* Assn. charged State had no power or right to license Christian schools. Constitutional attorney William B. Ball, representing schools, brought suit under federal civil rights law, and won.

In Pennsylvania, *Commonwealth Court upheld State's abortion-funding control law.* Lower had ruled law was unconstitutional (held it violated State's ERA statutes). Higher courts overruled that decision.

US Supreme Court has agreed to review decision by US 5th Circuit Court of Appeals that State's law permitting *prayer in school* was violation of First Amendment. *Other positive Supreme Court actions* (1983-84): tax breaks for parents sending children to Christian schools *do not violate 1st Amendment;* cities may display *nativity scene in public places* (a dubious victory since basis of decision was that such displays are "secular" and of similar status as Santa Claus and reindeers, etc.).

Supreme Court decision on *Grove City* (PA) *College v. United States* a toss-up. Good and bad. Federal govt demanded college comply with Title IX provisions and sign "non sex discrimination pledge." College had never discriminated on basis of sex, says such discrimination repugnant; further, *had never accepted federal funds*. Washington held that because *some individual students* at Grove City received govt educational opportunity grants, college was recipient of federal funds, had to comply. When college refused, *funds to individual students were halted*. College sued, claimed govt. with illegal assault on its independence. US Court of Appeals Court ruled that *all college's programs and activities were subject to govt. control because of financial aid to the several students*. US Supreme Court. subsequently modified that, ruled *sex discrimination laws are enforceable only on those programs and activities in which grant recipients were directly involved*. A step forward, but camel's nose still under independent college's tent.

Now, for the bad news.

US Supreme Court ruled against *Bob Jones University*. Held BJU ban on *interracial dating and marriage* disqualified university for tax-exempt status. IRS decreed BJU rules violated "public policy," revoked tax-exemption: Court agreed. (See below re "public policy" and religious freedom.)

County circuit judge in Portland, OR, *banned prayers from commencement* exercises at David Douglas High School, said prayer would violate principles of church and state.

New Jersey statute mandating a *minute of silence*

ous exercise. *Those who firmly hold to religious liberty argue that right to believe without freedom to practice is not liberty.* They emphasize First Amendment reads: *"Congress shall make no law . . . prohibiting the free exercise"* of *religion. Further, when Court did outlaw polygamy,* it held *"(it) is contrary to spirit of Christianity"* and *"Christianity has produced* (the civilization of) *the western world."* (136 US 1).

How far would some extend control of religious practices? US Senator Charles Mathias (MD) said, *"I don't think you can draw the line at race discrimination . . . we must consider how many examples of discrimination there are to cover . . . race, sex, religion, age or others."* Senator Mathias believes 1964 Civil Rights Act is open-ended, broad enough to facilitate complete control: "when we start enumerating we run into danger that . . . something is overlooked." Apparently Caesar's reach has no limit.

Opponents to such open-ended interference and control ask:

"Would Jewish seminary be forced to admit Moslems, or forfeit tax-exemption?" "Would Catholic seminary or convent be compelled to admit Black Muslims?" "Would a Christian college be forced to accepted avowed atheists — or practicing homosexuals?" (In Washington, DC, Georgetown University (A Roman Catholic institution) was forced to defend itself against charges of discrimination and violation of DC Human Rights Act. Why? Because University refused to provide funds for on-campus *homosexual* club.)

As John Baker, Baptist Joint Council on Public

Affairs warned: *"If you allow the IRS to force you to choose between your tax exemption and your theology, it would have the power to destroy many churches . . ."*

Those who seek to use tax policy to force social revision and "reform" raise three arguments: (1) Tax exemption is a form of *subsidy,* (2) Tax exemption should be granted *only to organizations that "further national policies,"* and (3) Agencies of federal govt (such as IRS) *Have authority to decide/interpret what national policy is and who or what does and does not conform to the policy.*

1. To argue that tax exemption is govt subsidy is to assert *that ~~all~~ property belongs to govt* and that individual who produced property *may keep only that which govt permits,* and to *spend it only on what govt approves.* Thus, both the power to tax and the power *not to tax would be power to control. Previous US Supreme Court has held that granting tax exemption is act of neutrality,* not a subsidy *(Walz v. Tax Commission,* 1970).

2. Purpose of tax exemption (IRS Section 501 (c) (3)) is to exclude from taxation institutions organized exclusively for "religious, charitable, scientific, literary or education purposes . . . (and to) foster (amateur) sports . . ." To suggest that exemptions and deductibilities) should go only to those who support "federal policies" is *to require all such groups to be propaganda agents for* (extensions of) *federal govt.*

Treasury officials have affirmed that "IRS is without legislative authority to deny tax-exempt status . . . on ground that their policies or practices do not conform to notions of national public policy."

And, just what is "national public policy?" Rep.

Phillip Crane (IL) observed, "It is significant to note that many of the favored, established religious groups that would be allowed to retain their tax exemptions advocate *abortions, homosexuality, and witchcraft.*" And, the late Rep. John Ashbrook once charged that the IRS seeks to deny tax exemption to Christian schools *"while leaving unhampered tax-exempt organizations which practice or promote witchcraft, homosexuality, abortion, lesbianism, and euthanasia."*

3. Constitution *does not give agencies power* (authority) to rule by administrative fiat. Agencies are created (commissioned) by *elected representatives* of the people and as such are *answerable to the representatives. They were never intended to become a "fourth branch"* of govt. *Congressional oversight and control is vital;* otherwise, what is left of the republic will be dominated by techno-bureaucrats. Supreme Court has held "(c)ourts are not arbiters of scriptural interpretation." Is IRS or any agency to be vested with such power?

CONSIDER THE BIBLICAL PRINCIPLES   1. *The principle of God's sovereignty. "I am The Lord your God, which have brought you . . . out of the house of* (civil) *bondage. You shall have no other gods before me" (Ex. 20:1-6).* The Lord God's words in that instance have a direct reference to civil governance. See also *Dt. 4:39; 10:17, II Sam. 7:22; Jer. 10:10.* For the State to demand that a person who has made Christ Jesus King of all life must deny God and obey it is to violate that individual's *freedom of worship.* And, to demand that the person who holds to the *total sover-*

eignty of God must put the State above God is to seek to abrogate God's dominion — *thus putting itself above God.* Such action by the State, or any of its agencies, does in fact force the individual to render unto Caesar those things that belong only to The Lord God.

"One is your Master, even Christ" (Mt. 23:8-10). We must live according to His word *(Eph. 1:22; Acts 5:29)* For there is, indeed, only one true King" *Christ Jesus.* The affairs of Christ's church — *including the peaceful and godly* (God-serving) *activities of its members* — are not to be abridged by the rudiments of man *(Col. 2:6-8).*

2. *The principle of personal property* (that which has been entrusted to the individual by The Lord God Who is the true owner of "the earth and the fulness thereof.") *"All the earth is mine"* said The Lord *(Ex. 19:5). "Behold, the heaven and the heaven of heavens is The Lord your God's, the earth also with all that therein is"* (Dt. 10:14). *"All things were created by Him and for Him,"* (Col. 1:16).

The Lord gives His property to whom He chooses (*Jer. 27:5);* it is to be used to glorify Him, *not the self, not the State — Him.* The individual gains temporal ownership (title or deed) of personal property by vesting *time and labor and resources and talents* in the development and fruition of that property; thus, the property is consigned (by The Lord) *to the individual as God's steward;* it is not consigned to the group, not to the State. The individual has control over that property *and is answerable to The Lord God* for his or her stewardship. In that context, it is the God-given liberty of the individual (in free concert with others) to determine what portion of his property (earnings, holdings) he will contribute to the State for God-ordained (commissioned) functions of civil government *(Rom 13:6, 7)*. God holds the individual accountable for the obedience (or disobedience) involved in the determination he or she makes. For the State to decree that property belongs to government, or to determine what the individual may keep, *violates not only the individual but more importantly violates God's sovereignty and the God-commission principle of personal property.* (It is the individual who decides what will go to the State, not vice versa.) The State creates no property, produces no property, should have only that which is voluntarily granted to it by its citizens (but today goes beyong that to confiscate what it unilaterally demands—such a State is tyrannical, and ungodly.

Conscience is the most sacred of all property. Christians must seek always to have a conscience *void of offense toward God.* Only then can they have a conscience that is truly void of offense toward men of good will. (Should one's conscience be void of offense toward God but be offensive toward men, it is because such men are ungodly and perhaps to be counted God's enemies). If, for example, we seek to have a conscience void of offense toward men by taking a position offensive to The Lord God, we sin against God. As the Apostle Paul said, it is better to please God than men *(Acts 4:19)*.

Those (including the State or its minions) who demand that the individual decide between obedience to God or prosecution by the State are offensive to God *(Mt. 18:7)*. Those who stand firm in The Lord are blessed of and to Him *(Lk. 7:23; I Pet. 5:6-9)*.

3. *The principle of individual/family/church responsibility.* Christian should need *no middle man* (no Caesar's agency or agent) to do The Lord's work. We as His are charged as individuals, as family members, and as members of His Body (church) to care for our own and for strangers *(I Tim. 5:8; James 1:27; Mt. 25:31-46; Lk. 10:25-37)*. To invite, or permit, the State to assume these responsibilities, or to proscribe them, is to be *guilty of forsaking Christ's teachings and God's commandments.* We must stand firm in the faith, put faith to His works, and resist the encroachments of government.

4. *The principle of separation.* We are not to use our liberty in Christ as a cloak of maliciousness or slothfulness or greed but as servants of God and followers of Christ (Christian) *(I Pet. 2:16)*. We are to be in but not of the world; to glorify Him in body and spirit *(I Cor. 6:20)*, even if the world hates us for doing so *(John 15:19)*.

We are to be separate from those things of the world that conflict with (deny) His word *(Gal. 5:1; II Cor. 6:14)*. The affairs of Christ's church are to be attended to *by members of His church,* not in secular courts *(I Cor. 6:1-4)*. The works of faith are to be attended to *by those in the faith (James 2:14-26)*. Our unity in Christ is to be the unity of faith in the work of His ministry. It is not to be based on thesis or anti-thesis or sin-thesis but *on His word (Mt. 4:4);* not on compromise *but on consecration and prayer* (Ps. 1:1-3).

RECOMMENDED READING: *A Defense of Liberty Against Tyranny,* Junius Brutus (1689), Peter Smith, Gloucester, MA; *Judicial Supremacy,* Hon. Robert K. Dornan and Csaba Vedlik, Jr., Nordland Publishing; *Separation of Church and Freedom,* Kent Kelly, Calvary Press, Southern Pines, NC.

22

"ROCK 'N ROLL": DRUGS, SEX AND REBELLION

BACKGROUND BRIEFING Estimated that some *80% of nation's teenagers* have a steady diet of "rock" music. Latest expansion—*rock 'n roll cable television* (MTV—Music Television): beams blood-curdling, sadistic sex and visual violence along with frenetic "rock" music. In one MTV feature, "rock" star turns self into werewolf to prey on women; in other MTV videos, hostile sex relations between men and women, torture and murder are steady diet. MTV transmits horror violence and "rock" music 24 hours a day to some 15 million cable subscribers. "Rock" and MTV are a billion dollar industry, a part of the sordid, destructive counter-culture.

How deeply has "rock" music permeated contemporary society? *Some churches now using "gospel rock" to woo young people.* Vitally important that godly Christians shun rock, that they know its origins, nature, influences and purpose.

"Rock" has roots in jungle tribes and cults; is kin to voodooism and demon worship. Term, "rock 'n roll," originated in ghetto as a descriptive sexual expres-

sion. Many forms of "rock:" hard rock, acid rock, folk rock, jazz rock, country rock, soul rock, "Jesus" (or gospel) rock—even "death" rock—touting suicide.

Some see "rock" as passing fad ("every generation has its music"). Those who have studied "rock" are convinced it is "international anthem" for dark forces; an integral part of satanic effort to destroy tradition, eradicate morality, and lure youth into depraved and enslaving culture of drugs, illicit sex, prostitution and revolution.

"An influx of 18-to-34 year olds, many of them confused relics of the drug culture of the 1960s and '70s, has started refilling the nation's mental hospitals." That according to the *Washington Post.*

Dr. Joseph Crow, Univ of Seattle, wrote that "rock" is use of music to *condition the mind* through calculated frequencies and mathematical formulae; vibrations of music are designed to *modify body chemistry, make mind susceptible to modificaton and indoctrination.* Thus, rock can be (and is) employed for "mind-bending, re-education and re-organization."

"Rock" is key weapon in revolution for moral and social change. Bob Larson, former "rock" star and composer who is now a Christian, reported that "Lyrics of today's rock songs are a large part of the cause of the tidal wave of promiscuity, venereal disease, illegitimate births and political upheaval."

Frank Zappa of "Mothers of Invention" is blunt about it: "Rock music is sex. The big beat matches the body's rhythms."

USA and England, where rock is most prevalent,

have highest incidences of juvenile delinquency, teenage abortions, venereal disease, and youth suicide. (16 to 17% of sexually active teenagers have *chlamydia,* a little-known venereal disease that is raging across the nation in epidemic proportions. It is spread from person to person when infected tissues come in contact with mucous membranes. In its wake chlamydia leaves hundreds of thousands of infertile women.

Calculated rhythms and anti-syncopations of "rock" spring from mind-altering techniques developed by Russian psychologist and father of "conditioned reflexes," *Ivan Pavlov.* Pavlov demonstrated he could change flow of dog's saliva by changing speed of metronome. Further, by subjecting dogs to both slow and rapid metronome beats at same time, Pavlov found he could create *artificial neuroses;* in other words, manipulate the mind. (Recently, a prominent "rock" star boasted that his group had the ability to "turn minds any way we want them. *We'll brainwash them and they will brainwash the world.")*

"Rock music caused a great evolution in the relations between parents and children. Its success was the result of an amazing cooperation among lust, art, and commercial shrewdness. Without parents realizing it, their children were liberated from them": Professor Allan Bloom, Univ. of Chicago. Prof. Bloom went on:

"The most powerful formative influence on children between 12 and 18 is not the school, not the church, not the home, but rock music and all that goes with it. It is not an elevating but a levelling

ABBREVIATED COMPARISON OF ROCK 'N ROLL WITH GODLY MUSIC

"Prove all things; hold fast to that which is good. Abstain from all appearance of evil" (1 Thes. 5:21, 22).

GODLY MUSIC	ROCK 'N ROLL
RHYTHM Rhythmic (based on the flowing rhythm of the pulse); well-organized patterns of rhythm and natural accents; may incorporate a variety of rhythms. In sum: *orderly & systematic.*	Little or no rhythm; uses a steady, continuous pounding (beat); usually has no organized rhythm but employs "wild" (erratic) and constantly repeated beat with unnatural accents. In sum: *disorderly, chaotic, jarring.*
HARMONY Uses many harmonious chords; has accurate, well-organized pitch patterns; employs modulations (changes in key) and accurate pitch.	Repetition of same chords (which are often dissonant); extreme & frequent use of high pitches ("screaming," often incoherent sounds); seldom modulates (stays in same key); usually slightly under true pitch.
MELODY Well-constructed, harmonious melody that runs throughout and builds to purposeful conclusion (i.e., is a complete score).	Seldom has an intrinsic or inherent melody running thru-out; uses bits and fragments over and over; no conclusion, only an abrupt ending that leaves listener handing.
INTENSITY Controlled sound & sound levels; employs deft changes in dynamic levels; makes use of contrasts between loud and soft passages; utilizes natural sounds (complementary) of variety of instruments—percussion, strings, woodwinds, etc.	Uncontrolled, wild sound (often as loud as 125 decibels); relies on powerful electronic hi-fi equipment to achieve maximum and sustained intensity to "overcome" listener; usually employs drums, electronic guitars & amplified voices to create frenzied atmosphere.
LYRICS Honor God (praise, adoration, thanksgiving, repentance); theologically accurate; offensive to satan and the ungodly. In sum. *Exalts The Lord.*	Anti-God; distorts, twists, and "uses" Scriptural passages of key words to snare unsuspecting Christian teenagers; utilizes ambiguous (coded) words and phrases (terms) to promote drugs, illicit sex, rebellion; invites demons and depravity. In sum: *blasphemes God and promotes ungodliness.*
THE MESSAGE Holiness, righteousness, propriety; purity; peace & well-being; cleanliness of mind & body. One with Christ.	Depravity, wickedness, sensuality; promiscuity; dependence on carnal stimuli; hedonistic; rebellious.

influence. The children have as their heroes banal, drug and sex-ridden guttersnipes who foment rebellion not only against parents but against all noble sentiments. . . . *One thing I have no difficulty teaching students today is the passage in the "Republic" where Socrates explains that control over music is control over character and that the rhythm and the melody are more powerful than the words."*

"Rock" generally distinguished by its trademarks: "a constant repetition of high pitches, almost no melody except oft-repeated fragments, repetition of the same chords, slightly under true pitch, breaking up of rhythms, unnatural accents (and) a constant driving beat evoking unnatural, sensual gyrations. *(See chart for comparison of rock and godly music.)*

Technically, "rock" is not music. Wendell K. Babcock points out, "Music is . . . a succession of tones with the components of melody, harmony, rhythm, plus variable dimensions of volume, all pleasing to the ear." Little, usually none, of that in "rock."

There are those, including some professing Christians, who insist music is "neutral" . . . neither moral or immoral; thus they assign it a sort of "situational ethics." They suggest that "rock" without its often subtle but always insidious lyrics is harmless. Dr. Howard Hansen, Eastman School of Music, warns against such ideas: "According to the proportion of those components, (music) can be soothing or invigorating, ennobling of vulgarizing, philosophical or orgiastic. *It has the power for evil as well as for good."* But, it is never "neutral."

Dr. David Noebel, who has studied rock for 20 years, also warns that such assertions of "neutrality" are totally false and manifestly dangerous. He reports scientific experiments on animals, plants and humans that clearly demonstrate "rock" music has definite and harmful effect: plants die, animals sickened, humans developed neuroses (tension, anger hyperactivity).

Consider the physcial and psychological impact of rock music: *Physical*—impairment (sometimes complete loss) of hearing, hysteria, heightened biological drives, stimulation of hormonal secretions, decline in body calcium, vascular restriction; *Psychological*—weakens (removes) inhibitions, excites desires, invites permissiveness, establishes sensual thought patterns, toys with (often succumbs to) mysticism and demonology.

Finally, *to evaluate the product, consider the producer* (Mt. 12:35). Most "rock stars" use and promote the use of drugs, advocate "free sex," engage in illicit sex relations (often perverted), are anti-social and denigrate traditional values and morality. *John Lennon,* of the Beatles rock group, was widely hailed as a purveyor of peace and love and lionized after he was shot down in New York. In fact, Lennon was a drug addict, a drug pusher, a wife-beater, a fornicator and adulterer, *and a blasphemer* (who once referred to The Lord Jesus Christ as a greasy, garlic-eating, illegitimate fascist Spaniard).

CONSIDER THE BIBLICAL PRINCIPLES   *Music is from God.* At Creation, "the morning stars sang together for joy" *(Job 38:7). Why did The Lord God cre-*

ate music? His word tells us. Music, song, is to be
used basically for three purposes: *To praise Almighty
God* (to glorify Him, to magnify His Holy Name, to
thank Him for His goodness and mercy, and to proclaim His Kingship); *To refresh the soul* (to express the
joy and peace that comes with walking with God and
the blessed assurances of His promises); and, *To
bring sinners face-to-face with The Holy and Living
God* — Blessed Trinity (conviction, repentance,
redemption). We also know *(I Sam. 16:14-23)* that
sacred music heals both the body and the soul (and,
in that we see a major distinction between godly and
ungodly music).

Johann Sebastian Bach, great Christian composer
and organist, wrote, "The aim and final reason of all
music should be nothing else but the glory of God
and the refreshment of the spirit." Leonard Seidel, in
his book, *"God's New Song,"* points out that sacred
music is a normal result of Christian growth. Seidel
demonstrates that as we grow in Christ our music
also develops so that, as the Apostle Paul wrote, *"I
will sing with the spirit and I will sing with the understanding, also"* (I Cor. 14:15).

God's word tells us there are, basically, three
types of sacred music: *"psalms, hymns, and spiritual
songs,* singing and making melody in your heart to
The Lord" *(Eph. 5:19).* "Let the word of Christ dwell
in you richly in all wisdom, teaching and ad-
monishing one another in *psalms* and *hymns* and
spiritual songs, singing with grace in your heart to
The Lord" *(Col. 3:16).*

Psalms are "Scripture set to music." The word

24

SEPARATION OF
CHURCH AND STATE

BACKGROUND BRIEFING *Religion, and freedom to worship God according to dictates of one's conscience —* that was what prompted most early colonists to come to this land. It was also a major cause of break with Great Britain. *"It is indeed time we repossess the important historical truth that religion was a fundamental cause of the American Revolution"* (Carl Bridenbaugh, *Mitre & Sceptre,* 1962). Americans forget, or were never taught, *that a final straw in colonists' decision to separate from Great Britain was Parliament's attempt to establish the Church of England as the "state religion" in American colonies.*

Deeply mindful of oppressions and persecutions state religion combines (church-State) had forced upon them and their fathers, committed to freedom of conscience (most sacred of all property), and *persuaded that the central (Federal) government had no jurisdiction in matters of faith,* framers of US Constitution (50 or 55 being orthodox Christians of various sects) purposefully omitted any reference to religion in that document. It was, they believed, completely out of its proper concern or function. None-the-less, colonies-turned States felt so strongly on the issue that *they refused to ratify Constitution until religious freedom was specifically spelled out and guaranteed* (In First Amendment).

There is nothing in *First Amendment* (or in entire Constitution) — *no word, no phrase, no concept* — to support idea of or demand for "separation of church and State" or to give legal standing to phrase "wall of separation." *What was clearly intended was "hands-off" religion by federal govt.*

As a matter of historical fact, at least one-third of original 13 States ratifying Constitution had predominant faiths which they desired to leave unchallenged or unmolested by central (Federal) government. The Amendment begins, "Congress shall make no law. . . ." Then, as it generally is now, term "Congress was synonymous with "the Federal government." Thus, Amendment is saying, *"The Federal government shall make no law respecting an establishing of religion, or prohibiting the free exercise thereof."*

It is clear that intent and purpose of First Amendment was this:

> *First,* to prohibit establishment of a national religion (such as the Church of England), and
>
> *Second,* to guarantee free exercise of religious belief void of any meddling or entanglement by federal government.

Joseph Story, foremost historian of his day, wrote (in *Commentaries on the Consitution,* 1833):

"... (the First Amendment) was not intended to withdraw the Christian religion as a whole from the protection of Congress . . . (at that time) the general if not universal sentiment in America was, *that Christianity ought to receive encouragement from the State so far as was compatible with the private rights of conscience and the freedom of worship.*

"An attempt to level all religions, and to make it a matter of State policy to hold all in utter indifference would have created . . . *universal indignation.*"

In fact, one of first acts of Congress following drafting of Constitution was *Northwest Ordinance of 1787* which specifically stated that "religion and morality" were essential to good government.

Over the years and more rapidly and pervasively in recent times, US has veered sharply from original intent and purpose of religious liberty clause of First Amendment. This has occurred primarily *via court decrees* based on historically inaccurate information — accidental or otherwise. There can be no doubt that *humanist-controlled State education* encouraged distortion; it was *seed bed* of such deviation and revisionisms.

Under guise of "separation of church and State," courts have led shift from encouragement of Christianity *to indifference* (1861), to declaring that *"humanism" is a religion* (1940), *to levelling religious faiths* (1961), *to protecting and favoring humanism,* and now to position that Christian sects are to be confined to "thought/faith" pursuits and any application of faith must be under State surveillance and control.

So it is US Supreme Court *banned posting of God's Ten Commandments in schoolrooms, took position that The Bible could be read in State-schools only as an historical doc-*

ument or included in a study of, held that States could not approve of prayer in public schools, held that *Nativity scenes and Christmas carols* (in public schools and civic displays) were allowable if given *the same secular status as such frivolities as "Jingle Bells," mistletoe and "Rudolph The Red-Nosed Reindeer."*

By court decree, Christ The King was put on same level as Kris Kringle. In addition, a continuing drive to control Christian ministries and missions through ever-narrowing definitions of tax-exempt status and taxation of churches and church employees via Social Security (FICA taxes), etc.

All the while, *humanism* — defined by Supreme Court as a "religion" — was not only permitted in State schools and other institution, *it was promoted and abetted.*

Constitutional attorney John W. Whitehead stresses fact that phrase "wall of separation" is nowhere to be found in US Constitution and "in fact, the term church and state is lacking in the First Amendment."

Wrote Whitehead in *The Separation Illusion,* "The phrases had their origin in a letter written by (Thomas) Jefferson in 1802 to a group of Baptists in Danbury, Connecticut, in which he maintained that it was the purpose of the First Amendment to build 'a wall of separation between church and state.'" *It is important to note, as Whitehead points out, that Jefferson had nothing to do with drafting the First Amendment and was, in fact, in Paris when the First Amendment was written.*

More importantly, Whitehead emphasizes, is the fact that in his Second Inaugural Address in 1805,

Jefferson stated that *Federal government had no business meddling with or controlling religious liberty:*

"In matters of religion I have considered that its free exercise is placed by the Constitution independent of the power of the General Government. I have therefore undertaken on no occasion to prescribe the religious exercises suited to it, but have left them, as the Constitution found them, under the direction and discipline of the church or state authorities acknowledged by the several religious societies."

Thus, Jefferson brought his views in line with Constitution. Constitutional law authority Edward S. Corwin summed up Jefferson's 1805 statement:

"In short, the principal importance of the amendment lay in separation which it effected between the jurisdiction of state and nation regarding religion, rather than on its bearing on the question of the separation of church and state."

Mr. Corwin concludes with observation that purpose of First Amendment was "to exclude from the national government all power to act on the subject of religion." And, Whitehead adds, "The First Amendment, therefore, provides freedom *for* religion, not freedom *from* religion."

Is it abysmal ignorance of history or rank malfeasance for courts, and legislators and executives to continue to suggest that "separation of church and state" is a part of Constitution of this republic—or that separation of God from government was intent of writers of First Amendment and States which ratified it.

Government is not alone in distorting purpose of the Amendment and using phrases such as "wall of separation" and *"separation of church and State"* to seek to justify their twisting of First Amendment and flagrant usurpation of power never given. Many in educational establishment reverse very purpose of First Amendment in an effort to attack Christians and their religious liberty. Some, even while professing to be Christian believers, demand "religious neutrality" in public affairs, national policies, and political action. They label as "extremists" and "zealots" those Christians who hold The Bible to be textbook for all of life, and Christ as King of all (as did our founding fathers).

While freedom of other groups to expound their dogma, and actively pursue and promote their beliefs, is jealously guarded and zealously promoted, *Bible-believing Christians are told they must be neutral* (i.e. to assume a neutered position on public affairs—spectators excluded from arena of politics and government but not participants) "because of First Amendment." To which Pastor Joseph C. Morecraft, III, responds:

> *"Neutrality in politics is rebellion against The Lord Christ."*

Aside from fact that such "neutrality" denies *sovereignty* of God, and ignores *both the cultural* (dominion) *mandate (Gen 1:28)* and *Christ's Great Commission*

(Mt. 28:19, 20), and is *violation of First Amendment and deprives Christian of his full rights as a citizen,* there is a blatant and serious deceit involved:

The "neutrality" they would impose is not neutral!

What humanists and National Council of Churches *et al* would deny to Bible-believing Christians, *they demand for themselves.* While demanding a divorcement of God's word from civil affairs, they press to put their god(s)—modern man or his "revised gospel" —*into civil orbit.*

They demand, for example, right to press for support of Communist-supported satellite regimes in Africa and South America; right to work actively to impose a oneway nuclear freeze, right to use taxpayer-funded grants to further their programs, and right to blame United States for all of world's ills . . .

. . . but they rise up in (self)righteous anger when other Christians oppose taxpayer support of Communist regimes, or warn that unilateral nuclear freeze and/or disarmament program could make this republic vulnerable to attack, etc., *or take a pro-American stand when nation is belittled by foreign powers.*

Theirs, then, is an ungodly and a double standard: the coin they use to determine to whom we must pay tribute *(Mt. 22:19)* is counterfeit—*it bears the image of Caesar on both sides!*

CONSIDER THE BIBLICAL PRINCIPLES The State is *not* above God *(Acts 5:29)*. The State is not equal to or with God *(Ex. 18:11)*. The State is to be "servant" of God to the people for good through its ministry of justice *(Rom. 13:4)*. The State is accountable to God for its actions *(Job 34:24)*.

The Lord God, He is the *governor* of all nations *(Ps. 22:28);* He is the *Head* above all *(I Chron. 29:11, 12)*. He is *The Supreme Ruler* over all the kings of the earth *(I Cor. 10:26); Rev. 1:5)*. man is to have *no other gods* before Him *(Ex. 20:3)* — *none*: not self, not other men or institutions, *and not the State*. When man hates God, and places himself or his State above God, he writes his own destruction *(Ps. 5:10; Pr. 8:36)*.

"Has a nation changed their gods, which are yet no gods? but My people have changed their glory for that which does not profit. Be astonished, Oh, you heavens, at this and be horribly afraid, be very desolate, says The Lord. For My people have committed two evils: they have forsaken me, the fountain of living waters, and hewed them out cisterns, broken cisterns, that can hold no water" (Jer. 2:11-13).

(Note: In additon to holding no water, broken cisterns permit filth to seep in and pollute any waters that might enter.)

There is *One God,* and one absolute moral order; that is God's law-order and God's law-word *(Dt. 4:6-9)*. To abandon God's law-order for another law results in coming under God's wrath *(Ps. 2:1-5; Isa. 59)*. God is our judge, He is our lawgiver, He is our King (chief executive) *(Isa. 33:22)*. Only His law is perfect and just *(Dt. 4:8);* only his word will stand forever *(Mt. 24:35).*

God, not man, *ordained and established civil government* (the corporate body politic) *(Gen. 9:4-6; Dan. 4:17; Rom. 13:1).* Government (the State) is, in the final analysis, the flow of *God's* power and force *(Job 12:23; Jer. 27:5).* All power is His *(Mt. 6:13; Rom. 1:20).* All power in heaven and earth was given to Christ Jesus *(Mt. 28:18);* He is Lord of all and King of Kings *(I Cor. 15:27; I Tim. 6:15).* Government rests on His shoulders *(Isa. 9:6, 7).* Thus, the powers (authorities) that be are ordained (commissioned) of Him as long as they employ that power in keeping with His will and law *(Rom. 13:1).*

When we understand that government is the flow of (His) power and force *through the individual* (created in His image) *to the State,* and when we know and believe that all is under Him and answerable to Him, then we understand this:

> The division between church and State is *one of function;* it is *a division of labor in God's world* — the church is to be a minister of *grace,* the State is to be a minister of *justice.* Both are branches of His government and both are to serve The Lord God.

God is the Supreme Sovereign. To seek to place man or state above God, or apart from God — or to place man's law above God's law — is to seek to limit the sovereignty of God. God holds such attempts — and such attempters — in derision *(Ps. 2:4-5).*

You shall love The Lord your God with all your heart,

and with all your soul, and with all your might" (Dt. 6:5; Mt. 22:37). *"This is the first and great Commandment."* That is total, totality: *God above all; God over all.* It means putting a lock on our personal desires and thoughts, our affections, our understandings and our action — *and then handing the key to The Lord.*

"If you love Me," says Jesus, *"You will keep My commandments."* Obedience, then, is the manifestation of *love.* And, seeking to obey Him, totally, is seeking to love Him, totally. Thus, what is involved is a total commitment, embracing all of life — excluding nothing, *including civil affairs and the State.*

Those who seek to be His — all His — *cannot ever be "neutral." A "neutral" Christian is a contradiction in terms;* when one accepts Christ as King, any thought of neutrality must end: we are His, we are *commissioned,* we are *mandated* to stand for Christ in all things. Our Savior and our King warned us about neutrality: those who are luke-warm, He will spew out of His mouth *(Rev. 3:16).*

In the final analysis, then, the demand for "separation of church and State" — the ungodly "wall of separation" — is at its root and purpose *a snare and a delusion and a deceit.* The crux of the matter, and the battle, is what it always has been:

man against God, humanism versus Christ.

"Choose you this day whom you will serve."

RECOMMENDED READING: John W. Whitehead, *The Separation Illusion,* Mott Media, Milford, MI 1977.

24

SEX EDUCATION AND VALUES MANIPULATION

BACKGROUND BRIEFING Regarding "sexual mores" in USA, *the revolution was* started in 1960s, raged during '70s, has slowed but still spreading in '80s. Revolution spawned, in part, by *radical rebellion,* rising tide of *nihilism and "Me-ism"* (both facets of humanism) and *"cultural pathology"* (a rejection of traditional values and cultural restraints that results in tosses everything "up in the air" or out the window.). Also, sex revolution is companion of *"rock" music and drugs.* Research find drugs and sexual promiscuity/ perversion go hand-in-hand; observers believe drug problem will not be solved until "free sex" attitudes are curbed.

But, one major instigator of "sexual revolution" *sex education in public* (State) schools. Sex ed courses filling many young people with ideas (1) that *traditional values and Christian morality are "junk,"* (2) that most *parents are "ignorant, intolerant, irrational and old-fashioned,* (3) that *Scriptures are "moralizing crap"* and (4) that the old *" 'shalt nots' simply are no longer relevant."*

Prior to 1960s — *when some semblance of Christian*

morality was still alive and in force in American classrooms, there were almost no teenage pregnancies under 16, and very little veneral disease among teenagers of any age. Today, after years of sex "education" (values manipulation), *both are rampant* (Gloria Dei Enterprises).

Sex education has — in sum and substance — become a *rogue elephant that tramples on individual privacy, runs rough-shod over parent-child relations,* seeks to *root out absolutes of right and wrong* . . . has left millions of wrecked homes, families and lives in its wake.

Sex educators claim programs are "value free," deal only with biology and physiology. *Course audits show clearly that is not true:* programs deal more with "sociology" than biology and are largely concerned with *values manipulation.*

"The purpose of sex education is to eradicate Christian values and Christian behavior relating to sexual activity and to replace them with Humanist values and behaviour." *(Barbara Morris* in *Change Agents In The Schools.)* After infamous *Roe v. Wade* decision on abortion by US Supreme Court, Dr. Alan Guttmacher, past president of Planned Parenthood boasted, *"The only avenue in which Planned Parenthood has to win the battle is sex education."*

One signer of *Humanist Manifesto, II,* Dr. Thomas Szasz, agrees that "What sex educators want is not to impart information but to influence behaviour." Dr. Szasz charges that "so-called sex education as practised is a mass of misinformation and outright fraud." Dr. Szasz might have added, *"disinformation"*

—a prime tool of the change agent.

Thus, underlying purpose and thrust of sex ed programs cannot be fully comprehended unless seen as one phase of a humanistic attempt to alter values of American youth. And, that goes hand-in-hand with promulgation of socialism. "It is no accident . . . they supplement each other . . . The socialist project of homogenizing society demands that the family be vitiated or destroyed. This can be accomplished in good measure by profaning (marriage love) and breaking monogamy's link between sex and loyalty." (Joseph Sobran, "What Is This Thing Called Sex?" *National Review*, 1/1/81.)

Margaret Sanger, founder of National Birth Control League (which became Planned Parenthood Federation), and "Humanist of The Year" in 1965, is often called the mother of sex education. Mrs. Sanger was one of the most radical feminists of all times. Her numerous extra-marital affairs was basis for Wm. Sanger's divorce. Her "creed" was free love, birth control, abortion and the sterilization of those she considered inferior. (Margaret Sanger: *A Biography of the Champion of Birth Control,* by Madeline Gray.)

"The full legacy of Sanger's philosophy has been the sexual revolution of the 1960s and 1970s: *Abortion on demand, multiple divorces, serial marriages, and a soaring rate of child abuse in all countries where abortion is legal, and epidemics of venereal and sexually transmitted diseases.*" (Bower & Kippley, *Not In The Public Interest: The Planned Parenthood Version of Sex Education.*)

"When Margaret Sanger's International Planned

BIBLICAL PRINCIPLES vs THE EVILS OF HUMANISM

GOD'S WORD

"Teaching us that, denying ungodliness and worldly lusts, we should live soberly, righteously, and godly in this present world" (Titus 2:12). "Because it is written, Be ye holy; for I am holy" (1 Pet. 1:16). "Let us hear the conclusion of the whole matter: Fear God, and keep His commandments: for this is the whole duty of man" (Ecc. 12:113, 14).

SEXUAL CONDUCT

"Therefore shall a man leave his father and his mother and shall cleave unto his wife: and they shall be one flesh" (Gen. 2:24; Mt. 19:5). "What? know ye not that he which is joined to a harlot is one body? for two, saith He, shall be one flesh" (1 Cor. 6:16). "I beseech ye, therefore . . . that ye present your bodies a living sacrifice, holy, acceptable unto God" (Rom. 12:1). "Know ye not that ye are the temple of God . . . if any man defile the temple of God, him shall God destroy" (1 Cor. 3:16, 17). "That every one of you should know how to possess his vessel in sanctification and honor" (1 Thes. 4:4, 5). See also 1 Cor. 7:2-4; Pr. 5:1-23; Eph. 5:25-29; 1 Thes. 5:22; Heb. 13:4; 1 Pet. 3:7.

MORAL VALUES

"Thy word have I hid in my heart, that I might not sin against Thee" (Ps. 119:11). "Let this mind be in you which was in Christ Jesus" (Php. 2:5). "And herein do I exercise

TENETS OF HUMANISM

"Yeah, hath God said . . . ?" (Gen. 3:1). "And, even as they did not like to retain God in their knowledge, God gave them over to a reprobate mind, to do things which are not convenient" (Rom. 1:28).

"In the area of sexuality, we believe that intolerant atti-tudes, often cultivated by orthodox religions and puritanical cultures, unduly repress sexual conduct . . . '" "Sex is fun and joyful, and it comes in all types and styles all of which are okay. Do what gives pleasure and enjoy what gives pleasure, and ask for what gives pleasure. Don't rob yourself of joy by focusing on old-fashioned ideas about what's 'normal' or 'nice.'" (Planned Parenthood booklet for teenagers).

" . . . moral values derive their source from human ex-perience. Ethics is autonomous and situational, needs no theological or ideological sanction."[2] "Parents with tradi-

myself, to have always a conscience void of offense toward God, and toward men" (Acts 24:16). "Beware lest any man spoil you through philosophy and vain deceit, after the tradition of men, after the rudiments of the world, and not after Christ" (Col. 2:8). "But, put ye on The Lord Jesus Christ, and make not provision for the flesh to fulfill the lusts thereof" (Rom. 13:14). See also Num. 15:38 and 3 John 11. "Having therefore these promises dearly beloved, let us cleanse ourselves from all filthiness of the flesh and spirit, perfecting holiness in the fear of God" (2 Cor. 7:1).

PARENTS & FAMILY

"Train up a child in the way he should go: and when he is old he will not depart from it" (Pr. 22:6). "Ye fathers, provoke not your children to wrath: but bring them up in the nurture and admonition of The Lord" (Eph. 6:4). "And ye shall teach them (The Lord's commandments) to your children, speaking of them when thou sittest in thine house, and when thou walkest by the way, when thou liest down, and when thou risest up" (Deut. 11:19). See also Deut. 6:8, 9.

CHILDREN

"Children, obey your parents in The Lord, for this is right. Honor thy father and mother; which is the first commandment with promise" (Eph. 6:1-3). "My son, keep thy father's commandments, and forsake not the law of thy mother; bind them continually upon thine heart" (Pr. 6:20-23, Also Ex. 21:17).

tional values are 'intolerant, ignorant and bigoted' . . . Sex educators approach the following with an 'openess' to 'relieve' the child's anxieties: non-marital sex, homosexuality, masturbation, abortion, contraception and incest. Noticeably missing are God's plan for reproduction, the beauty of marital sex, and the value of abstinence until marriage."[3] "Schools must not be allowed to continue the immorality of morality. An entirely different set of values must be nourished." (Sexuality and the School, Marianne & Sidney Simon.)

PARENTS & FAMILY

Parents are the worst source of factual information regarding sex. (Human Sexuality, textbook) "DOP (Dimensions of Personality, a course used in some 4th, 5th, & 6th grades) demotes and patronizes the parent when it isn't showing them to be mean, lacking in sensitivity to the child's feelings . . . parents hold foolish and false values. Children are told their parents lack the skills to be good parents."[4]

CHILDREN

Planned Parenthood calls for compulsory state sex education, K-12th grades.[5] "No religious views, no community moral standards, are to deflect (the child) from the overriding purposes of self-discovery, self-assertion and self-gratification."[6]

FORNICATION/ADULTERY

"Thou shalt not commit adultery" (Ex. 20:14). "Abstain from fleshly lusts that war against the soul" (1 Pet. 2:11). "For this is the will of God, even your sanctification, that ye should abstain from fornication. . . . For God has not called us unto uncleanness but unto holiness" (1 Thes. 5:22). "Now the works of the flesh are manifest, which are these: adultery, fornication, uncleanness, lasciviousness . . . that they which do such things shall not inherit the kingdom of God" (Gal. 5:19-21). See also Mt. 5:27, 28; Pr. 6:20-35; 7:1-27; Acts 15:20; 21:25, and 1 Cor. 5:1-8.

"Youth is led (through school sex-ed programs) to believe that carnality need not be sublimated; governing factors responsible for normal maturation are thereby excluded from their lives."[7] ". . . teachers must be alert to keep 'moralizing crap' (Christian morality) out of their work with values."[8] ". . . a lengthy list of reasons why young people have sex . . . included such reasons as 'they want to prove their masculinity or femininity,' 'everybody else is doing it,' etc. without once mentioning love or marriage."[9]

SODOMY

"In the image of God created He him; male and female created He them" (Gen. 1:27). "Thou shalt not lie with man-kind as with womankind . . . Defile not yourself in any of these things" (Lev. 18:22-24). "For this cause God gave them up unto vile affections: for even their women did change the natural use into that which is against nature: And likewise the men, leaving the natural use of the woman, burned in their lust one toward another . . . receiving in themselves that recompense of their error which was meet" (Rom. 1:26, 27).

"The prevailing theme . . . children from sixth grade on must come to accept it (homosexuality) as normal" . . . "a good experience (is to) have two 10-yr-old girls 'role play' two male lovers. Parents who quote Scriptures against homosexuality are 'irrational,' their minds are perverted . . ."[10]

ABORTION

"Thou shalt not commit murder" (Ex. 20:13). "If a man strive and hurt a woman so that her fruit depart from her (i.e.

Abortion is touted to young people as one more form of birth and population control. Planned Parenthood centers arrange

miscarriage) . . . and if any mischief (harm, loss of life to mother or child) follow, then thou shalt give life for life" (Ex. 21:22-25). See also Deut. 22:6, 7; Isa. 59:1-9).

"Wherefore God also gave them up to uncleanness through the lusts of their own hearts, to dishonor their own bodies between themselves" (Rom. 1:24, 28-31). "While they promise them liberty, they themselves are the servants of corruption: for of whom a man is overcome, of the same is he brought into bondage" (2 Pet. 2:19). "Thus they were defiled with their own works, and went a whoring with their own inventions (ideas). Therefore was the wrath of The Lord kindled against His people, insomuch that He abhorred His own inheritance" (Ps. 106:39-41).

for teenage abortions without parental knowledge or consent.[11] "What happens . . . if you get pregnant, what are the choices? Well, you can carry the baby or abort . . ."[12]

PERVERSION

". . . the many varieties of sexual exploration should not in themselves be considered evil . . Individuals should be permitted to express their sexual proclivities and pursue their life-style as desired."[1] "Perversion is a word that should be discarded."[13] "The influence of sex educators has the same effect as seduction, which can lead the young person into all kinds of sexual aberrations."[14]

Notes

1. *Humanist Manifesto*, II, 1973.
2. *Idem.*
3. Report on Sex Educators' Workshop, Washington, DC, 11/81, by Mrs. Daren Davis, *Christian Women's National Concerns*, Ft. Worth TX.
4. Dr. Rhoda Lorand, as quoted in "Weep For Your Children," Dr. Murray Norris, *Christian Family Renewal*. Clovis, CA.
5. *Family Protection Report*, Washington, DC, 1/81.
6. Prof. Jacqueline Kasun, "Turning Our Children into Sex Experts," *Sex Education and Mental Health Report*, 1979.
7. Dr. Melvin Anchel, "A Psychiatrist Looks At Sex Education," *Up With Families*, Clovis, CA, 8/81.
8. Dr. Sidney Simon, as quoted by Farnum Gray in "Doing Something About Values."
9. Prof. Kasun, *op. cit.*
10. Mary Lee Tatum, Sex Educators' Workshop, *op. cit.*
11. Janis Sumpter, "A Mother Reports From The Battle Front," *CAPSULE*, Caravans for Christ, Stewartsville, MO, 1/81.
12. Mary Lee Tatum, *op. cit.*
13. Lars Ullerstam, MD, "The Erotic Minorities."
14. Dr. Melvin Anchel, *op. cit.*

Parenthood sexologists first attacked America's . . . Christian foundation of moral ethics, there was only one divorce in every 11 marriages. Now, 50% of all marriages end in divorce. . . ." ("Where There's God's Will There's A Way," Gloria Dei Enterprises.)

Current impetus for sex ed sprang from 1961 conference on *Church and Family* called by *National Council of Churches*. Delegates from 28 Protestant churches met with scientists and educators to discuss sex and marriage, came up with assertion that "sex codes requiring too high a level of ethical sensitivity are harmful," called for "Understanding, tolerance and reform as a meaningful Christian ethic of sexual behaviour was developed." *Any reference to Biblical mandates and principles was absent.* Conference birthed *SIECUS* (Sex Information and Education Council of the US). Today, SIECUS is major purveyor of "value free" sex ed programs in public schools along with Planned Parenthood, the National PTA, and National Education Assn. (NEA).

". . . the dominating characteristic of the programs (pushed by those agencies) is their obvious promulgation of the philosophy of humanism. Thus, there has been the elimination of any established moral base, any traditional values, any Scriptural principles that support a belief in absolutes declared by God in His word. All this is in a philosophical attitude of permissiveness." ("Sex Education," THE CAPSULE, 1/81.)

Consider the assist given to teenage and preteenage "sex education" by American Library Assn. (1978 resolution): "ALA urges librarians and library educators to re-examine existing policies and practices, and to assume a leadership role in seeing that information is available to children and adolescents . . . to assure that comprehensive sex-related education materials, programs, referral and health services for youth are available and publicized."

Promoters insist sex ed in schools is necessary because most parents won't or don't teach their children at home. *Surveys indicate otherwise.* National poll reported 87% of parents want to teach their teenage sons about sex, 91% their teenage daughters. Only 7% wanted schools to do the job; some opted for church or doctor. More than 50% said children should not be burdened with such information before they reach their teens — *yet, some sex ed classes begin in first and second grades!*

"Sex education programs cause particular harm to children between the ages of 6 and 12," warns *Dr. Melvin Anchel,* psychiatrist. During those years, he points out, latent sex drive is sublimated into seeking personal achievements and feelings of compassion; when that latency is stimulated and diverted through sex ed programs it can do irreparable harm and *in later life often results in sex cruelty or perversion.* (Sex educators maintain there is no such thing as sex perversion; that the term is a manifestation of the "hang ups" caused by "religious bigotry and puritanical cultures.")

Sex ed promoters (SEICUS, Planned Parenthood, etc.) claim sexual activities among youth is natural and inevitable and should be made "safe" by arming children with information, contraceptives and access to abortion. Studies show their claims are totally false. Opponents of State-controlled sex ed cite the record of damage and despair in *Denmark and Sweden;* such sex ed programs have been compulsory in those nations for well over a decade:

> "Denmark and Sweden experienced a 200% to 500% rise in VD, teenage pregnancies, abortion, divorce and suicide since sex education was made compulsory."

In 1949, USSR outlawed classroom sex education as a "detriment to society;" decreed such training must be handled in the home.

Professor Philip Cutright, Indiana Univ., observed: "In these younger groups we find no evidence that (sex ed) programs reduced illegitimacy . . . Veneral disease is actually found to increase . . . the reason for negative results is that the programs stimulate much higher rates of sexual activity." Other studies show that when teens are "given information and access to contraceptives, they assume 100% freedom and safety in sex, and activity increases." In addition to seeking to replace traditional values with a "there is no 'right' or 'wrong' but only what feels good for you," sex ed programs often fail to stress to young girls the dangers of IUD and "the pill" and the higher incidence of cervical cancer caused by premature sex and promiscuity.

When does sex education start in State (public) *schools?* How long does it continue? Generally, it is a K-12 continuing program conducted under a variety of classes: Family Planning, Health, Biology, Life

Sciences, Social Science, Human Sexuality, Home Economics, etc. In first grade, sex ed may start with a "mixed-group" tour of restrooms and an explanation of male and female genitals. By fourth grade, many students receive a detailed description of human sexual intercourse. In many schools, seventh and eighth graders may spend one-fifth of the day for four weeks on sex ed. Discussions center primarily around "values clarification." In all but a few instances, *traditional values are debunked, sexual activity* (how and with whom) *is presented as "strictly a matter of personal preference," sexual deviation (homosexuality, incest, etc.) is viewed as acceptable* (see accompanying chart). Love and marriage are largely ignored.

Who foots bill for sex ed? Taxpayers, mostly. Millions of tax $ from Federal govt. (Title X grants) go for sex education and contraceptive programs. However, large foundations (Rockefeller etc.) pour millions into sex ed through such organizations as Planned Parenthood.

RECOMMENDED READING: "Sex Education," The CAPSULE, 1204 W, 5th Street Terrace, Cameron, MO 64429; *Weep For Your Children,* Dr. Murray Norris, Christian Family Renewal, Box 73, Clovis, CA 93613; *Turning Our Children Into Sex Experts,* Christian Family Renewal; *Sex Education in the Public Schools & Planned Parenthood,* Karen Davis, Christian Women's National Concerns, P O Box 18489, Ft. Worth, TX 76118. For additional information regarding sex education in the State schools and what you can do about it, contact your local Pro-Family Forum, or write *PACT* (Parents and Children Together), 522 Hilaire Road, St. Davids, PA 19087.

25

SOCIAL SECURITY AND THE TAXING OF CHURCHES

BACKGROUND BRIEFING Congress passed *Social Security Act* Aug. 14, 1935. Benefits were not intended as full-scale retirement program; only a partial replacement of wages lost due to retirement. In 1937 1% of worker's first $3,000 earnings went to federal old age insurance fund ($30/yr matched by tax on employer). Since 1937, Congress has *expanded* program *13 times; tax rate* has been increased *seven* times, *taxable earnings* have been *upped $30,000—for a net Social Security tax increase at the top of 670%.*

At start, Social Security paid only retirement benefits; now, *21 general types of benefits* provided by *Old Age Survivors and Disability Insurance* (OASDI). This yr *Federal Insurance Contributions Act* (FICA) tax on both employee and employer is *7% on wages up to $37,500* (9.35% for self-employed). Maximum annual employee-employer tax is $5,250; *will increase to 15.3% of wages up to $57,000 by 1990.*

51% of all Americans pay more FICA taxes than federal income taxes. 13 + % of national payroll goes to OASDI. In 1970, OASDI expenditures took 18.7%

of federal budget; today, more than 27%. In 1970, OASDI took 3.8% of gross national product (GNP); *now, 6.5%.*

From 1935 to 1982, Social Security taxes totalled $1 trillion. $1 trillion in OASDI benefits will be paid out in the four years, 1983-1986, OASDI is voracious. It can aggravate fiscal crises (a 1% hike in inflation ups OASDI payouts $1.5 billion/yr; 1% increase in unemployment reduces OASDI revenues by $2 billion). *OASDI tax hikes worsen unemployment.* Estimated social security tax increases since 1977 have cost at least 500,000 jobs (funds could have gone for plant expansion/equipment instead of OASDI). Higher FICA taxes starting in 1984 may cause additional unemployment through 1990. *OASDI lessens ability and incentive for Americans to save* (economists estimates a loss of 35% in savings); thus, private sector being decapitalized and GNP lowered.

Yet, with increases in taxes, and reforms of Social Security Amendments of 1983, OASDI is *still fiscal nightmare.* System's *unfunded liabilities* (to cover those now under the program) *is $5.6 trillion* — about 5 times greater than rest of federal debt. *System's future solvency even more unsettled: when baby-boomers of '40s and '50s* reach retirement age, workers then will be even more heavily taxed to fund system. Economist Michael Boskin warns: *unless honest solutions are found and commitments honored, US faces "greatest tax revolt and age warfare in (its) history."*

What caused crisis in Social Security program? *Politics*, mostly. Congress *bought votes with "liberalized" benefits,* depleted reserves (average Social Security beneficiary receives about five times as much as he/she paid into system). In face of increased longevity of American workers, politicians okayed *earlier retirement* (at age 62 at 80% of maximum benefits), eased requirements for *disability benefits,* added *hospital insurance, special student benefits,* etc. Also, ratio of workers to recipients has declined drastically. In 1940, 16 workers funded each social security recipient; *in 1984, it's 3-to-1 with a projected decline to 2-to-1 by yr 2,000.* (By then, at present trends, OASDI expenditures will take 10% of GNP, 43% of federal budget—and 30 + % of average worker's wages.)

Is OASDI a good deal? *For some, yes.* Those who have been in it since start will benefit from being in the "legalized pyramid club." *For example:* a 65-yr-old retiree as of Dec. 1981 would have paid in (at most) a total of $14,760 and would get that back in just 19 months.

But, for the young worker, it's a lousy investment (thus, participation mandatory rather than voluntary). Worker entering system in 1980, earning average wage all his life and retiring at 65, will probably pay more than $335,000 over the length of his working years (the actual amount will depend on future wage trends since tax base is now indexed). But, he would receive OASDI benefits of *about $15,000/yr* for himself and spouse and thus would have to live to be almost ninety to have benefits equal tax paid. If, however, deposits equal to FICA taxes were put into *private fund at 6%,* he could retire at 65 on *$45,000/yr or could draw $28,000/yr and bequeath an estate worth*

$500,000. OASDI is now virtually a full-scale tax-funded welfare program; *97% of all Americans over age 65 depend on it for large part of income.* (Each yr *$60 million* in social security benefits go to *felons behind bars* and *between $500-700 million goes to aliens* — many of whom made minimal contributions to OASDI *and have returned to their native lands.*)

In 1982-83, system teetered on bankruptcy. *Social Security Amendments of 1983* (Public Law 98-21) intended to solve problems and prevent system going broke: *payroll taxes increased* starting 1/84, *more hikes* to come; cost of living adjustments on benefits *delayed;* middle-upper-income retirees will be *taxed on benefits* they receive; full-benefits *retirement age* to be *raised* from 65 to 67 by 2027; *benefits reduced for early retirement* (before age 65), benefits increased if later retirement taken (after 65).

Revisions estimated to save Social Security system about *$160 billion,* 1983-89, plus some long-run savings. Authors say this will insure system's solvency for many years. Others challenge that, *say it falls short of meeting needs* by about one-third; point to Medicare's rapidly growing financial crisis which was not addressed.

So much for dollars and cents. Consider more important impact: Section 102 of 1983 law, passed by Congress and signed by President Reagan on April 20, 1983. It *mandates employees of non-profit organizations must be covered by OASDI and must pay tax.*

It meant for first time in nation's history, federal govt. taxes religion.

Church staff (secretaries, sextons/janitors, etc.

and church school teachers) *must join Social Security, must pay FICA tax.* Original provision compelled churches to collect employee's FICA tax and *also pay employer's tax.* Estimated social security *taxes* under that law would have *cost Christian schools about $240,000 a day.*

Tax on religion brought storm of protest. Senator Tom Eagleton (MO) told Senate Finance Committee ". . . mandating participation of religious organizations in tax system *violates Constitutional principles of religious liberty* required by First Amendment . . ." Foremost Constitutional atty William B. Ball warned "(Congress) has not only said in effect that *churches and other religious bodies must pay if they are to carry out thier God-given mandate* or else suffer persecution and penalties; *it has also set the stage for further taxation.*" Forest Montgomery, counsel to Natnl. Assn. of Evangelicals, urged Congress to rescind tax on church and halt what he sees as "an inevitable confrontation between church and state."

(*National Council of Churches and Lutheran Council in USA, support mandatory tax.* Many NCC member churches joined social security voluntarily in past yrs. NCC says solvency of social security system is "*a state interest that may outweigh any claims of religious liberty* . . ." *Atty. Ball disagrees,* says no evidence whatever that "whether churches are in or out of the program will affect the health" of Social Security program.

Dr. Gerald Carlson, American Assn. of Christian Schools, insisted (1) *govt. does not have power to tax church;* (2) *Christian school is inseparable part of church ministry;* (3) mandated payment of social security

(FICA) *tax violates time-honored principle of separation of church and state. Pastor Kent Kelly,* Calvary Memorial Church, Southern Pines, NC, and pres., Christian Schools of NC, argued *it is not ministry of church to collect taxes for State,* and to do so would give IRS access to church records (excessive entanglement).

More than 8,000 pastors vowed not to pay tax. Christian attys warned *IRS has power to put liens and levies on church property* and hold *individually responsible* pastors, deacons, elders, or trustees involved in refusal to pay tax.

Pastors across nation stood firm: they *could not* and *would not* pay the tax because of religious and Biblical convictions. President Reagan adamant: stated Social Security Act of 1983 was *"untamperable,"* churches must pay the FICA tax.

However, faced with possibility of thousands of pastors, church officers and employees being indicted or jailed, or church properties being seized, Congress had second thoughts. On July 17, 1984, *Congress passed so-called "Dole Amendment" and repealed direct FICA tax on church and church-controlled organizations* (i.e. Church schools). *But, Amendment shifts entire tax to church employee* and renders that person "self-employed." In other words, FICA tax is lifted but SETA (Self Employment Tax Act) is enforced. (Churches have until Oct. 15, 1984, to make one-time irrevocable election to opt out of Social Security system and shift tax to its employees.)

Must all church employees pay? *No.* Members of "religious orders" (*nuns* and *priests*), and *Christian Science* practitioners are exempted (ministers are considered "self employed," thus pay on that basis).

Christian leaders see switch an unfortunate and unsatisfactory compromise. Clearly, Dole Amendment simply *switches OASDI levy on church from direct to indirect taxation: and they argue, a tax is still a tax*—direct or indirect.

Some churches refusing to exercise "election for exemption" option, or require employees to pay SETA. They plan to press test case in court. *Dr. Richard Harris,* pastor of Bethel Baptist, Sellersville, PA, and pres. Keystone Christian Education Assn. explained why his congregation has agreed to take lead battle:

1. Congress continues in its purposes to tax churches, even if indirectly. 2. Since church employees are part of church, indispensable to church, tax on them is tax on church. 3. If church accepts "exemption," it permits federal govt. to change relationship between church and its employees (i.e. church staff member to be considered "self-employed"). This would constitute federal entanglement in the affairs of the church. 4. The Bethel Baptist case (to be argued by atty. William B. Ball) will test both constitutionality of taxing church or church employees. And, 5. "To accept this provision (i.e. the "election of exemption") the church is further silenced instead of raising its voice in opposition to the continuing and expanding intrusion of the Federal Government into (God's mandated way of) family affairs." (See "Biblical Principles" that follow.)

Should Christians go to court in such matters? Yes! Purpose of civil government is to be a servant (minister) of God through ministry of justice. And,

The Lord God, through Moses, ordained and established system of courts to administer justice (*Ex. 18:21, Dt. 6:18; 7:8, 9*). The Apostle Paul, a citizen of Rome, when charged with sedition because he preached the word of God used litigation to defend himself (*Acts 22:25-20; 25:10-12*).

CONSIDER THE BIBLICAL PRINCIPLES "Social Security" (OASDI, its related programs and problems) is one more example of *rejection of God's sovereignty and disobedience to God's* laws regarding the tithe, the family, care of elderly, and "welfare programs." By accepting Caesar as major source of care for the aged, disabled, and survivors (widows & orphans), nation attempts to escape Biblically-mandated *personal and family* responsibilities. OASDI makes Caesar "the great provider;" *that will not work* (*Mt. 7:24*).

According to God's word (and The Word), individuals, families, and congregations are responsible for care of elderly and needy. Is heavy and intrusive hand of Caesar punishment upon people who refuse to obey God? *The lighter we take God's commandments, the heavier God permits Caesar's hand to weigh upon the land (Dt. 28:15-68; I Sam. 8:15; Mal. 3:8, 9).*

Parents are to care for and provide for children, including an inheritance (*Dt. 21:15-17; 2 Cor. 12:14*). In this manner, Godly culture/society is perpetuated through the generations, and God's will on earth is dynamically developed and extended. At same time, children are to honor parents (*Ex. 20:12; Eph. 6:2, 3*); this includes caring for them in their old age if need be (*Mt. 15:1-9*). That does *not* mean handing them over to Caesar's tax-supported and often dehumanizing care. The son or daughter who fails to care for parents in need is *cursed;* considered worse than an infidel (*Dt. 27:16; 1 Tim. 5:8*). One of "bloody abominations" of ancient Jerusalem was failure of the people to obey The Lord God in that respect (*Ezek. 22:7*).

In God's order, family is basic unit, the foundation of society (*Gen. 2:24; Num. 1:1-3; Mt. 19:4-6*); its God-ordained functions are *both spiritual and material* (economic). Consider the words of Christ: children who view care of the parents to be an option or a "gift" rather than a God-mandated responsibility, *deny the word of God*. And, consider His words on the cross as a good son keeping His Father's law: Jesus made sure His earthly mother would be cared for after He departed (*Jn. 19:26, 27*).

When the family cannot provide care of elderly, widowed and orphaned, needy or disabled, responsibility rests with congregation, the local assembly of believers (*Gal. 6:2; Rom 5:1; James 2:8*) — thus, *it falls on each one of us as a part of our life-work for Him* (*Mt. 25:31-36*). It must be a *personal* work, an *individual* responsibility, as Jesus commands — *not* a program under Caesar. in a very really sense, expecting the State to assume duties which our King has assigned to His own is to "render unto Caesar" those things which belong to God and His people. (In strict economic terms, Caesar's legion of horrors *cost four to five times as much* — thus taking in taxes those funds which could better be spent to serve others and do our work for The Lord.

Those who preach/teach a "dialectical gospel" in which State and its institution are instruments of first resort for "welfare" are at odds with God's word (*1 Sam. 8:7, 18*). They magnify Caesar and diminish flow of God's bounty in and through the lives of those whom He expects to fulfill His royal law (*Mt. 22:37-40*). Thus, *tithing* (of time and money) is a rudimentary requirement if we will obey the Lord and seek to serve Him by serving others (*Lev. 27:30-33; Dt. 14:17-29*). Should any one question the sufficiency of His funds, let them remember God's promise in *Mal. 3:10*. Who dares to suggest the hand of The Lord waxes short (*Num. 11:23*)?

Consider now the most basic principle: God's supreme and total sovereignty.

Taxation is assertion of sovereignty; the assumption of power to control. it is a claim of *pre-eminence*. Thus, when State taxes the church, as it does under Social Security Reform Act of 1983, *it asserts its sovereignty over Christ's church* and takes unto itself the right to control it. Congress and Chief executive have placed State (federal govt) *above the sovereignty of God*. They have made of the State ("public policy") a god and put it above The One True God; thus they violate God's First Commandment (*Ex. 20:3-5*).

Even pagan Artaxerxes, king of Persia, acknowledged the sovereignty of God and sanctity of God's house and holy servants. Mark these words in the letter of authority and credit which king Artaxerxes gave to Ezra (an able scholar in the law of Moses who was chosen by God to restore the temple):

"Whatever is commanded by the God of heaven, let it be diligently done for the house of the God of heaven: for why should there be wrath against the relm of the king and his sons? Also, we certify to you, that touching any of the priests and Levites, singers, porters (door-keepers), Nethinim, or ministers of this house of God, *it shall not be lawful to impose toll, tribute or custom upon them"* (Ezra 7:23, 24).

That which is *"devoted"* to The Lord (i.e. established/operated/maintained by tithes and gifts to worship and serve God) *is "most holy unto The Lord"*—it is *not* to be taxed, incumbered or decapitalized (*Lev. 27:28-34*). To tax such property—such holy estate—is to tax The Lord God just as the State taxes the individual when it taxes his property. For the church to pay tax to the State is to agree that it exists by the grace of the State *(rather than the grace of God)* and is a subject of the State *(rather than of The Lord God).* That the church of Christ cannot do; for, *the church is Christ's body, not Caesar's.*

What does the Psalmist say of those who would appropriate God's property? *"O, my God, make them like a wheel; as the stubble before the wind. As the fire burns wood, and as the flame sets the mountain on fire; so persecute them with Your tempest and make them afraid with Your storm. Fill their faces with shame; that they may seek Your name, O Lord. Let them be confounded and troubled forever; yea, let them be put to shame, and perish: that men may know that You, whose name alone is Jehovah, are The Most High above all the earth"* (Ps. 83:13-18).

God's people cannot accept any law, any regulation, that places the sovereignty of man or State above the sovereignty of

God. Those who accept or condone such laws that are illegitimate in the eyes of God are as guilty as those who originated and enforced the illegality. Thus says the word of God (*Ps. 50:18*).

What, then, shall we do? The proper course is not anarchy, not revolution, *but a revival of tithe while using God-ordained court system to end the violation.* The tithe advances God's kingdom on earth; God means it to be used to create His order. It is incumbent upon individual and congregation to be about His works and to enlist others in them . . . *keeping in mind always that all we do must honor and glorify Him.* Consider this concerning Ezra, used mightily of God: "*For Ezra had prepared his heart* to seek the law of The Lord, *and to do it,* and to teach in Israel statutes and judgments" (*Ezra 7:10*). *Thus could The Lord use Him . . . even as he would use us, now.*

References & Sources

1. John W. Whitehead and Tedd Williams, "The Social Security Amendments of 1983: Impact on and Response By Churches," *The Rutherford Institute,* Manassas, VA, January 1984.
2. "Social Security Tax on Churches," *Freedom Defender,* Pennsylvanians for Biblical morality, Harrisburg, PA, January 1984, p. 3.
3. Bill King, "Churches Battling Social Security Tax," *Washington (DC) Times,* December 14, 1983.
4. William Bole, "Evangelicals Warns Congress on Social Security Reforms," *Christian News,* December 26, 1983, p. 19.
5. "Social Security: Changes and Choices," ALERT, National Christian Action Coalition, Washington, DC, October 1983.

6. "School Leaders on Social Security Issue," ALERT, National Christian Action Coalition, Washington, DC, December 1983.

7. Jack Clayton, "Social Security Options," *The CS Newsletter,* American Association of Christian Schools, Normal, IL, October 1983.

8. Dr. Gerald Carlson, "The Social Security Threat," *The CS Newsletter,* American Association of Christian Schools, Normal, IL, January 1984.

9. Pastor Kent Kelly, "A Minority Report," Christian Schools of North Carolina (undated, c December 1983).

10. Hobart Rowen, "Ducking Social Security,' *Washington (DC) Post,* February 27, 1984.

11. Peter Germanis, "Social Security 'Lousy'," *Manchester (NH) Union Leader,* February 1, 1984.

12. Micket D. Levy, "Social Security: Vast Improvement, but Major Problems Remain," *The Economist,* American Enterprise Institute for Public Policy Research, Washington DC, April 1983, pp. 1-8.

13. Senator Jesse Helms, "Social Security Guarantee and Individual Retirement Security Act of 1983," *Congressional Record* (S1418), February 21, 1983.

14. Walter W. Williams, "Social Security — A Bad Deal, A Lie, and a National Obstruction," *Newsweek,* New York, January 26, 1983.

15. "Reagan: Locking The Social Security Exits," *Human Events,* January 29, 1983, p. 4.

16. "Greenspan Panel Ignored Conservative Solution," *Human Events,* January 29, 1983, p. 4.

17. "Social Security for Illegal Aliens?" *Review of the News,* December 21, 1983, pp. 68-69.

18. "Religious Groups Employees Protest Social Security Requirements," *Family Protection Report,* Washington DC, January 1984, p. 5.

19. Robert G. Marshall, "A Program for Social Security," *ALL About Issues,* American Life Lobby, Stafford VA, December 1983, pp. A-D.

20. Peter G. Peterson, "Can Social Security Be Saved?"

Reader's Digest, March 1983, pp. 49-54.

21. Backgrounder: Social Security Financing, Republical Study Committee, US House of Representatives, Washington DC, II-87.

22. "Freeloading Aliens Milk Social Security for $700m A Year," *Globe,* January 4, 1983, p. 2.

23. "Slammer Security," *Keene (NH) Shopper News,* November 20, 1983, p. 4.

24. "Social Security Debt Far Greater Than Was Thought," *Manchester (NH) Union Leader* (UPI), February 5, 1984, p. 2.

25. Social Security, a debate between Rep. J. J. Pickle, MC and John A. Svahn, *New York Times,* May 31, 1981, p. 4E (Op-Ed).

26. Harry Anderson, "The Social Security War," *Newsweek,* May 25, 1981, pp. 40-41.

27. Harry Anderson, "The Crisis in Social Security," *Newsweek,* June 1, 1981, pp. 25-27.

28. Robert M. Bohon, "Reagan Exposes Inequities of Social Security," *Human Events,* Sept. 1, 1984, p. 14.

29. Dr. Richard Harris, "Memorandum," *The CS Newsletter,* August 4, 1984, pp. 1-3.

30. Robert McCurry, "Congress Repeals Mandatory Tax On Churches," *Temple Times,* August 4, 1984, pp. 1, 2.

26

SODOMY

BACKGROUND BRIEFING In US, the opposition to homosexual ideology and lifestyle is widespread, crosses all social, economic and ethnic groups. Rejection is based mainly on religious/moral grounds. *A nationwide poll found 71% believed male homosexuality morally wrong; 70% held that female homosexuality was morally wrong.* (The higher the level of "religious commitment," the stronger opposition to homosexual behavior.)

Estimated that about 4% of nation's adult population are sodomites. Yet, despite that and in face of society's overwhelming disapproval of sodomy, *sodomites becoming increasingly militant.* (And, as homosexuals become more brazen, while disapproving but timid majority remain silent, other sexual deviates become more daring. *Example:* emerging campaign to gain acceptance of incest and child seduction [some gay psychologists prescribe incest as "healthy & good" for the child]. *Example:* NAMBLA [North America Man Boy Love Assn] openly procuring and seducing young boys as homosexual partners/prostitutes.)

Greatest political advancement for gays made during

Carter administration. Under Carter administration, gay rights groups gained tax exempt status (501 (c) [3]). Doors of White House were then "wide open" to sodomites. In 1977 Dade County, FL, campaign against "gay rights ordinance," White House sent chief of its liaison office to work with and for sodomites. In 1982 election campaigns, *about 90 "gay-PACS" in 40 states raised more than $1 million* and openly supported candidates for state and federal offices. All 54 US Representatives who had co-sponsored federal gay rights bill were re-elected. More gay-panthers now being activated for 1984 campaigns.

Are sodomites making "progress" in campaign to force acceptance of immoral lifestyle? Dr. Howard Hurwitz points out that 20 years ago most states had anti-sodomy laws. *Today 27 States* have lost anti-sodomy protection either by legislation or court action. And, more than 30 of the nation's major cities have enacted pro-sodomy laws, or executives have issued orders including gays with other minorities. In New York, Mayor Edward Koch decreed barring sexual orientation as basis for job discrimination would result in loss of city contracts to companies and groups. As a result, Salvation Army and Catholic Charities refused to sign contracts that help subsidize their day care centers, foster care homes and adoption programs.

Democratic Natnl. Committee elected and supports lesbian and gay men party caucus, gives it equal status as black and Hispanic caucusses, etc. In 1984 presidential primary compaigns, Senators Cranston (CA) and Hart (CO) boasted of sponsorship of gay civil rights bill. *Walter Mondale* keynoted gay fund-raising events. Mondale boasts "We are including and recruiting openly gay and lesbian candidates on our delegate slates . . . *(and my campaign has) openly gay and lesbian staff members."* Some political observers express suspicion that *one reason for Mondale's tirades vs "religion and politics" is to accede to demands of homosexual leaders angry at "religious right."*

Republicans have not embraced sodomites. Said *Vice President George Bush,* "I don't think American society should be asked to accept that homosexuality is a sta..dard which should be held up for acceptance." GOP candidates do not endorse "gay rights" bill.

Democratic party moved to make itself the party of the gays. Ann Lewis, *party vice chairman* asserts, "Human rights, and that includes gay rights, is no longer a debatable issue within the Democratic Party."

Democrats' platform, adopted at 1984 National Convention, supports gay rights legislation and calls for "equal" treatment of sodomites. Vice presidential nominee *Geraldine Ferraro (Vaccaro)* was chairman of Platform Committee that calls for "federal legislation to prohibit discrimination in the work place based on sexual orientation." Also calls for immigration laws to permit "homosexual immigrants" to enter the US, and laws to make sure that homosexuality, per se, does not bar service in the military. Democrat delegates also adopted party rules *to attract and recruit sodomites* to "full participation" at all levels of party affairs. Would establish quotas for inclusion of gays.

As columnist James Kilpatrick asked: *"Will school*

boards be required to certify that they have hired an 'assured percentage' of lesbian and gay men to teach in the classrooms?"

One of the gay-PAC top priorities: *federal gay rights legislation.* Two bills now before Congress: *HR 427* and *HR 2624 and S.430.* Would require sodomites be given preferential treatment in *hiring, housing and education;* make it illegal to "discriminate" on basis of "sexual orientation"; mandate that state/public school and other institutions receiving federal funds *not only hire but actively recruit* sodomites. Endorsers of bills include Natnl. Council of Churches, United Presbyterian Church and United Church of Christ.

Proponents of gay rights bill say it's strictly a matter of civil rights. *Opponents* counter: civil rights not based on sexual appetite, do not include license to promote perversion or corruption of children. Further, opponents insist govt. has no right to force employers and home-owners to accept sodomites as employees or tenants if that violates their religious beliefs or moral values. Taxpayers, they say, should not be coerced into subsidizing sexual deviates. *Federal, state & local taxes now fund about 46% of all homosexual organizational budgets.* US Dept. of Human Services has granted sodomites $11.3 million for one forthcoming [1984] project.)

Proponents of gay rights bills demand favored status as a "minority." *Opponents* retort that is insult to those legitimately deemed to be minorities (on basis of color, national origin, religious conviction, etc.). Sexual perversion, they insist, is a sin—not grounds for special treatment.

Some avid backers of gay rights legislation profess

to be Christians. They say: "God made us the way we are." Say it may be wrong for heterosexuals to indulge in homosexual acts but it is OK for homosexuals to do so. Further, they label anti-homosexual Christians as *homophobic* and *unChristian*, accusing them of rejecting God's handiwork. By accepting the homosexual and his lifestyle without judgments, they argue, one may "move into the full light of God's love and grace." (San Francisco Roman Catholic archdiocese took position that "homosexual orientation is *not* held to be a sinful condition. . . ." Report encourages homosexuals to resist promiscuity by forming a *"closer relationship with* [only] one person.")

Friends of sodomy cite Christ's forgiveness of woman taken in adultery *(John 8:4-11)* as reason Christians should not judge or reject sodomites. Opponents point out Bible makes it clear God created humans to be heterosexual; that The Lord God consistently and specifically (and through His prophets and judges and apostles) condemns sodomy, often as a capital sin. As for *John 8,* they underscore Christ's parting words to the women: "Go, and sin no more." Thus, The Savior, while forgiving the woman her past sins, admonished her to repent — *to put an end to her adultery:* He loved the sinner but hated the sin.

Just as gay panthers push political clout they also push for influence in mainline religious groups *(see insert at end of chapter).* About 330 homosexual congregations now reported in USA: 93 Roman Catholic, 37 Episocpal, 21 Jewish, 16 Lutheran, etc. Core of homosexual "ecclesiastical community" is *Universal Fellowship of Metropolitan Community Churches* with about 100 congregations. New Way Ministry works within Catholic church. Gays have caucusses in United Methodist, United Presbyterian, Episcopal, Friends Society, American Baptist, and Unitarian churches, plus United Church of Christ, Natnl. Council of Churches, Natnl. Federation of Priests' Council, Union of American Hebrew Congregations and General Convention of Episcopal Church.

Sodomites argue their sexual tastes are their own business, do not hurt others, and should not hurt others. *But, homosexual "reproductive" process depends on recruitment.*

As Rev. Enrique Rueda emphasizes in his landmark book, *The Homosexual Network,* "The transformation of the schools according to the needs of the homosexual leadership." Rueda points out that Gay Rights Platform demands "federal and state encouragement and support for sex education courses, prepared and taught by Gay women and men, presenting homosexuality as a valid, healthy preference and lifestyle as a viable alternative to heterosexuality." Call for textbooks to encourage students "to explore alternative lifestyles including lesbianism."

Also, after a study of "sexually flavored" mass murders, Dr. Paul Cameron of Institute for Scientific Investigation of Sexuality, reports homosexual murder rate is 15 times higher than that for heterosexuals. The likelihood that a murderer is a homosexual are 12 times greater in most mass homicides.

And, this: *Emerging spectre of rampant homosexually-transmitted disease gives public great cause for concern.* With only 4% of adult population, sodomites account for

71% of aids fatalities, 49% of all syphilis, 51% of throat gonorrhea, and 53% of intestinal infections.

AIDS (*Acquired Immunity Deficiency Syndrome* — "gay cancer," also called "the gay plague") has higher than 50% mortality rate. With no known cure physicians fear rate could near 100%. Every sodomite known to have AIDS in 1979 is now dead. More than one-half of those who had AIDS in 1980 are now dead. *AIDS spreads thru homosexual colonies with geometeric progression.* Columnist Jeff Hart writes: "The homosexual's lifestyle may turn out to be his 'deathstyle.' " Hart also reports that one reason for rampant growth of AIDS among sodomites may be incredible number of "partners" average homosexual male may have during his active sex life (*often more than 1,600!*) Homosexual acitvities — and incidence of AIDS and other venereal diseases are more prevalent in states and cities where sodomy has been legalized. San Francisco (Sodom-by-the-Bay) passed "gay rights" ordinance in 1978; *since then, "sex diseases" have risen some 2,400%.*

What causes mounting concern among disease control experts? Many sodomites "sell" their blood thus endangering purity at blood banks — *AIDS can be transmitted through blood transfusions.* In San Francisco, one "gay rights" leader urged sodomites sell their blood "to get even with the straights." At Cedars-Sinai Medical Center in Los Angeles, woman had blood transfusion during surgery. Male blood donor had had AIDS. As a result, patient has contracted AIDS. Centers for Disease Control states *it's "clear-cut . . . (her) case demonstrates clearly that trans-*

mission (of AIDS) could take place via a blood transfusion."

AIDS can even be spread by casual contact at public gatherings, etc. The prestigious *New England Journal of Medicine* cited diseased homosexual food handlers as major cause of increase in amebiases and hepatitis in San Francisco and Minneapolis.

"Make no mistake about it—AIDS is one of the most serious incurable disease we've come up against." So warned Dr. Leonard Feldman of Centers of Disease Control in Atlanta. Because of that fact, Dr. Cameron was prompted to ask: *"By what logic does the (federal) Health Service not condemn homosexuality even as it condemns smoking?* Why do they not immediately warn homosexuals to stop homosexual activity?

"We are paying our taxes to be protected and they are risking the lives of the rest of the citizenry not to offend homosexual activities . . . *that is patently criminal."*

CONSIDER THE BIBLICAL PRINCIPLES Sodomy (homosexuality, lesbianism) is an abomination in the sight of The Lord God—a perversion of the creature He made in His image: "male and female created He them (heterosexuals)" *(Gen. 1:27)*. Sodomy is a sin of the gravest and most serious consequences. In *Rom. 1:28* Paul wrote that sodomy is one of two sins for which God abandoned sinners— the other being the sin of blaspheming the Holy Ghost *(Mt. 12:31, 32)*.

God warns man against the sin of sodomy: "Thou shalt not lie with mankind, as with womankind: it is an abomination" *(Lev. 18;22)*. "Defile not

yourselves" in this sin, commands The Lord God
(*Lev. 18:24;* see also *Deut. 23:17*). "If a man also lie
with mankind, as he lieth with a woman, both of
them have commited an abomination: they shall
surely be put to death; their blood shall be upon
them" (*Lev. 20:13*). In setting forth God's laws of
human relations, Moses made it clear there were to
be no sodomites in Israel (*Deut. 23:17*).

Sodomy brings catastrophic consequences upon
city or nation that approves of it, or condones it, or
fails to stand against it: "The land is defiled: therefore I do visit the inquity thereof upon it, and the
land itself vomits out her inhabitants" (*Lev. 18:25*).

Did God really mean what he said? This
nation—and many cities and states—would do well
to consider the fate of Sodom and Gomorrah (*Gen.
19:1-29;* see also *2 Peter 2:6-10; Jude 7*). The wickedness of sodomy brought forth the wrath and curse of
The Lord God. Because sodomy was so prevalent
("all the people, from every quarter"—*Gen. 19:4, 5*),
God destroyed both cities ("all the inhabitants of the
cities, and that which grew upon the ground" (*vv. 24,
25*), "and lo, the smoke of the country went up as the
smoke of a furnace" (*v. 28*). Jude wrote that the
destruction of Sodom and Gomorrah (and adjacent
towns that likewise gave themselves over to sensual
perversions) was not only a punishment but also *"set
forth as an example"* (*Jude 7*).

The people of ancient Canaan were completely
submerged in depravity (*Gen. 13:13*). Homosexuality
was so prevalent it was made a religious rite. For
such abominations God sentenced the Canaanites to

death *(Lev. 18*—esp. *vv. 22-29; Deut. 9:1-3).* God warned the Israelites that when He had delivered the wicked Canaanites before them *(Deut. 8:5)* they were to make no covenant with them *(Deut. 7:2-4).* Israel's failure to execute the judgment God demanded ultimately became its own judgment *(Deut. 7:1-5; Lev. 18:28, 29; Judges 2:9-15; 4:1-3).*

Sodomy promotes idolatry, invites false gods, nurtures apostasies. It spawns additional perversions; it gnaws at the vitals and rots the soul—*first,* the souls of those who indulge in its lusts and evils and, *finally,* the soul of the nation that permits it to continue unchallenged. Historically, rampant homosexuality has been one of the social malignancies that preceded the fall of nations/empires (Greece, Rome, etc.).

So final and so awful are the consequences of sodomy that The Lord God, in His grace, grants time for cleansing; and, he commends and rewards those who work to rid the land of the evil. "And Asa did that which was right in the eyes of The Lord, as did David his father. And he took away the sodomites out of the land, and removed all the idols that his fathers had made" *(I Kings 15:11, 12; see also I Kings 22:46 and II Kings 23:3, 7).*

The Apostle Paul minced no words about sodomites. He wrote to believers in Rome that if sodomites refuse to repent and change their wicked ways, God abandons them to "uncleanness through the lusts of their own hearts, to dishonor their own bodies between themselves."

"Who changed the truth of God into a lie (a false religion) and worshipped and served the

creature more than The Creator, Who is blessed forever. Amen! For this cause God gave
them up to vile affections: for even their women
did change the natural use into that which is
against nature (exchanged their natural function for an unnatural and abnormal one): And
likewise also the men, leaving the natural use of
the woman (turned from natural relations with
woman) buried in their lust for one another;
men with men working that which is unseemly
(committing shameful [indecent] acts with
men), and receiving in themselves that recompense that was meet (suffering in their own
bodies and souls the inevitable consequences
and penalties of their wrong-doing). And even
as they did not like to retain God in their
knowledge (since they did not choose to acknowledge God or consider Him worth knowing) God gave them over to a reprobate (base)
mind to do those things which are not convenient (things not proper or decent but loath-
some) . . . Who knowing the judgment of
God, that they which commit such things are
worthy of death, not only do the same (persist
in doing such things) but have pleasure in (approve and applaud) them that do them" *(Rom.
1:25-32).*

In *I Cor. 6:9, 10,* Paul includes homosexuals —
"abusers of themselves with mankind (sodomites)" —
among those who shall not inherit the kindgom of
God. In his first letter to Timothy *(I Tim. 1:9-10),*

Paul writes that the law is made for the lawless, the disobedient, and the ungodly sinner including "them that defile themselves with mankind (sodomites)."

Is there a cure for sodomy, a way in which to break the bonds of appetite and passions of this awful and unnatural desire? There is, indeed! *Through the redeeming love of Jesus Christ.*

As *Dr. Rod Mays of Family Counseling & Resources* minds us: The homosexual can experience the forgiveness of God. But, repentance is mandatory. Those who will turn to Christ, and accept Him as their Savior and their Lord, will find power to repent and resist *(Phil. 4:13; Col. 1:13)*. The power of Christ can cleanse the vilest mind, cure the most evil heart *(I John 1:7; I Thes. 5:23)*. The individual who scorns and rejects Christ is lost, dead in sin. But, whoever shall turn to Christ, and believe on Him, shall become a new person, redeemed, born again, justified and sanctified. *Praise God!*

"WHO CHANGED THE TRUTH OF GOD INTO A LIE . . ."

Leaders of the "gay rights" movement see religious beliefs (traditional Christian teachings) as greatest single force causing universal disapproval and rejection of homosexual behavior. Thus, their all-out effort to overcome, subvert, or discredit religious organizations that hold fast to Biblical truths. They seek to do this by (a) revision ("modernizing") the Scriptures and (b) subverting mainline denominations and then using them as launching pads for attacks against Bible-teaching churches.

Rev. Cecil Williams, of far-left, pro-gay Glide Memorial Church, San Francisco, testified before a Congressional hearing *"There are no absolutes. All absolutes have to be . . . reinterpreted, revised. That is why you have revised versions of the Bible."* Williams: *"The Bible is not the word of God but the word of men in which the con-*

temporary word of God comes to men." . . . *a Bible passage is to be interpreted in terms of experience."* How far will homosexuals and pro-gay groups go to revise God's word? Wm. R. Johnson, first ordained homosexual minister in United Church of Christ proclaimed *"gay liberation is a movement of the Holy Spirit."* Gay Bible "scholars" suggest (a) David and Jonathan were homosexuals *(I Sam. 18:1-4; 20:16-18),* and (b) the apostle Paul's "thorn in the flesh" was his homosexuality *(2 Cor. 12:7).* Finally, they infer (even assert) that Jesus and St. John the Apostle were homosexual lovers because John is referred to as "the beloved apostle" *(John 13:23; 20:2).*

RECOMMENDED READING: *The Homosexual Network: Private Lives & Public Policy,* Enrique T. Rueda, Devin Adair, 1983 (available through The Free Congress Research and Education Foundation). Also, *Restoration* (Mar-April, 1983), Dr. Rod S. Mays, Family Counseling and Resources, Inc., P.O. Box 4032, St. Albans, WV 25177, and *Gay Isn't Good,* Darlene Bogle, Issues & Answers, Student Action for Christ, May 1983, p. 7. US Press, June 15, 1984, p. 2. *Salt Shakers Newsletter,* March/April, 1984. *Manchester (NH) Union Leader* (UPI), March 19, 1984, p. 2. *Globe,* April 19, 1983, p. 6. Dr. Howard Hurwitz, *Hurwitz on Education,* Jan. 30, 1983 and May 29, 1984. James Kilpatrick, August 1, 1984. *Christian News,* January 23, 1984, p. 14.

27

TAXATION

BACKGROUND BRIEFING Existing federal progressive income tax system is *disgrace*. A complex and unfair *crazyquilt* of *loopholes, dodges, tax shelters and exclusions*. Its abuses fall most heavily on *middle class*. Adding insult to injury: *complicated reporting* forms drive taxpayers up the wall.

On top of all that, taxpayer faces *huge tax increases in yrs just ahead*. Pay hikes to offset rise in cost of living could push wage earner into *higher tax brackets* ("bracket creep")—*indexing, if not deferred/repealed, would prevent that* by adjusting (indexing) federal income tax to inflation). Mandated future *Social Security hikes* (on both tax rates and income-base) are set in law for rest of this Century. Thus, workers will continue to have greater portion of earnings taken by FICA taxes. If trend continues, per employee Social Security taxes in 1990 will be *at least $4,200 per year*.

Unfair taxation (rates and impositions) *promotes cheating and evasion*. Estimated some $299 billion in "underground economy" (cash transactions, etc.) "escape" the tax collectors; General Accounting Office reports *problem grows 10% each yr*.

Thus, increasing demand for tax reform.

Danger: what is labelled "tax reform" may turn out to only be a "shift" bringing increased taxes rather than reform and reduction.

Democratic tax reform plank calls for tax simplification, for tax increases in 1985, broadened income tax base and increased taxation of businesses and "wealthier individuals." Would "partially defer" tax indexing. Calls for taxation in "fair, progressive fashion." *Republican* platform opposes any attempts to increase taxes (President Reagan says "tax increase only as last resort"). GOP opposes move to repeal or defer tax indexing, and pledges to work for a modified flat rate income tax on broad base while maintaining deductions for mortgage interest, etc.

Two "reforms" at top of list: *Value Added Tax (VAT) and Flat Rate federal income tax.* Tax battles in near future may well revolve mostly around those two plans.

VALUE ADDED TAX Legislators figure *Value Added Tax* (VAT) would pour about $150 billion a yr in the US collection plate. VAT proponents say part of that new revenue could be used to reduce Social Security taxes (and, perhaps, increase personal exemptions in federal income taxes). Thus, VAT would provide *multi-billion dollar tax windfall* for Uncle Caesar during first years.

VAT would (probably) place *10% tax* on spread between cost and price *(value added at each stage of production* (i.e. raw materials, etc.), *manufacturing* (or processing), and *sales.* Processor, manufacturer, and retailer would calculate VAT and send to IRS. Total (cumulative) VAT would be added to consumer's purchase price. Basically, *VAT might work like this:*

Mining company sells ingots to mill for $100 plus 10% ($10) *for value added* to raw ore by its mining and processing operations. Mill processes ingots and sells metal (in sheet or rod form, etc.) to table mfgr. for $150 plus $5 VAT (since *value added* by mill was $50). Table maker sells finished table to wholesaler for $225, *plus $7.50 VAT;* wholesaler warehouses and distributes table to retailer for $250 *plus $2.50 VAT.* Retailer sells table to consumer for $300 *plus $5.00 VAT.* All along the line VAT is added to cost of the table (is included in price of the materials, manufacturing, distribution, sales, etc). Altogether, *consumer pays Value Added Tax of $30.* (One way or another, *consumer always pays every tax* regardless of form or gimmicks.)

Opponents charge VAT is nothing but *regressive federal sales tax.* That it is a *hidden* tax. That because it is hidden it is designed to be "painless" and "painless" tax is most dangerous tax of all (the less "painful" the tax the more easily it is raised and the more rapidly it increases. Also, say VAT would be costly and difficult to administer for both private and public sectors *(Great Britain was forced to triple its tax bureaucracy to handle paperwork, etc., when it adopted VAT).* Further, warn opponents, once VAT's nose was under the tent, no guarantee that it would stay at 10%.

FLAT RATE INCOME TAX *President Reagan* has called flat rate "tempting." OMB director *David Stockman* thinks a flat rate proposal could be part of future budget/revenue proposals. At least *9 different flat-rate tax bills have been introduced during recent yrs.*

What is flat-rate tax? Picture this: A federal income tax applied at the same rate on all taxable income. Basic exemptions for head of house and dependents but *no other loopholes or exclusions.* And, a simplified tax return that would be about four or five lines long and fit on a postcard. *Theory:* because exemptions would be eliminated and tax base broader, tax rate would be relatively low but would produce revenue at least equal to that gained from present inequitable system.

In its simplest form, flat tax would replace existing 12 (progressive) income tax rates (from 12% to 50%) with *single rate that would apply to all income above a set level* (i.e. a "zero tax" on taxable income up to $5,000.) Proponents say flat *11% tax rate* on personal and business income would provide about same fed revenue as now collected. (Former US Treas, Sec. *William Simon* once suggested *16%* flat-tax rate on personal and corporate income *would balance federal budget.)*

Big question: under flat-rate tax, *what happens to which deductions and exemptions?* (The more deductions permitted, the higher must be the flat rate to produce same revenues.) Critics warn that ending deductions for mortgage interest and property tax *would virtually kill home purchases by middle-income groups and wreck the housing industry* which is already in tough straits because of high interest rates.

Charitable institutions fret that elimination of deductions for contributions might curtail or even end their operations. And, some religious organizations express concern over potential loss of income (does that mean their *reliance on tax deductible* gifts is *greater than their faith* in the providence of The Lord God?).

Among flat-rate proposals: Rep. George Hansen (R-ID) would establish *14%* rate. Deductions for interest, taxes and depreciation would be repealed. Deductions would be allowed for religious contributions and medical bills greater than 10% of gross income.

Rep. Phillip Crane (R-IL) would set *flat rate at 10%.* Special tax deductions, credits and exclusions would be ended. Personal exemptions would be increased to $2,000 ($8,000 for a family of 4). Crane's proposal was companion to one introduced by Sen. Helms (R-NC).

Rep. Ron Paul (R-TX) would apply *flat 10% tax rate* on all taxable incomes and repeal all deductions, credits and exclusions. Would set $10,000 for personal exemptions.

Sen. Bill Bradley (D-NJ— and Rep. Richard Gephardt (D-MO) *propose 4-tiered version* (thus, not really flat-rate tax). Would apply 14% rate to taxable incomes up to $25,000 single ($40,000 on joint returns). Then 3-tiers of surtaxes on higher incomes to max of 28% at $37,000 single ($65,000 joint). Brandley-Gephardt would keep deductions for interest, contributions, state and local taxes, etc.

Proponents believe flat tax would curtail present *diversion of investment capital* into non-productive tax shelters (tax free govt. bonds, etc.) and invite more investments in productive private sector. Also, they contend flat rate would *end tax "bracket creep"* . . . and, importantly, flat-rate system would give *new vitality* to *nation's floundering economy* (encourage investments, stimulate expansion and development and new jobs, greater productivity and thus *rejuvenate sagging GNP*).

Opponents say flat-rate tax is *unfair*, that taxes should be based on *"ability to pay"* . . . *that govt. should take greater percentage* from larger incomes via progressive rates (in WWII top income tax rate was 91%, dropped to 70% in 1965, now 50%). Opponents suggest govt. has right (responsibility) to use tax system as tool for social reform *(redistribution of wealth, etc.)*.

Advocates of flat tax insist all citizens should share in cost of govt, that taxing incomes at same rate is *fair way*, that progressive rates are unfair (legalized plunder) and *destroy seed capital* that provides jobs and more goods and services at lower prices. Further, they maintain taxes should be used only *to raise revenues* needed for legitimate govt. programs — not to coerce social reforms.

In all of this, *some fiscal watch-dogs urge caution*. Warn that many sins can be hidden under cloak of "tax reform" — in this case under guise of flat-rate tax. There is now great pressure from some quarters to *increase tax take* ("revenue enhancement") to offset *increasing federal deficit*. They point out a straight revenue-increase (tax) bill would meet with strong resistance; but, *hiding behind* promised relief of a flat-tax, big spenders might try to maneuver through "sleeper" provisions that would actually *increase* tax take.

TAXFACS

Total tax take in US *more than* tripled *1970-83* . . . taxes now cost consumer more than 35% of all goods and services produced (not including the "tax" of inflation) . . . all told, fed, state & local govts spend $1.07 trillion (67% goes to Washington); that averages out to about *$10,500 per working man and woman* . . . tax take increases at rate of *10% per yr;* average annual increase in govt deficits in 9% (at that rate, tax take could double in less than 7 yrs . . . there are *80,000 govt. bodies* in USA, financed by *68 different types of taxes* (income, property, sales etc.) . . . Indiana taxes ice for alcoholic beverages, but not for soda pop or watermelons . . . New York taxes caramel-popcorn, not salted or buttered variety . . . in 1895, federal income tax was declared *unconstitutional* . . . during 1913 congressional debates on 16th (income tax) amendment, opponents warned that *tax rate might go as high as 10%!* . . . federal withholding of income taxes was instituted in 1943 as *temporary measure* to help finance WWII . . . in 1960, *"tax freedom" day* came on April 15 (from Jan. 1 until then worker's total earnings equalled amount taken by taxes); *in 1984, "tax freedom" day fell on May 1* (one-third of the yr) . . . Look at it this way: *first three hrs of every working day* go to Uncle Sam and his nephews.

Opposition to any plan that increases total Federal tax take argue *there is a better way to handle nation's fiscal woes:*

Continue to *reduce federal income tax* by stages, thus economy by encouraging initiatives/investments; *put lid on federal spending via a Constitutional amendment;* require gradual *reduction of federal debt* (x% per yr), invoke discipline of *gold or silver standard,* wrest control of nation's money (and economy) from privately-owned *Federal Reserve System.* As for "uncontrollable" items in federal budget, "what congress has done congress can undo." Said then-congressman David Stockman: Over the past decades Congress has created a "perpetual motion machine . . . a self-propelled, half-trillion spending machine that is simply out of control."

CONSIDER THE BIBLICAL PRINCIPLES   The *godly* Christian *(and the godly nation)* will consider taxation within the context of God's total sovereignty. He will seek to pattern tax laws and systems after God's laws and precepts and principles. If the individual (or nation) acknowledges *God is God* (and He is — *Ex. 3:14; Isa. 44:6)* then he must know Him and worship God for what He is *(The God of all — Isa. 42:8).* God's sovereignty prevails *in every sphere of life.*

Taxation is an *application of sovereignty;* an exercise of power. Power is an attribute of The Lord God Who is The Source of all power — The Supreme Sovereign. (Ref. Plymouth Rock Foundation's course, "Fundamentals for American Christians" *(FACS 1) Lesson Three,* "The Flow of Power and Force.")

When the State demands a greater tax than God requires through the tithe, the State seeks to *usurp* the sovereignty of God; it reaches to gain dominion over that which belongs only to Him. *By the same token,* when God's people fail to obey Him in the matter of the tithe, which is part of honoring Him, they also deny (reject) His sovereignty over their lives and property. Thus, whether they like it or not — and whether they realize it or not — they hand Caesar *an open invitation* (a) to assume an expanded and ungodly sovereignty and (b) to take dominion over those affairs that are the personal and congregational responsibility of God's people (vice regents).

Christians are instructed by God's word to support the proper and necessary functions of civil government. Thus, Paul could write *(Rom. 13:6, 7)* that we are willing to pay tribute (taxes) to support the persons and the programs that exercise (wield) the civil authority ordained by The Lord God. (Mark these key words in Paul's passage on civil authorities: *"for they are God's ministers."* As such — and as long as they are true to their "commission/authorization" — they are to be honored, supported and obeyed. But, when the civil authorities cease to conduct civil affairs (including taxation) in accord with the laws of God *(The Source of their authority)* Christians must work lawfully to remove them from office and to restore adherence to Biblical principles of government. To do so is to honor God and welcome His sovereignty; to fail to do so, especially under a representative form of government, is to be a party to dishonoring God and denying His sovereignty.

Our Lord commands us *not to covet our neighbor's property (Ex. 20:17)*. We are not to covet on a personal basis *(self government);* we are not to covet or be a party to covetousness on a corporate body politic level *(civil government)*. Thus, the godly Christian must oppose, lawfully resist and seek to change, any tax system that plunders a person's property (whether it is his own or his neighbor's *(Lev. 19:18; Mt. 22:39)* or even a stranger's *(Lev. 24:22; Deut. 10:19)*. We are not to steal *(Ex. 20:15): stealing is stealing* whether it is done on an individual or a collective basis under the aegis of the State. *The anonymity of the gang* (even an elected gang) *can not legitimize crime* or excuse sin.

Withholding of wages to pay taxes is antiBiblical. The firstfruits of our labors belong to, and should go to, The Lord God *(Ex. 22:29, 30; Rom. 11:16.* See also *Ex. 23:16-19; 34:26; Num. 18:8-13; Dt. 18:3-4).* We are not to give God our left-overs. As Mark Rushdoony points out *(Chalcedon Report, #203,* July 1982), "The redemption of the firstborn and the offering of the firstfruits to God are symbolic offerings of a part of our substance which represents the whole" . . . *and the whole belongs to The Lord God (Ps. 24:1; 1 Cor. 10:26, 28).* Withholding of the individual's earnings before he can tithe puts The Lord God *in second place—* behind the State. Thus, the sovereignty of God is denied (rejected), the State is deified (resulting in a modern form of *Moloch* worship *(Ex. 20:3; John 19:15).*

May we not take *the tithe* (a flat-rate tax) *as a basic principle of taxation?* Each individual giving (returning) to God a set portion (the sum of the *three types of tithe* is approximately 16%) of that which The Lord has provided. God does not demand a greater *percentage* for tithe from a wealthy man than he does from the one who may be poor. We are told to *neither thwart nor favor* any person simply because of his or her economic status; we are to be even-handed *(Ex. 23:2, 6).* In *Exodus 30:14, 15,* when The Lord was instructing Moses regarding the collection of atonement money, (a type of head or poll tax) we read, *"The rich shall not give more, and the poor shall not give less . . ."* Progressive taxation would seem to be unscriptural.

1 Sam. 8 seems to make it clear that, under God, the State's power to tax is to be restricted (to the tithe on income and to a head tax) lest it seek to magnify itself rather than serve God. When the Israelites rejected God and "demanded a king to judge us like all the nations," Samuel could accurately warn that the people would not only be compelled to pay a simple tithe to such a king, they would also be forced to give the "king" a tenth of virtually *everything* they had (and even their sons and daughters). In fact, warned Samuel, it would become so oppressive that the Israelites would cry out because of the king they chose over The Lord God *(1 Sam. 8:9-18).*

Is there not a modern-day parallel here? Has not this nation rejected The Lord God? Have we not, like Israel, run after other gods and other laws and standards? And, like Israel of old do we not now pay a horrendous price? Is not part of that price the *malignant* tax system and the *corrosive* Babylonian debt-economy that robs the individual of his liberty and deprives the nation of seed corn (investment capital)? In a very real sense the tax system in this land today may be seen as part of the fruitage of fiscal rebellion against The Lord God *(Malachi 3:7-9).*

Some additional Biblical principles of taxation:

Hidden taxes (those that are not readily and consistently apparent) are deceitful and abominations. The individual should always know when and how much he is being taxed *(Ex. 30:12-14). Hidden taxation (deceit) is the companion of fraud and injustice (Ps. 10:7)* and leads to oppression *(Jer. 27:28); it is a thief in the night that robs (Job 24:16, 17; John 10:10a).*

Capital property (tangible and intangible) is not

to be taxed. Rather, what the capital (property) produces is to be the basis for taxation. Taxes that
destroy a person's capital (or, property) must be considered antiBiblical. The property tax is an attack on
the family. That property which God has entrusted
to a family is to be preserved and to remain in the
family, handed down from generation to generation.
Thus, it is clear that inheritance and estate taxes are
also antiBiblical *(1 Kings 21:3)*.

"Sin taxes" are a no-no; taxes on gambling, prostitution, drug and alcohol traffic, etc., are unacceptable
(Dt. 23:18). To tax sin is not only to profit from it but
to condone it and promote it.

Institutions and individuals in full-time ecclesiastical service (work for The Lord) are not to be taxed
(Ezra 7:23, 24). Included under this are God's houses
of worship and education (churches, schools, seminaries, colleges, missions, etc.). At the same time, this
places an unyielding responsibility on the part of
such institutions and individuals: *They must serve The
Lord God and only Him* lest they be found guilty of taking improper advantage of this Providential provision (and taking the name of The Lord in vain).

Maintaining the proper Biblical equation
(balance) between God and Caesar in the area of
taxation is *part of the total charge of holiness (Col. 1:22; 1
Pet. 1:16)*. We are to submit (render) unto God all
that which is His—including our selves. By submit-
ting (rendering) unto Caesar that, and only that,
which is his rightful due *(for a ministry of justice and
civil protection)*, we glorify God and magnify His

name while keeping Caesar's reach and role to its proper (Biblical) purpose.

True tax reform will come (Caesar's oppressions will cease) when we begin to obey *God's tax system* — the tithe He commands to finance His works in His name and for His sake here and now. *Then our taxes will serve to advance His kingdom, not Caesar's! Mark this as true:* the more niggardly God's people are in their tithes and offerings, the more He permits Caesar's hand to dig deeper into our pockets and pocketbooks . . . and lives.

When a people obey The Lord God in the payment of tithes and offerings, His immeasurable blessing are poured out upon them — both as individuals and as a nation *(Dt. 28:1-14; Mal. 3:10)*. When a people disobey God, and thus rob Him, they are cursed with a curse and so is their nation *(1 Sam. 8; Dt. 28:15-68; Mal. 3:8, 9)*.

RECOMMENDED READING: *Law and Society,* R. J. Rushdoony, Ross House Books, 1982; *The World Under God's Law,* T. Robert Ingram, St. Thomas Press, 1962; *Christianity As A Life-System,* Abraham Kuyper, Christian Studies Center, 1980; *To Harrass Our People,* Rep. George Hansen, Positive Publications, Box 23560, Washington DC 20024.

28

TUITION TAX CREDITS AND CHRISTIAN EDUCATION

BACKGROUND BRIEFING About 5 million students are enrolled in some 21,000 private schools (K-12) — *4.3 million (85%) are in 16,000 sectarian (mostly Christian) schools.* Average tuition at church-related day schools, $900/yr (slightly higher at private Christian day schools — $1,000-$1,500). Estimated *$12.8 billion spent in 1982 to send students to church-related and private Christian day schools (K-12).*

Parents turning from state (tax-funded) schools in increasing numbers. Parochial schools (mostly evangelical/fundamental Christian) grow at rate of about 100,000 students per yr. Recent Gallup Poll found *47% of public school parents would shift* children to pvt school if cost were not a factor. A second Gallup Poll reported *49% of public believe increase in non-public schools is "good thing"* — 30% thought it a "bad thing," 21% had no opinion.

In 1981, *$148 billion went to tax-supported schools, $105 billion for K-12.* Parents sending children to private schools helped pay those billions. Thus, *they carry double burden:* pay taxes for state-controlled public schools and tuition for private (Christian) school. For several yrs, private groups have pushed *for tax relief for double costs*. Mostly, effort has been for *federal tuition tax credit (TTC)*—an amount to be subtracted from bottom line of income tax form.

One of first in Congress to seek TTCs was *Rep. Phil Crane* (IL). He introduced bill in 1969. In 1976, both major party platforms supported TTCs. Political support for tuition tax credits continues. President Reagan makes tuition tax credits a campaign promise. His proposed legislation went before Congress in 1983 (*S. 529, Educational and Opportunity Equity Act—Dole (KS)*. Bill passed Senate Finance Committee (11-7). *Sen. David Boren* (OK) opposes TTC, calls bill "most damaging legislative proposal I have seen." Bill also opposed by *House Speaker O'Neill* and *Rep Dan Rostenkowski*, chairman of Ways & Means Committee.

S. 529 would have permitted *tax credit for tuition paid by parents of child attending tax-exempt private school (K-12) that does not follow a "racially discriminatory policy."* Credit would be for *one-half of tuition with maximum credit of $300 per child;* credits would be phased in ($100 max in 1984, $200 max in '85 and $300 max in '86), could not exceed tax liability, would apply to families with *adjusted gross income under $40,000* and be reduced and phased out at $50,000. Bill stipulates tax credits *"shall not constitute federal financial assistance to educational institutions or to the recipients."*

Backers of S. 529 believe US Supreme 5-4 ruling upholding Minnesota's state tax deductions for parents' school expenses may enhance their cause (about 95% of pvt schools in Minnesota are sectarian). However, Court pointed out Minnesota law provides tax deductions for *both public and private school* expenses (tuition, textbooks, gym clothes, transportation, etc.); thus it dealt with *secular* nature of education. Opponents emphasized S. 529 would have provided tuition tax credits for parents of private school children, *only.* And, Court did *not* disturb its 1973 ruling that New York statute providing tax benefits to parents of pvt school children was unconstitutional — many of pvt school beneficiaries were sectarian.

Proponents of TTC argue that by sending children to private schools they *reduce tax (cost) for state schools.* If all K-12 students in pvt. schools were to enroll in public schools, would up cost to nation's taxpayers by *$12 billion;* if just students in parochial schools (K-12) descended upon public schools, *additional tax cost would be $11 billion.*

Opponents retort TTC *would cost fed govt. millions in lost revenue* at time when deficit is mounting and more funds are needed. *Sen. John Chaffee, RI,* argues such diversion of funds to pvt. schools flies in face of fiscal crisis in public school. Joint Congressional Committee estimated *TTC would have cost $229 million in fiscal '84, $491 million in '85, and more than $700 million in '86, '87, & '88.* Supporters of TTC contend that even $800 million/yr represents *only .8 of 1% of money spent on* State *education;* that, they say, is small compared to billions pvt school parents save the public system.

Backers of TTC believe plan would promote

(make possible) *freedom of choice;* that credits would enable many more families to send children to pvt school; *that nothing in the law gives state exclusive educational fiat.* Compulsory education, coupled with economic burdens, virtually hands state education monopoly that destroys choice, smothers competition, strangles pursuit of excellence (*Php. 1:10*).

Opposition insists most private schools are primarily effort to escape govt mandated integration of schools; that pvt schools are *"subterfuges of segregation."* Pvt school supporters reject argument, say few Christian schools were started for that reason. According to 1982 survey (Coleman Report) *there is less segregation* (racial and/or economic) *in religious schools than in public schools.* Pvt. schools were started, they emphasize, *because public* (state) *schools are unsupportable.* Most private schools (especially Christian day schools) are run for and by parents who seek *quality education* for their children. If they seek to escape anything it is *violence, drugs and sexual promiscuity; low moral and academic standards, lack of discipline, biased and humanistic curricula that deny/belittle God; and the subtle drumbeat that works to separate child from parental values.*

(In 1940, according to a report by the Mel Gablers [Educational Research Analysts], the most prevalent offenses in public schools were *talking, chewing gum, making noise, running in the halls, and getting out of turn in line. In 1982,* wrote the Gablers, most prevalent offenses in public school were — *rape, robbery, assault, burglary, and arson.* In Montgomery County (MD) high schools, *teen-age pregnancies* are now "not only acceptable *but fashionable"* — in that suburb of Washington, its *"baby chic!"*

Opponents of tuition tax credits assert State has *responsibility to set "minimum standards,* that TTC would encourage growth of schools without/below such standards. Supporters of TTC reject that; say centralized standards *destroy diversity* (pursuit of truth and excellence); are *usually bureaucratic, often humanistic—and by measurable criteria most Christian schools not only meet but surpass academic standards* set for state schools.

Groups against TTC charge plan would *violate First Amendment;* that it would use govt. funds to subsidize religious schools.

(*Liberals use double standard* in this argument. *Example:* When demanding tax monies to subsidize abortions for poor women, liberals insist use of federal funds does not imply approval of abortion *but simply guarantees (allows for) freedom of choice.* Apparently what's good for pro-abortion is not good for pro-TTC.) Those who support TTC argue tuition tax credit is in same league with *tax deductions allowed for contributions to church, missions, etc.* Further, argue proponents, food stamps are not restricted to govt. stores, and medicare benefits are not confined to govt. hospitals. *Why should benefits of taxes paid for education be available only at govt. school?*

Opposition claims *TTCs would benefit only the upper-middle and upper classes* but advocates say *contrary is true.* Of those parents who send their children to private schools, *62% have an annual income of $25,000 or less.* And, in the inner city, where minority parents send their children to pvt. schools, *72% earn less than*

$15,000 a yr. CORE (Congress On Racial Equality) charges state school monopoly locks black parents into inferior schools in the ghetto.

Teachers' unions charge tuition tax credits would destroy state school system. Say it would take away funds and reduce support for tax-funded schools at a time when they are struggling to make ends meet. TTC advocates respond, *Not so!* TTC is not tied to reduction in funds for public schools (those tax monies have increased during recent yrs even while enrollment had decreased). Loss of support for state schools, say TTC groups, was brought on by State bureaucrats and union establishments. They suggest experience in other nations indicates *TTCs bring competition* to education and forces state schools to be more responsive to public and parental desires. They point to Western Europe and English-speaking nations; claim govt support of dual educational system (public and private schools) has forced state schools to seek excellence.

Not all opposition to tuition tax credit comes from groups hostile to private or Christian education. Not all support is without reservation.

US Sens. Orrin Hatch (UT) and Jesse Helms (NC) both support TTCs. But, *both express concern that tax credits might become "a lever" for federal control of private education.* Bill Billings, National Christian Action Coalition (NCAC), warns of proposed amendments to any tuition tax credit bill. Billings urges caution lest a bill is passed that opens door to federal control of Christian education: *"It would be better to have no bill than a bad bill."*

Advocates of tuition tax credits insist their legislation would not seek to control private education, lightly dismissed *Section 3 (c) (1)* of Senate Bill 529 that provided TTC will be denied if educational institution *"follows a racially discriminatory policy."* Concerned educators argue issue here is not approval or disapproval of racial discrimination (most disapprove). *Issue is control.* If prohibition of racial discrimination is not a control then question arises: *"When is a control not a control?"* Answer seems to be: *"When a control enforces 'public policy'."* In view of recent Court actions, what new "public policies" lie ahead?

Federal court decisions do raise questions and do cause concern that TTCs could become bait used to snare Christian schools into federal trap. In 1982, US Supreme Court unanimously held *Amish employers must pay Social Security tax* even though that violated longheld Amish religious belief *(1 Tim. 5:8).* Chief Justice Warren Burger wrote: *"religious belief in conflict with the payment of taxes affords no basis for resisting the tax."* In *Bob Jones Univ.* case, majority on US Supreme Court held *"entitlement to tax exemption depends on meeting certain common law standards . . . namely that an institution seeking tax-exempt status . . . not be contrary to established public policy."* Justice Powell concurred with decision but expressed fear it *might invest IRS "with authority to decide which public policies are sufficiently 'fundamental' to require denial of tax exemption."* Some caution that fear should also concern supporters of tuition tax credits.

Ominous court order came recently from federal

Judge George Hart in *Green v. Regan* (revocation of tax exemption for certain church schools in Mississippi on allegations of racial discrimination). Judge Hart refused to acknowledge church school education is first and foremost religious. *Hart insisted reading, writing, and arithmetic are strictly "secular" subjects; thus, basic education is secular;* therefore *government control and interference with Christian education does not violate First Amendment.* If ruling withstands appeal it will be clear signal that freedom to "bring up a child in the nurture and admonition of The Lord" is in serious jeopardy in USA.

Barbara Morris, in *TAX TUITION CREDITS: A Responsible Appraisal,* "TTCs are the camel's nose under the private school's tent" . . . *with public funds goes public control,* that's what Supreme Court has said. She emphasizes that since TTCs concern federal income tax, *TTCs will be concern of Internal Revenue Service.* On-going IRS harrassment of Christian churches and schools should be big red flag to supporters of tuition tax credits.

As for Western European nations, Mrs. Morris reminds that France recently took over all private schools *and integrated more than 9,000 religious schools into the public school system — because the schools receive state aid.* In *Netherlands,* extolled by TTC advocates, govt supports private schools — & determines curriculum, teacher qualifications.

According to Mrs. Morris, supporters of Minnesota law providing tax deductions for parents (*see above*) admit *"it was designed primarily to rein in a rash of tiny 'home schools' set up by fundamental Christians . . ."*

Citizens for Educational Reform, major TCC supporter, also suggests tuition tax credits will reduce number of home schools.

CONSIDER THE BIBLICAL PRINCIPLES The responsibility to educate children rests not with the State but with parents. Is responsibility of parents to bring up children in the fear and love of God *(Pr. 22:6; 1 Pet. 2.2)*. *Parents* are to make sure that children receive an education based upon God's written word *(Isa. 28:10;* in "the nurture and admonition of the Lord" *(Eph. 6:4)*. See also *Dt. 6:5-9; Pr. 1:7; Mt. 4:4*.

Albert Shanker, president of American Federation of Teachers, asserts *"In short, public schools exist to create citizens."* That was also Hitler's view; it is USSR plan. It definitely is *not* purpose of education for godly Christian parents; those parents know children are to be educated so they will grow to be God's servants and first and foremost citizens of His kingdom. Thus, Christians (and especially Christian parents) must resist, must avoid, must be apart from, anything that will or even might interfere with such a God-given blessing and responsibility *(Job 8:14)*.

We must shun that which might spoil not only ourselves but also our children (Col. 2:8). *If it appears that tuition tax credits might be a carrier of such seeds we must shun it.* We dare not risk any venture, any alliance, any gift (real or false) that makes us wards of the State *(Isa. 42:17)*. Paul warns us, in *Eph. 5:6, 7*—"Let no man deceive you with vain words: for because of these things comes the wrath of God upon the children of disobedience. Be ye not partakers with them."

We must never forget: the Caesar that grants tax credits is the Caesar that levied improper tax in the first place. The Caesar that bears "gifts" is same Caesar that banned our God from schools we are compelled to support with our taxes—the same Caesar that opened public schools to the gods of humanism.

Consider purpose of taxation. As set forth in God's word, it is to support civil authorities (powers) in their proper duties as magistrates (ministers) of God so that we may live peaceful, productive and godly lives *(1 Tim. 2:2; Rom. 13:6, 7).* God's word does not tell us to pay taxes for social reform; it does not give Caesar power to tax for education of our children; such work is to be done by the church and to support that work we are to tithe. We may be compelled to pay taxes for programs that are ungodly, but we must never voluntarily seek or support tax programs that invite or enable Caesar to trespass on areas not his. That would be to place a very small price on our faith. To do so would be to trust in man, rather than God. If we are persuaded that He is able to keep that which we have committed unto Him *(2 Tim. 1:12)* we will not seek gimmicks or gadgets or favors from the State (Php. 4:19; Ps. 118:8, 9). Rather we will tithe to educate our children in God's house, work to redress the proper balance between church and state, and realign man's laws with God's. Only then, when we obey God, will Caesar stop infringing upon those rights and duties which belong to Christians.

RECOMMENDED READING: TUITION TAX CREDITS: A Responsible Appraisal, Barbara Morris, The Barbara Morris Report, Box 756, Upland CA 91786.

29

UNITED NATIONS AND WORLD PEACE

BACKGROUND BRIEFING *Moscow, October 19-30, 1943:* Agreement for United Nations Organization is reached by big four allied powers: United Kingdom, United States, USSR, & Republic of China. *Yalta, February 4-11, 1945:* Voting arrangement for UN reached by Churchill, Roosevelt, and Stalin (*five major powers* — France included — to be permanent members of 11-member Security Council, each of the five to have *veto power.** / Also, Soviets to have *three votes in General Assembly* — one for USSR, and one each for Ukraine SSR, and Byelorussia SSR). *San Francisco, June 26, 1945:* Representatives of 50 nations sign UN Charter. *July 28, 1945:* US Senate ratifies UN Charter, *89 to 2* (Senators *William Langer* (R-North Dakota) and *Henrik Shipstead* (R-Minn) vote "Nay" — Langer warns Senators, *"(UN) is fraught with danger to the American people and to American institutions." October 15, 1945:* UN charter ratified by majority of signatory nations.

Mindful of horrors and devastation of World War II, nations saw UN as *"man's last best hope for* peace," ignored implicit dangers. In US, vast majority welcomed organization. Even in 1959, Gallup reported 87% of Americans thought UN was doing good job. Since then, *public has lost confidence:* in 1970, *50%* thought UN was effective; in 1971, *35%*; 1973, *34%*; 1980, *31%* (with 53% saying *UN does poor job*). *In 1981, Roper poll found only 10% thought UN effective.* 1983 survey found Americans highly critical of UN operations; negative opinions ran *higher than 90%*. Recent ABC-TV poll asked viewers, *"Should the UN leave US?"* Response was *"Yes" by more than two-to-one* (125,340 to 60,970). On 9/22/83, US Senate voted 66-23 to *cut US contributions to UN* by 21% for fiscal 1983-84, and 10% more in each of following three yrs.

Some say if US Senate were acting on UN membership today, *vote would be negative.* After drawing up "balance sheet" on UN, Dr. Juliana Geran Pilon concluded *"There are questions . . . as to whether the U.S. is benefiting from its U.N. membership, given the paralysis of the Security Council and the anti-American, anti-Western, anti-industrial, anti-capitalist majority in the General Assembly."*

Purpose of United Nations? To keep world peace. (What is "peace?" To Soviets, peace is not absence of war; peace is absence of resistance. *In each of past 15 yrs, 52 million free persons have been taken over by anti-Christian communists.*) Has UN achieved its purpose? *Supporters say "Yes."* Boast "because of UN no major wars have been fought since 1945." Call Korea and Vietnam *"police actions."* *Critics disagree.* Say charter calls for UN to uphold right of self-determination of small nations. Absence of "major" wars due to restraint between super-powers, not because of UN. *Say as peacekeeper, UN has been mostly all mouth and no muscle.* British prime Minister *Margaret Thatcher* pointed out (6/82) that *since 1945 there have been "140 conflicts in which up to 10 million people have died."* UN did little to prevent those or restore peace while spending $3 billion on "peacekeeping." Between 1945-77, UN totally inept and ineffective in regard to *93 conflicts.* UN did little or nothing about *Soviet invasion of Hungary* (1956), *war between Netherlands and Indonesia* (1962); *Soviet invasion of Czechoslavakia* (1968); *Vietnam wars* (1945-1975); *Ethiopian war vs Somali* ('77); *Vietnamese invasion and slaughter in Cambodia* ('77 to present); *Soviet invasion of Afghanistan* ('79-present); *Iran-Iraq war* ('80 to present); *Qadhafi's invasion of Chad* ('83) or *war in Lebanon,* etc.

*/In first 20 years of UN, Soviets used veto more than 100 times; half of them to reject memberships of nations with non-communist govts. Latest Soviet veto: *to kill UN Council resolution censuring USSR for shooting down Korean Air Lines Flight 007.*

Pro-UN groups insist it is important for world dialogue — "talking is better than fighting." UN Ambassador Jeane Kirkpatrick says "UN is forum for airing ideas." But, say UN opponents, most ideas at UN are anti-USA; UN is forum for attacking US. Phyllis Schlafly reminds: Japanese emissaries were *talking* even as their planes headed for Pearl Harbor. Stalin wrote, *"Words must have no relation to action."*

Critics say UN *maintains double standard;* has " consistent record of exploiting and exaggerating the problems of the West while remaining silent regarding the flagrant, often heinous violations of human rights by the Soviet bloc nations." Bloc of 93 Third World nations branded USA as "only" threat to peace and prosperity in the world. Critics charge *UN fuels violence by supporting wars of "national liberation" and by fanning regional disputes into global conflicts and legitimizes terrorist groups such as PLO and SWAPO* (South West Africa People's Organization). PLO was virtual non-entity until UN invited *Yassir Arafat* to address UN General Assembly (11/13/74). Non-member PLO has observers in General Assembly and representatives on UN agencies (a courtesy extended to no other non-member, *including founder-nation, Free China*).

Burton Pine, Heritage Fndtn. UN Assessment Project, *charges UN increases tensions, politicizes non-political issues and provides US base for USSR espionage.* (Arkady Shevchenko, ex-KGB agent and UN Under-Secretary for Political and Security Council Affairs defected to the West in 1978. He revealed that high percentage of Soviet UN delegates work for KGB.) Opportunity for spy nest cited as one reason USSR always insisted UN be located in USA.

Supporters say UN is needed to protect human rights throughout world. UN said little or nothing of *Idi Amin's policy of genocide in Uganda,* little or nothing about *Pol Pot's slaughter of 3 million in Cambodia,* or the *continued violation of human rights in USSR and Soviet bloc nations.* UN has said little, done nothing, about Soviet use of *germ and biochemical warfare in Afghanistan, Cambodia.* UN does little *to halt terrorism,* a most blatant violation of human rights. Critics also point to UN's vicious war against the black, anti-Communist govt. of *Katanga;* call it horrible example of gross violation of human rights: *UN forces bombed hospitals, shelled ambulances, destroyed churches, murdered non-combatants, slaughtered women and children.*

Observers insist UN had built-in *bias against* free world (and US) *from beginning.* From *Alger Hiss to Kurt Waldeim, UN Secretary-Generals were either communists or socialists.* (Hiss, FDR's key UN adviser, was quietly selected at Yalta to act as interim Secretary General until UN charter was ratified.) Andrie Gromyko, then USSR Ambassador to UN, led campaign for *Trygve Lie,* first elected Secretary-General. Lie was high-ranking member of Norway's Social Democratic Labor Party, *spin off from Communist International.* Lie was succeeded by *Dag Hammorskjold,* Swedish Socialist and admirer of Red China's Chou Enlai. (Hammerskjold once wrote, *". . . I was 12 years old when I had a very strong feeling that I am a new Jesus."*) He was succeeded by *U Thant* of Burma, avowed Marxist and vocal anti-American. U Thant appointed Soviet KGB officer his personal aide; was followed by *Kurt Waldeim,* Austria's Socialist representative at the UN. Waldeim, a Nazi lieutenant during WW II, appointed KGB agent as UN personnel director.

Also, communists have always held most sensitive post in UN Secretariat: *Under-Secretary for Political and Security Council Affairs.* Of 13 who have held post, 12 were Soviets, one a Yugoslav. How sensitive is that office? *It handles all matters concerning military, territorial and jurisdictional disputes; thus it virtually controls way in which UN Secretariat approaches regional conflicts, deploys and directs the use of military forces, etc.* (UN officer in charge of military operations in Korean war—thus, privy to UN plans and strategies vs communist North Korea—was a communist from Soviet Union.)

UN's total budget for 1983 is about $1.4 billion. Maximum assessment for a member nation: 25% of budget, about $371 million. *Only USA pays it.* USSR assessment *less than 13%;* Japan's, 10%; West Germany, 8%; Great Britain, 5%. Rest of member nations (153) pay remaining 39% of budget. *Three-fifths (95) of 158 UN member nations pay from .01% to .03% each.* Oil rich Saudi Arabia pays UN just over one-half of 1% (.58%). Bloc of 120 Third World and non-aligned nations contributes 9% of total budget, has 3.4 of the vote in Assembly.

In 1981, in addition to membership assessment of $370 million, US paid $562 million in voluntary contributions to various UN agencies and projects. (from 1945 to 1965, US taxpayers paid *40% of UN budget;* assessment was gradually reduced to 25% by 1974. *During yrs 1946-1980, UN cost US taxpayers about $10 billion.*)

In UN General Assembly, it's *one nation, one vote. That means 44,404 inhabitants of St. Kitts-Nevis* (newest member nation) *have vote equal to USA with population of 234 million.* Small nations, *paying only 3% of UN budget,* are majority in General Assembly.

Heritage Fndtn. points out, *US also shortchanged re staffing of UN Secretariat and its agencies.* Third World nations vastly over-represented. *Example:* US payments and contributions total more than 25% of all UN spending; *only 11% of UN's professional staff is American*. African nations pay 1.6% of UN budget, *have 13.6% of high level posts;* Latin Americans pay *3.88%, hold 9% of posts;* Middle East countries pay 2.36%, *hold 7% of senior top-level spots.* "Tone and thrust and strategies" of UN set by Secretariat bureaucrats. *Truism of govt:* "Those who administer/enforce policy end up making policy." Thus, US is locked into minor role.*/

More indications of *anti-USA, anti-free world bias:* UNESCO (United Nations Education, Science & Cultural Organization) *now pushing "New World Information & Communication Order"* (NWIO). Sponsored by Soviets and Third World, *NWIO would end free flow of information, license journalists, censor Western-owned international news and information services.* NWIO assault on Western media is seen as one front in the *major UN push vs. Western free market economy.* Underway in UN (by bloc of 120 nations) is drive for *New International Economic Order* (NIEO). Call it *global socialism.* Among NIEO's stated goals: *to redistribute US wealth on global scale, regulate US business and industry* (use of raw materials, production, etc.), *force US to share technologies, weaken protection provided by patents, allocate ocean floor mining sites, levy taxes on ocean mining, regulate per capita consumption, make World Health Organization* (WHO) *enforcement agency superceding US Food and Drug Agency, etc.*

As *Senator David Patrick Moynihan,* former US Ambassador to the UN, warned, United Nations is *"a dangerous place."* There, the US is becoming *"an endangered species."*

/Heritage Fndtn poll, 1/1-3/2/83, found 80% approved reducing US share of UN budget; 91% favored reducing its 25% share of UN agency budgets where US did not have fair representation, and 90.8% wanted US contributions to UN agencies reduced or cancelled if that agency engaged in or sanctioned terrorism.

CONSIDER THE BIBLICAL PRINCIPLES   *The Lord God* is man's best (and only) hope of peace. *Christ Jesus is the Prince of Peace (Isa. 9:6)*. World peace is a condition to be desired. But, neither the prince of this world, nor all his agents or agencies—human and inhuman—can bring it to be. A messianic state, national or supranational, is not an instrument of peace; it can only be an instrument of coercion. Unless *The Lord God* build the house, politicians, diplomats, all labor in vain (*Ps. 127:1*). Men would make of the United Nations a god. It is, in a sense, the ultimate expression of humanism; as if man could save the world. Yet, men would lift it above The Lord God; His sovereignty is spurned (*Ex. 20:3*). In the UN "meditation room" other gods are placed on a par with The One True God. That individual or institution that denies God will be denied by The Lord God (*Mt. 10:33; 2 Chron. 7:19*).

Men may reject God, they may seek to create a god-State and worship it, *yet even in their hardness of heart some desire what only He can provide (Isa. 26:3)*. In the UN park across the street from UN tower this Scripture is writ in the marble. ". . . they shall beat their swords into plowshares, and their spears into pruning hooks. Nation shall not lift up sword against nation. Neither shall they learn war any more." *Consider what was omitted on that UN wall.* Ignored, rejected, is the very basis, the central, unyielding requirement, of that blessed hope. Here is what goes before and what follows after that passage from *Isa. 2:2-4* (italics added for emphasis):

"And it shall come to pass in the last days, that the mountain of *The Lord's house shall be established* in the top of the mountains (i.e. above all other nations, above all other kingdoms) and shall be exalted above the hills; *and all nations shall flow into it*. And many people shall go and say, Come ye, and let us go up to *the mountain of The Lord, to the house of the God of Jacob;* and *He* will teach us *His* ways, and we will walk in *His* paths: for *out of Zion* shall go forth *the law,* and *the word of The Lord* from Jerusalem. And *He shall judge among the nations,* and shall rebuke many people, and . . ." Then, after verses 2-4, follows verse 5: "O house of Jacob, come ye, and *let us walk in the light of The Lord."*

Man may seek to pick and choose what they desire from God's word, but it won't work. *God's word is a seamless whole.* Man's spiritual and geopolitical myopia not withstanding, it is *The Lord's* house, to which the nations shall come; *The Lord* God that shall establish peace; God's law, and God's word that shall prevail, and *God's* ways, and *God's* paths (not the UN's) that nations shall travel to find true and lasting peace.

We are not to follow false gods or make idols of institutions; we are to stand firm in the faith, meek (obedient) before Him. Then, surely, we shall delight in the abundance of peace (*Ps. 37:11*). *Blessed are such peacemakers for they do love The Lord (Mt. 5:9).*

Consider the tower of Babel (*Gen. 11:1-9*). It, too, was an affront to God; a rebellion vs God by those who thought themselves wiser than God. Did not Nimrod seek to establish *a universal monarchy,* to challenge the Supremacy of God—even as the UN seeks to be a god and establish *one world government?* And, did not The Lord God confound the language of those who would have built a high tower to be on a level with Him? Does not controversy and strife and babble rage in the UN today? Never have so many words accomplished so little. And, even as the builders of Babel quit building because of confusion, is not the UN self-destructing because of confusion and stalemate and hostility? Those who would have built the tower of Babel had no rock, *they made their own brick. They used slime for mortar.* Those who would build the UN have no rock, they have rejected The Keystone; they use hatred for mortar and they build on the sands of man. They are destined to despair and destruction (*Mt. 7:24-27*). "Come out of her, My people, that ye be not partakers of her sin and ye receive not of her plagues" (*Rev. 18:4*).

RECOMMENDED READING: Heritage Foundation, BACKGROUNDER series, *A United Nations Assessment Project,* Washington DC; Robert W. Lee, *The United Nations Conspiracy,* Western Islands, Belmont, MA; Archibald E. Roberts, *The Emerging Struggle,* Betsy Ross Press, Ft. Collins, CO.

30

USURY

BACKGROUND BRIEFING Will U.S. Institutions (economic, social, religious, political) sink in sea of debt and usury? Economists and forecasters warn *it could happen*. R. E. McMaster, Jr., says mounting debt and compounding interest is "time bomb" that could "decimate" nation's "religious/social/political/economic order." Says existing debt/usury situation appears to be an "insurmountable problem." Robert E. Record writes "We have legalized a debt money system that has . . . transferred the wealth of the nations into the hands of the bankers who hold the mortgages on their property."

Total debt at close of 1983 was *$6.2 trillion* — up $600 billion from 1982. (That's all debt — govt., corporate, personal — and $850 billion owed US banks by Iron Curtain and 3rd World countries.) *That does not include "contingent liabilities" of US govt.* — Rep. Ron Paul (TX) figures them to be about *$11 trillion*.

Here's quick picture of debt for past 10 years:

	1974	1984
Fed. Govt. debt*	$543 billion	$1.573 billion (+190%)
Personal debt	671 billion	1.832 billion (+173%)
Business debt	900 billion	2.589 billion (+188%)

*Tip of iceberg, see below

National Taxpayer's Union claims total federal debt is $12.3 trillion. That means that each and every taxpayer is on the hook for *$153,338*. And, says NTU, that gets bigger by the minute.

Mortgage debt was $1.63 trillion in 1982; $109.5 billion-plus on *farms* (total farm debt has more than tripled in past 10 yrs). And, total *personal debt* (loans, credit cards, etc.) hit $1.8 trillion in 1983, up 173% from 1974. All told, about 6 million credit cards in circulation. Nation sinking in a sea of plastic. Color it red! Mortgage debt was *$1.5 trillion in 1981;* $100 billion-plus on farms (total farm debt in '81 was $195 billion, *three times 1971*). Total credit (over & above mortgages) was $405 billion in 1981, *double 1971.* More than *600 million* credit cards now in circulation in US.

In 1983, just the *interest on debt was more than $900 billion.* That's 35% of nation's total personal income. Equal to 30% of gross natnl. product. Just interest on debts was *four times* total corporate profits; $200 billion more than federal budget (not including "off-budget" items), *three times federal income taxes collected in 1982!*

(*Interest on debt* is fastest growing item on *federal* budget: $149.5 billion. About six times what it was in 1974. Comes to *15% of total budget.* That interest on federal debt costs taxpayers about $277,000 each and every minute; $16 million an hour; about $2.8 billion a week. Meanwhile, deficit increases at rate of *$3.7 billion/wk.* And, projected deficits for '84 and '85 mean interest on debt will take even bigger chunk of federal taxes and budgets in future.)

How serious is all this? Fred J. Russell, writing in *The Reaper* (11/13/83) describes the trauma: *"The seriousness of interest expense on US government debt is that interest alone will* double *the US national debt in* 5 years *and will* quadruple it in 10 yrs. (A trillion dollar debt becomes 2 trillion dollars the fifth year and 4 trillion dollars in the tenth year.)" *That's the cancer of compounded interest!*

And, *Congressman Ron Paul* measures the magnitude of "the crime of deficits": "Between 1960 and 1980, it took 20% of Americans' savings to finance the federal debt. *But, in 1983 alone, the US government was forced to borrow an amount equivalent to 98% of all the money saved by Americans just to finance* (i.e. pay the interest on) *the debt.*"

Where does all the money go? The profits from *$150 billion in interest* on the federal (taxpayers') debt? *A big chunk of it goes to foreign investors.* They hold *$170 billion* (17%) of the $1.4 trillion US public debt held outside govt. Office of Management and Budget reported that *13.8% of all Federal spending in 1983 went to international banker-owners of the Federal Reserve System* (to class "A" stockholders of the System)!

Small wonder economy is a basket case! Take *1971-81* for quick look-see at a critically ill patient: Money supply almost tripled as supply of money (mostly fiat; i.e. paper) increased, interest rates [cost of money] went up. *Prime rate* rose from 5.5% to 21.5% then dropped to 18%; *Federal Reserve discount* rate up from 4.8% to 13.4%; *conventional mortgages* from 7.6% (1971) to 14.23% (12/81); *consumer credit* to 18% and higher. Consumer price index almost doubled (i.e. purchasing power of $ cut in half); rate of business and personal bankruptcies more than doubled; unemployment up from 5.5% ('71) to 10.8% (11/82).

And, the cause? Years and years of (Babylonian) debt/ usury money system controlled by the international bankers and their puppets, the taxers and spenders. Robert B. Record in *The National Message* bells the cat:

"We (the people) are the unwitting victims of a col-ossal fraud. We have legalized a debt money system that has impoverished the nations and which has transferred the wealth of the nations into the hands of the (international) bankers who hold the mortgages" on our personal and public property." (11/28/79)

Yet, in face of what some warn as *impending disaster,* calls continue for more *debt and increased usury.* One major credit card company, in state with 18% lid on usury, sold its accounts to Midwestern banking conglomerate. Why? *Because,* said company, *18% usury rate was not enough.* Banking group, chartered in state with no lid on usury, can charge more (20% +), make more. (In Arkansas, bankers demanded state abolish law controlling usury or banks would take credit/loan money elsewhere. In Maryland, major banks threatened to move operations to Delaware if legislators did not remove 18% lid on consumer loans, credit cards and 2nd mortgages. *Politicians responded by lifting lid to 24%.*)

Some argue debt/usury system *fueled nation's econ-*

USURY AND $50,000 MORTGAGES*
(Impact of varying rates and spans of years)

	10%	14%	18%
10-yr term	[$660]	[$776]	[$900]
	$79,000	$93,120	$108,000
15-yr term	[$537]	[$666]	[$805]
	$96,660	$119,880	$144,900
30-yr term	[$438]	[$592]	[$753]
	$157,600	$213,210	$271,000

*$ amounts in [brackets] indicate approximate monthly payment at that interest rate and term of years. $ amounts in bold face and not in brackets indicate approximate total payment of $50,000 principal loan during full term of contract.

on.y, spurred its growth during past decades, and accelerated rise in standard of living. Others respond: perhaps, but cost of that system was (and will be) *devastating!* What may have seemed a benefit is now an *economic cancer* that has matastisized. *"We are a nation of economic slaves; the usurers are the slavemasters."*

Consider the cost of usury: Suppose family obtains $50,000 mortgage (home loan) at 14% for 30-yr term. If mortgage goes full 30 yrs, payments on mortgage will add up to some *$213,120, principal and interest—more than 4-times the amount borrowed.* (See chart below.) Mortgages seldom run full term; according to Financial Publishing, average life of mortgage is *8 yrs.* Suppose our family ($50,000 at 14% for 30-yrs) sold the house at the end of seven yrs. What was the cost of their loan? Over those 84 months *they would have paid $49,728 on the mortgage* ($592 a month for 7 yrs). How much did that reduce their loan principal? *$3,760!* The rest of their seven-yrs of payments ($45,968) went to pay interest/usury. *They still owe $46,240* on that $50,000 mortgage. *That is economic slavery!*

What has emerged, say forecasters, is *just tip of volcano* that is about to erupt. *For example:* figure that interest on $5.5 trillion of debt averages 10%, compounding quarterly. *That means debt-load doubles every 7 yrs.* Add to that debtors' difficulty/inability to pay interest let alone principal (e.g. Poland, Mexico, Brazil, Zaire, Argentina, etc. as well as increasing number of consumers and businesses in USA). *Magnitude of problem, social, economic, political impact of problem, begins to* become clear.

ACRES, USA, thinks possibility of *debt pay-off is bleak,* suggests compound interest will consume everything. ACRES says: "If we were to adopt a plan to repay this $5.4 trillion of public and private debt that

pay this $5.4 trillion of public and private debt that prevails in the economy today at 13% interest with annual payments over 100 years, *it would cost $70.2 billion per year for 100 yrs, principal and interest,* a total of $70.2 trillion. If we postpone it one year, the cost goes up to $78.3 billion per year, *a total of $78.3 trillion . . ."*

Such are the deadly fruits of debt usury system. Yet, some (congressmen, bankers, economists, special interest groups) continue to call for increased govt. spending and more lenient debt/credit/banking laws. Take *Monetary Control Act of 1980,* for example: gives Fed Reserve power *to monetize debts* owed to major US banks by Iron Curtain, 3rd World and other foreign nations (i.e. it would allow banks to use debts as *collateral* to print more Fed Reserve notes even though repayment of some if not all of those loans seems highly doubtful). *Thus, US taxpayers could end up paying the debts* — to prevent defaults and to keep banks "solvent." Critics insist such monetization (money creation) can only increase debts, deficits, inflation, usury, and cause eventual economic, social, cultural, and political disruption in USA. Congressman Paul warns "(Monetary Control Act) will surely lead to a disastrous end for American dollar."

CONSIDER THE BIBLICAL PRINCIPLES God's word makes it clear: *we are not to engage in usury.* We are not to charge interest on our property (money or goods) when we loan to a brother in need. *We are not to oppress or extort* if we loan (money or goods) to a stranger (non-believer) (Lev. 25:17; Ex. 33:9). "Usury" as unrevised in The Bible means *any* gain (taking of *any* interest) *whatsoever.* This principle was held by the early Christian church and persisted in many sects, even into the reformation yrs. Today, term "usury" is *erroneously* used to signify taking exhorbitant or excessively high interest or gain on the loan of property (money, goods, etc.).

Early Christian church forbade usury (interest). St. Augustine denounced interest as unjust appropriation. Thomas Aquinas asserted usury was theft and contrary to justice. Common law of England held that taking of any interest was mortal sin. During reign of James I, usurers ranked with murders (under Edward III, usury was a capital crime). *Early protestant leaders condemned usury:* MARTIN LUTHER — "Whosoever eats up, robs, and steals the nourishment of another commits as great a murder as he who carves a man or utterly undoes him. Such does a usurer . . ." JOHN CALVIN — "For we altogether condemn usurers, we shall impost severer restrictions upon the conscience than The Lord Himself desired; while if we make the least concession many will use it as a pretext and will snatch at a bridgeless license . . ."

Gradually, "distinction" evolved between loans *for consumption* (no usury) and loans for production and commerce (usury allowed). Over years Biblical principles were altered as church heirarchy sought approval and support of commercial-industrial-banking communities. Political and economic individualism switched emphasis from hand of God and His laws to Adam Smith's "invisible hand" and man's laws of economics. Secular humanist insistence prevailed (i.e. political and economic considerations take precedence over God's laws. Thus began rise of *apostate capitalism* and *corporate state* as men put his law and plan above God's. Godly Christians know that all property, all wealth, is God's (*Ps. 24:1*); that men are His stewards who are to manage His resources according to His laws and purposes (*Dt. 11:1; Luke 12:43*). "Today, State has become a god; in its self-appointed, messianic role it has determined it will create money out of 'official' paper, wealth out of politician's hot air" and credit/debt out of "fractional reserves" (Gary North).

Consider, now, some admonitions regarding usury as they are set forth in God's written word: "If you lend money to any of My people that is poor by thee, you shall not be to him a usurer, neither shall you lay upon him usury" (*Ex. 22:25*). "Take no usury of him, or increase; but fear your God; that you brother may live with you. You shall not give him your money upon usury, nor lend him victuals for increase" (*Lev. 25:36, 37*). "You shall not lend upon usury to your brother; usury of money, usury of victuals, usury of anything that is lent upon money: Unto a stranger you may lend upon usury; but unto your brother you shall not lend upon usury; that The Lord thy God may bless you in all that your set your hand to in the land where you go to possess it" (*Dt. 23:19, 20*).

As God gave His chosen a land "to possess it" (above) so He also drove the rebellious Israelites out of it because they disobeyed His law. Among reasons for their expulsion: "You have taken usury and increase and you have greedly gained of your neighbors by extortion and have forgotten Me, says The Lord God" (*Ezek. 22:12-15*).

The prophet Ezekiel, in *chapter 18:8*, described as just and righteous the man who "has not given forth upon usury, neither taken any increase." Conversely, *in verse 13, the* wicked son who "hath given forth upon usury" shall not live. In *Psalm 15,* in answer to David's question "Who shall dwell in Thy holy hill?" Among those listed is he "that putteth not out his money to usury nor taketh reward against the innocent."

Remember how it was in Jerusalem when God used Nehemiah to rebuild the wall (*Neh. 5:1-13*). Famine ("dearth") forced the repatriates to *mortgage their lands, vineyards and houses* to buy food and pay taxes [vv 3-5]. Usury demanded by the moneylenders was so oppressive that families were forced to sell their sons and daughters into slavery to make payments on the mortgages. There seemed to be no hope of redeeming their children because interest was so cruel (12%/yr). They cried out to Nehemiah *"These, our own brothers, are doing this to us!"* In wrath, Nehemiah demanded that the nobles, rulers and priests cease taking usury and restore the property and money [v 11, 12]. (Is there not a *parallel,* of sorts, *with today?* Productive citizens are taxed more and more to "rebuild the wall" (repair the nation's defenses). Unemployment and high prices force more and more families to borrow to pay taxes, make ends meet, etc. Usury virtually consumes the payments they make. There seems little hope of ever getting out of debt. . . . and, the future of our children and our children's children is indentured [put into economic bondage] by a huge and ever-growing federal debt.)

Finally, did Christ our Savior and King condemn usury? He did indeed! Read His words in *Luke 6:34-36:* "And if you lend to them of whom you hope to receive, what thanks have you? for sinners also lend to sinners, to receive as much again. But love you your enemies, and do good, and lend, hoping for nothing again; and your reward shall be great, and you shall be the children of The Highest: for He is kind to the unthankful and to the evil. Be you therefore merciful, as your Father also is merciful."

In *Economics, Money and Banking, Christian Principles,* Dr. E. L. Hebden Taylor, describes Babylonian system of economics *based on debt and high rates of interest* (20%). Entire Babylonian concept of social control and imperialism *rested on usury* (as it does for today's international bankers). (Quoting R. J. Rushdoony's *The Politics of Guilt and Pity,* Dr. Taylor reminds us "it is not surprising that Babylon the Great, the harlot, is the type in the Book of Revelation of the one-world order which shall seduce all nations. . . ." (*Rev. 18:4 calls upon God's people to come out from such a world system, and not be partakers of such sin.*)

Dr. Taylor emphasizes *restrictions* God's law places upon usury: *No believer is allowed to profit from another believer's financial distress or poverty.* On the contrary he is to help with an interest-free loan. *Loans are to be sought or made only for necessities/emergencies* — not luxuries. When *commercial loans* are made, reasonable interest may be charged since it is equitable for lender to share in the profits earned through the use of his money (while also sharing the risk of loss). Dr. Gary North (in *An Introduction to Christian Economics*) writes that loaner is entitled to a return on his money because (1) he forfeits use of that money for length of loan, (2) there is a risk factor, and (3) he should be able to protect himself against eventuality of inflation (loss of value of his principal) during term of loan.

IN SUM: *Christian world-and-life system* places severe limits on debt and usury. We are to avoid debt if at all possible and avoid multiple indebtedness in any event. Duration (term) of debt strictly limited. Two types of loans recognized in God's word: *loans to believer without usury* (no interest); *loans to unbeliever with usury (Dt. 23:20).* (Views of Biblical scholars differ in regard to loans to a "stranger" (unbeliever). Some hold it is against God's word to levy usury on such loans (*Lev. 25:35-36; Luke 6:35, 36*). Insist there is distinction between term "stranger" ["gare" — an unbeliever who is citizen of community] and "foreigner" ["nakar"] who is neither a believer nor fellow-citizen but someone from a foreign land. Usury, they suggest, is permitted on loans to such foreigners but not to fellow-citizens.)

RECOMMENDED READING: E. L. Hebden Taylor, *Economics, Money and Banking; Christian Principles,* The Craig Press, 1978; Gary North, *An Introduction to Christian Economics,* The Craig Press, 1974; Elgin Groseclose, *America's Money Machine: The Story of the Federal Reserve*; Tom Rose, *Economics: Principles and Policy from A Christian Perspective,* Mott Media, 1977; and H. B. Clark, *Biblical Law,* Binfords & Mort, 1944.

31

VIDEO WITCHCRAFT

BACKGROUND BRIEFING Among the "hottest" items for youngsters (and many adults) are fantasy games and interactive video sports such as *"Dungeons & Dragons,"* "Tunnels and Trolls," "Chivalry and Sorcery," "Runnequest," "Hellpits of Nightfang," etc. Selection ranged from coloring books for younger children to high priced role-playing games complete with guide books for dungeon masters adapted for personal computer and home TV video cassettes (VCR) games involving hunt and chase and murder fantasies, etc. Sold through computer, department, and toy stores, games are merchandised as "fun and fantasy." Players compete to "summon *demons* to defeat opponents," to "employ *dark forces* to win battles," etc. Games also used in classes for gifted children *in some public schools*.

It's a big business. Millions of Americans (mostly teenagers and young adults) comprise growing market, are literally enchanted with "games." Industry grossed about $500 million (one-half billion) in recent years. But, is it all "fun and games?"

Some may think games harmless, strictly fun,

fantasy and entertainment. *Beware! They are not!* Parents who buy or allow such games are playing with dynamite — *and their children's souls.* They open their homes, and their children, to *subtle introduction to occult* and *malignant world of psychotherapy* (mind alteration, values modification). *There is nothing benign about these games:* they are part of the increasing spread of occult, a push that will increase in tempo and fervor as satan's time grows shorter. Facets of games include: death, deities, prayer and fasting, satanism, human sacrifices, murder, cannibalism, defilement and defecation, and constantly use Biblical terms and phrases blasphemously.

Consider this: ". . . *after years of study of the history of occultism, after having researched a book on the subject, and after having consulted with scholars in the field of historical research, I can say with confidence: these games are the most effective, most magnificiently packaged, most profitably marketed, most thoroughly researched introduction to the occult in man's recorded history."* (Dr. Gary North in *None Dare Call It Witchcraft.*

Thus, reasonable to assume that such interactive games (i.e. player not only plays role but assumes identity of character he creates and lives in a created "reality") are fraught with peril. They are or come very close to being part and parcel of a program to teach the (religious) principles and rituals of witchcraft (occultism).

Examine the *dangerous role-playing* (fantasizing) *component* of these games: role-playing is *subtle* (sugar-coated) *form of psycho-drama adapted to humanistic designs for sensitivity training and values modification.*

Some Christians may view role-playing as harmless. Fact is it is a *first-step form of psychotherapy* that seeks to destroy what humanists call *"the God syndrome"* (i.e. belief in God). In other words it is the *first step* toward *subtly inducing child to reject the religious training of home and church.*

Psychodrama used extensively in USSR to separate children from traditional religious values held by parents (substituting State for God, creating faith in all-powerful State while weakening and then destroying faith in God).

Highly directed and sophisticated *socio-drama or psycho-drama* (psychotherapy) can destroy traditional values and imprint subject's mind with "new" or no values. *Lavrenti Beria,* Soviet master-manipulator, used such methods to develop the USSR's psychopolitical warfare *(psychopolitics/brain-washing).*

Psychodramatic techniques (the root of role-playing) were introduced in early 1900's by *Dr. Jacob L. Moreno,* a contemporary of Sigmund Freud. Moreno wrote that his objective was to develop *"a positive religion"* (for evidence of how his work has been implemented and is being implemented, see *"Humanist Manifesto I"* [1933], and *"Humanist Manifesto II"* [1973]). Such a "positive" religion, wrote Moreno, would be expanded and improved by science while making use of "insights" of Marxism. In his 1932 book, *Who Shall Survive,* Moreno wrote that *through psycho-drama with role-playing "we will destroy the God syndrome."* He set forth his intentions: *"The idea was that if you can 'play a role'* — for instance, the role of God — *and develop that role and stop its playing at will, you*

*will begin to learn how not to be possessed of that role . . .
The only way to get rid of the God syndrome is to act it out."*

"Values clarification, "sensitivity training," role-playing, have been going on in USA for decades; part of *program to remold American traditions and values through generational-revision (Judges 2:10).* The seemingly innocuous games of "fantasy" would seem to be a part of that strategy.

CONSIDER THE BIBLICAL PRINCIPLES   *1. The Occult*: Trafficking (even trifling) with the occult—demons, witchcraft, dark forces (ouija boards, tarot cards, astrology, fortune telling, charms—is *paganism* (idolatry). *Such is an anathema, an abomination, to The Lord God.*

". . . *neither shall you use enchantment (sorcery), nor observe time (astrology) . . . Regard not them that have familiar spirits, neither seek after wizards, to be defiled by them" (Lev. 19:26).*

"*There shall not be found among you any one that makes his son or his daughter to pass through fire, or that uses divination, or an observer of times, or an enchanter, or a witch. Or a charmer, or a consulter with familiar spirits, or a wizard, or a necromancer. For all that do these things are an abomination unto The Lord . . ." (Dt. 18:9-12).*

"*And the soul that turns after such as have familiar spirits and after wizards, to play the harlot after them, I will even set My face against that soul and will cut him off from among his people" (Lev. 20:6).* See also *Isa. 47:12-14; Jer. 10:2,* etc.

Demons are unclean spirits *(Mt. 10:1),* evil spirits

(Acts 19:12), fallen angels who rebelled and are now in darkness unto judgment *(Jude 6)*; their power is limited but not ended *(II Peter 2:4)*, they serve the prince of darkness, the prince of this world *(Mt. 12:24; John 12:31)*.

Occult practices are *a sin that honors satan rather than God;* it makes God's enemies the guiding force, the hope and source of knowledge. How can we live in and for Christ Jesus and traffic with satan? *We must not depart "from the faith" or give heed to "seducing spirits and doctrines of the devil" (I Tim. 4:1)*. Once a person's delight (interest) is in the occult rather than in the love and law and prophets of the Lord God, a door is opened unto satan. *"Know not that to whom you yield yourselves servants to obey, his servants you are" (Rom. 6:16)*.

We must not be preoccupied with thoughts or fears of satan or his demons; but, certainly *we should be aware of and on guard* against such forces. How are we to shun, to overcome, such evil entities? God's word counsels us: (1) *"Submit yourselves therefore unto God,* (2) *Resist the devil and he will flee from you" (James 4:7, 8)*.

2. *Role-playing (psychodrama):* Role-playing (assuming another's identity and values as contrasted with legitimate dramatic arts) is *ungodly, dangerous — deadly. First recorded case of role-playing?* Eve, in Garden of Eden when satan tempted her into trying to play the role of a god *(Gen. 3:5)*.

Mrs. F. C. Bosworth, Pro-Family Forum, Cleveland, sets forth *two basic premises on which psychodrama* (role-playing) *must be opposed:* "(1) *The root determines the fruit (Mt. 7:17);* the root of role-playing is humanistic psy-

chology with the intent to 'play God out of one's life.'
(2) *The method is the message;* and there is no way to
use the psychodrama (role-playing) method in a
Christian way; the underlying message of role-
playing will always be *the message of humanism."*

"*The fool hath said in his heart there is no God*" (*Ps
14:1);* satan said he would be like God *(Isa. 14:14).*
Surely it must be clear that Christians must *have no
part of those who deny God or would play God;* surely we
must not fall prey to their schemes and devices.
"*Learn not the way of the heathen*" (*Jer. 10:12).*

In addition to its other, and insidious, evils, *role-
playing invites* (encourages) *escapism, nihilism, and
situational ethics.* It paves the way for *values modification
and manipulation.* It suggests that the *absolutes of God's
truth* must give way to the *"electives"* of humanism.
Against such things we are to be on guard *(Eph.
4:14, 15).*

RECOMMENDED READING: *None Dare Call It
Witchcraft,* Dr. Gary North, Arlington House;
Dungeons & Dragons Information, Handbook #23,
Education Research Analysts (The Mel Gablers),
P. O. Box 7518, Longview TX 76702 (send contribu-
tion of $5.00 to cover costs of production and mail-
ing). This section on psychodrama originally sug-
gested by *Mary Louise Reintjes,* Prairie Village, KS.

32

WOMEN AND "EQUAL RIGHTS"

BACKGROUND BRIEFING March 22, 1972, US Congress passed and sent to States the *"Equal Rights Amendment."* If ratified by three-fourths of States, ERA would become 27th Amendment to US Constitution.

Key section of Amendment contained 24 words: *"Equality of rights under the law shall not be denied or abridged by the United States or by any state on account of sex."*

Congress also set *7 yrs* as time-limit for ratification. 22 States ratified in 1972, another 13 by 1978: total, 35 — *three short of required 38.* States refusing to ratify included: AL, AR, AZ, FL, GA, IL, LA, MS, MO, NV, OK, SC, UT and VA. (Five of State that had ratified subsequently *moved to rescind ratification;* 5 other ratifying States indicated that, given another vote, they would not ratify.)

At end of 7-yr period, *ERA failed to gain necessary number of States.* In 1978, Congress — with 225 dissenting votes in House and Senate — *extended ratification* time by 39 months. That extension ended in 1982. Supporters of ERA in Congress, *resubmitted measure* in attempt to once again start ratification process. Bill, with many co-sponsors, was defeated in Committee in Nov. 1983 unders suspension of rules. Little doubt backers will try again next session.

Original ERA impetus stemmed mostly from *inequities in employment opportunities and pay scales.* However, militant feminists soon turned ERA drive into all-out movement for their cause; escalated demands to achieve not simply equality but *"liberation."* Many saw (and see) such positions and demands as clear indication of way in which "women's liberation" groups would press for *distorted and extreme enforcement* of the ERA should it become law of land.

ERA proponents began touting Amendment as *"support legislation" for pro-abortion* position ("Women should be 'free' to terminate unwanted pregnancies, should not be denied medical assistance because of sex"). That stance increased opposition to ERA, thus feminists switched positions and *"Played a dishonest game with Congress, claiming that ERA has nothing to do with abortions . . . while arguing just the opposite in the State courts"*—Douglas Johnson, National Right-to-Life Committee.

Pro-abortion decisions argued and decided on basis of state ERA laws make clear *passage of federal ERA would certainly be big push in pro-abortion direction.* In *Massachusetts,* State Supreme Judicial Court ruled in favor of govt. funding of abortion partly on basis of State's ERA law. In *Pennsylvania,* state court decision struck down abortion-funding restrictions on grounds of sex discrimination (3/9/84). Thus, taxpayers in that State will be forced to fund abortion on demand. In *Connecticut,* pro-abortion groups using State ERA law to challenge abortion-funding restrictions. In other States where courts have examined ERA-abortion link, courts have ruled on other grounds but did not reject ERA arguments.

ERA forces also expanded push to include demands that women be given jobs now held by men (*"affirmative action"* programs based on sex—job quotas, etc.). Further, argue that *"homemaking" is a demeaning role* that makes women "second-class citizens" deprived of equal rights. To pro-ERA forces, *traditional family unit is passe in an emerging egalitarian* (unisex) *society;* thus they urge women to shun home and motherhood in favor of "liberating" careers or—at very least—place children in care centers and strike out for new horizons. (*Bio-statistical studies indicate that in rush to achieve "total" equality with men,* feminists are closing gap with men in such areas as alcoholism, auto accidents, suicides, heart diseases, lung cancer, etc.)

Opponents of ERA at both Federal and State levels see it as (1) *threat to dignity, security and well-being of women;* (2) threat to *family and home;* (3) *anti-Biblical,* and (4) fear it would open *floodgates for laws and regulations extremely demeaning to women* (military conscription, pre-empting health and safety requirements, and other laws now protecting women).

Additionally, anti-ERA women see it as an *implicit anti-marriage/fidelity message;* divorce is not only to be condoned but encouraged and facilitated (*the more women assert their "rights" the more men feel free to abandon their responsibilities)*—thus men, not women would be "liberated." Its opponents contend ERA would be tantamount to legislating situations that could bring further disintegration of marriage and home, and security of wife and children. Also, warn of *dangers of close-contact, mixed-sex jobs* (shared work situations, especially under pressure and for prolonged periods, tend to create temptations and aphrodisiac influences).

Finally, those opposed to ERA argue that Federal amendment would by-pass States and be *one more slide toward lock-step centralism* (Sec. 2 of ERA reads: *"Congress shall have the power to enforce . . . with appropriate legislation."*). They suggest that where inequities do exist (unfair job and pay discrimination, tax laws, survivor benefits, etc.) *these should and can be rectified by State statutes and regulations.*

CONSIDER THE BIBLICAL PRINCIPLES According to God's holy word, woman are to be subordinate to men; *not inferior — subordinate (Gen. 3:16, I Cor. 11:8).* The wife is to be in submission to her husband *(Eph. 5:22).* As Christ is the head of the church, so the man is to be the head of home and family *(Eph. 5:23). Christ exercises authority over His church* to protect her, to save her from evil, and to supply her every good. *In like manner, the husband exercises authority over the home* to protect it, to guard it from evil, and to supply its good and proper needs (both spiritual and material).

Let it be clear that *subordination is not inferiority;* woman is not inferior to man. The man who assumes lordly superiority over woman is as much in error as the woman who refuses to be subordinate to man. The woman is the "rest" (the completion) of man; created out of man to be his helpmeet; *together, they make a completeness.* If woman were taken from the very substance of man, how can she be inferior? Subordination is in fact *a sign of authority* since the wife (woman) is not devoid of authority but *has authority as the helpmeet of God's appointed vice regent* and as such is to *work with him* to gain dominion for the honor and glory of The Lord God. The real tragedy of the so-called women's liberation movement is that it fails to restore women to their rightful place of authority beside men, and seeks to put them into competition with men; *thus, rather than completion and fruition, there is conflict and chaos.*

Paul *(I Cor. 11:2-12)* compares the line of authority between husband and wife to that between God, The Father, and Christ, The Son *("and the head of Christ is God").* Christ is not inferior to The Father *("I and My Father are one")* (*John 1:1; 5:18-23; 10:30; Php. 2:6);* yet, He was willingly *subordinate* to God, The Father, obeying Him and seeking to do His will in all things (*Lk. 22:42).*

The flow of power and force that is government originates with God and flows from Him to man. "Under every government, sovereignty must vest in some recognized head; in the family—which is constituted by God's authority, the prerogative of representing God's power is attached to the husband and father." It is the same in church and civil polity. (Note that in the Scriptures cited in paragraph one, above, the Biblical reference is to man.)

God's line of authority concerning the sexes is firmly established in His Book (*I Cor. 11:3; Col. 3:18, 19*). The woman who despises or disobeys her husband or who seeks to dominate him, violates Divine law and thwarts Divine judgment (*Gen. 3:16*). There is a vast distinction between offering wise counsel and seeking to dominate.

The sexes are not to seek to change places ("roles"). This applies to the man who fails to exercise authority properly and to the woman who would pre-empt the male authority (*I Cor. 11:9; I Tim. 2:12*). It is not God's plan that women be like man (*"man and female created He them"*) (*Gen. 1:27*). Both should seek to be like Jesus (*I Cor. 2:16b; II Tim. 1:19; Php. 2:5*). They should seek to glorify God rather than self (*I Cor. 6:20*). The woman who truly knows (loves) Jesus, and seeks to obey Him, is the woman who is truly "liberated" (*John 8:34-36*).

In *Pr. 31:10-31,* we find described the godly woman who is to be valued *"far above rubies."* (1) Her *integrity* is above reproach. (2) She is *industrious and competent.* (3) She is *strong in heart and mind* and imparts that strength to her husband (again, the fact of "completeness") and her children. (4) She *fears The Lord and is wise.* (5) She is *compassionate.* (6) She is a *good homemaker and mother.* (7) She serves The Lord *in words and works.* (8) She honors her spouse and *brings honor to him and to their home.* (9) She is *well-loved.* The wise woman builds her home and preserves her family; the foolish one destroys them (*Pr. 14:1*). Young women are to marry, have children, guide the home, and give no reason for reproach (*I Tim. 5:14*).

Can a woman serve The Lord in a career? *Certainly!* Consider Lydia *(Acts 16:14, 15)*. Women have served The Lord, and serve Him now, in many careers and profession (education, healing arts and sciences, missions, commerce, arts, social work) as well as in the home. Yet, in such work it is vital that The Lord's line of authority be obeyed and that it be kept in mind that *the greatest responsibility and privilege The Lord has bestowed upon the woman is her role as wife, homemaker and mother.*

As we consider the vital role of the woman in relation to *civil governance, the key verse is Pr. 31:23:*

"Her husband is known in the gates (where the affairs of civil government were conducted), *when he sitteth among the elders of the land* (those elected to civil authority)." It is not the wife who "sits among the elders"; it is because his wife brings honor to the home and fulfills her all-important duties so well and so faithfully that the husband is able to fulfill his responsibilities and duties in the civil governance of the community.

In *Isaiah 3,* we learn that one of God's punishments upon the nation that departs from obedience to His laws is that it is to be ruled by women. In Chapters 1 and 2, God recounts the sins of Judah and calls upon the people to repent. Then, in Chapter 3, He foretells of the judgment that befalls the nation for its sins and, in *Isa. 3:12,* this: *"As for My people, children* (e.g. immature, weak, "little" men of limited ability) *are their oppressors and women shall rule over them. O, My people, they which lead you cause you to err, and destroy the way of your paths."*

Letters from Plymouth Rock

Biblical Principles
of Government

"The law of the Lord is perfect, converting the soul; the testimony of the Lord is sure, making the wise simple. The statutes of the Lord are right; rejoicing the heart. The commandment of the Lord is pure, enlightening the eyes." Psalm 19:7-8

THE BIBLICAL PRINCIPLES of government, on which this nation was founded, are not very much in evidence these days. More and more we are being pulled in and down by the centralizing forces of socialistic humanism. Both man and State seek to deny and usurp God's sovereignty.

It is not that Biblical principles have ceased to be or that they are no longer imperatives: they are imperishable and immutable; their consistent application is essential for all who would obey The Lord God.

"Therefore, you shall love The Lord, your God, and keep His charge, and His statutes, and His judgments, and His commandments, always." (Deut 11:1)

Many professing Christians embrace Jesus Christ as their Savior but do not enthrone Him as their King. Could this be due, in part, to their failure to realize that God has handed down certain principles and precepts for both *internal* (self) government and *external* (civil) government?

IF WE ARE truly persuaded that God sent His Son into the world to be our Redeemer, if we believe that Jesus Christ is to be both our Savior and our King *(Acts 17:7)*, is it not reasonable to assume that

God has given us certain rules to guide us while we are here? A loving Sovereign does not leave His subjects to hunt and peck for indications of His will; He sets forth His institutes, clearly and firmly.

God's word leaves no doubt about it: He did, indeed, set forth certain absolutes to govern our lives and our institutions. The Bible also tells us that His Sovereignty is total (Deut. 4:39; John 19:11; Rom. 14:11). And, God warns His people that His Sovereignty is not to be abridged, not to be divided, not to be intermittent (Deut. 10:12; Matt. 22:37-38). We are not to be lukewarm about our God (Rev. 3:16). In every endeavor, in every area of our here-and-now, His principles and precepts are to serve as the fundamental rules of conduct (Col. 1:18). His word is to be the ultimate authority on which we are to form our decisions and base our actions and live our lives — for Him.

WHAT ARE GOD'S basic principles of government that should guide us in our civil affairs as well as our personal deportment? We may consider these to be "foundation" principles:

- the principle of *God's supreme sovereignty*
- the principle of *individuality*
- the principle of *personal property*
- the principle of *self government* (and personal accountability)
- the principle of *marital and parental responsibility*
- the principle of *voluntary association*
- the principle of *local autonomy*
- the principle of *limited civil government,* and
- the principle of *stewardship* (individual enterprise).

Each of these Biblical principles is important in itself and each is important to the whole of our Christian responsibility to maintain a self- and civil government that is in keeping with God's plan and purpose. These principles work together in and through Christ's perfect Laws of Love and Liberty *(Matt. 22:39; James 2:12; 1 Pet. 2:16).* They also combine to create the only true and effective alternative to the regressive, oppressive forces of humanism. (By reason of their origin and nature man's alternatives to God's principles must be humanistic.)

WHEN CIVIL GOVERNMENT is properly constituted and employed, there is no conflict between it and the faithful application of Biblical principles.

Consider the origin, and the originator, of civil government.

It was not man who ordained human government; it was God.

God established civil government after the great flood *(Gen. 9:5, 6)*. Through the Noahic covenant The Lord God reaffirmed the order of His creation and instituted civil government. Thus, the Apostle Paul could say, "the powers that be are ordained of God" *(Rom. 13:1)*.

It bears restatement that *government is necessary.*

Government need not (should not) be evil. The errors and excesses of fallen man in regard to civil government are abundantly manifested in this world. This may—and does, at times—cause us to view civil government with disfavor, yet, it is important to remember that it is the excess, the error, that is evil—not the institution.

Man's first constraint to obey his Creator and to maintain a proper relationship with his fellow men was, and still is, *internal:* God's Spirit working within man's heart and mind. That "voice of authority," that inner sense of right and wrong and personal responsibility called "conscience." But, because fallen man did not and does not always accede to that internal constraint and because there are those who reject the sovereignty of God, He added *external* restraint: civil government. *The external was not, and is not, a substitute for the internal.* The abiding purpose of government was, and is, three-fold:

- *to be a servant of The Lord God* (a ministry of justice)
- provide *protection* for the law-abiding, and
- to *punish* the law breaker.

The defensive (that is, the protective, non-aggressive) purposes for which God instituted civil government are made clear in The Bible. For example, Paul's instructions in *Rom. 13:3, 4,* and Peter's in *1 Pet. 2:13, 14:*

> *"For rulers are not a terror to good works, but to the evil. . . . Do that which is good, and you shall have praise of the same. For he is the minister of God to you for good. But if you do that which is evil, be afraid; for he bears not the sword in vain; for he is the minister of God, a revenger to execute wrath upon him that does evil." (Rom. 13:3, 4).*

Since God ordained civil government to protect those who seek to keep His laws from those who break His laws, it must follow that His are the laws by which government must be governed: *to the Cre-*

ator belongs the creation. If this were not so, there would be no constant absolutes, no abiding source and flow of godly authority. Civil government would be twisted and turned on the spit of human desire subject to the vagaries of passing passions. The history of man makes it clear that *only when the governed and the governors conduct themselves according to God's laws can the blessings of life, liberty and property be secured to each and every individual.*

IT IS CLEAR that our individual responsibility is first and always to God; always, including matters pertaining to civil government.

God did, indeed, delegate certain areas of His authority to man. We see that, for example, in *Gen. 1:28* and we see it also in *Gen. 9:5, 6.* However, the civil authority God granted to man is to be employed in keeping with His purposes and in harmony with His laws.

The Lord's delegation of certain powers to man, through civil government, was in no way an abdication of His authority; *it was an assignment.* Man, through properly constituted civil government, is to be God's vice-regent; man is to use that power to honor God and protect his fellow-man. When those in authority mis-use that power, when they violate the terms of God's proxy, there is contradiction and conflict between God's laws and man's institutions. *When such conflict arises, what are Christians to do?* The Apostle Peter wrote to the point:

"We ought to obey God rather than man" (Acts 5:29).

So it must be. And, so it was that even Paul, who urged that "every soul be subject unto the higher powers" would not and could not compromise or yield to those "higher powers" when they demanded, for example, that he stop preaching The Gospel.

When the laws of a nation—and the interpretation and administration and enforcement of those laws—are not in keeping with Biblical principles, then that government is not in harmony with God's plan and God's purpose *(2 Chron. 7:19-22).*

Thus, as our founding fathers understood, rebellion against the tyrant is obedience to God.

GIVEN TODAY'S STATE of the nation, how shall American Christians press forward to reform civil government? How shall we rebuild, or realign, our institutions? How shall we correct our political condition so that it is in keeping with Christ's perfect Laws of Love and Liberty? Surely, if Christ is truly our King, this is part of our task. As Verna M. Hall has written:

". . . God expects us to fight the good fight of faith for the Law of Liberty in the same degree as He expected the colonists to fight. We are as dependent upon God for the maintenance of individual freedom and liberty as for the actual gift of it in the first place."

Where do we begin the task of restoring the Christian foundation and character of our nation? How do we go about re-instituting the Biblical principles of government?

WE BEGIN, EACH ONE OF US, WITH OURSELVES. THE REGENERATION OF AMERICA MUST BEGIN AS AN INSIDE JOB!

First, we must understand Biblical principles . . . study them, know them, master them, "make them our own." If we are to change the world, if we are to "turn it upside down" as did the early Christians, we must first change ourselves. The sins that have separated this nation from God are not only sins of commission on the part of un-believers, they are also sins of *omission* on the part of those who call themselves Believers.

Second, we must apply Biblical principles conscientiously in our own lives, in all areas, in all things . . . in the home, the church, the school, the community, and the State. "If these are sound, the nation will be sound; conversely, if they are not sound, nothing can camouflage the nation's unsoundness." (We get the kind of government we *resemble*.)

Third, we must train up our children in Biblical principles and the Christian history of this nation so that they learn to govern themselves according to God's word. The seat of good government is (or, should be), first, the *heart,* second the *home,* third, the *church and school,* and—*then*—the State house.

THIS TASK WILL not be done with bumper strips and fancy stickers. It will not be accomplished through tinkling slogans and clanging symbols. The race belongs not to the spectacular, but to the steady; to those who keep The Faith. It goes to those who will pray, and study, and apply; to those who will make The Bible their "great political textbook"; to those who go about His work quietly, persistently, effectively. . . . *putting on the whole armor of God* and knowing that His is the glory, not their's.

All this we, as His, should do. All this we should commence to do—now. Not simply because His perfect Laws of Liberty and Love are the only positive and practical bases for individual liberty and responsible civil government (not unimportant benefits) but *because adherence to Biblical principles is obedience to God.*

The Sovereignty of God

"He rules by His power for ever; His eyes behold the nations: let not the rebellious exalt themselves." "For the Lord is our judge, The Lord is our lawgiver, The Lord is our King; He will save us." (Ps. 66:7; Isa. 33:22)

THE INCREASING MISAPPROPRIATION of sovereignty in today's world should be of deep concern to Christians—not only as it involves the affairs of state but especially as it relates to *obedience to The Lord God.*

By ignoring God, by denying His Supreme Sovereignty, and in seeking to be as gods, man trespasses on that which belongs only to God.

Consider, at this point, the words "sovereign" and "sovereignty."

Contemporary dictionaries tell us that a "sovereign" is one "possessing, or held to possess and exercise, supreme authority." "Sovereignty" we find defined as "a supreme authority, especially over a body politic."

Thus, lexicographers of this day define "sovereignty" in *humanistic* terms, measured on man's self-centered scale of things.

If we accept such definition (which, after all, is simply a citation based on common use and meaning) we are led to believe that man, in and of himself, is the ultimate sovereign; that sovereignty begins and ends with man—or, men.

In early America, sovereignty was *not* defined or viewed in such a light or from such a perspective. Noah Webster, in his *First American Dictionary of The English Language,* defined sovereignty at a different level:

"Supreme power, absolute supremacy; the possession of the highest power. Absolute sovereignty belongs to God only."

As for "sovereign," Mr. Webster wrote: *"God is the sovereign of the universe."*

There is a *philosophical grand canyon* between Mr. Webster's definitions (which reflected the Christian temper of his times) and those that are set forth today. That difference bespeaks the rejection of God and the spread of humanism—that malignant religion that holds man to be the center of all things. Thus it is that sovereignty is misappropriated, and misapplied.

THE QUESTION OF SOVEREIGNTY has to do with government: that which is sovereign, governs—both man and his State.

Government may properly be defined as "the flow of power and force." The "power" being the authority to exert the "force," i.e. to exercise control.

In that context, sovereignty is the source of the flow of power and force; that which is acknowledged to be sovereign is, in fact, the source of the power and the force. Further, the source of the flow of power and force determines the nature and quality of government. These facts apply to all government, whether it be self or civil.

For example: that which is sovereign *in the life of the individual* is the source of the flow of power and force that is the *self-government* (the self-control) within the individual. That source determines the heart-condition and the mind-set. It directs the thinking. It develops the presuppositions, sets the standards of deportment, determines the values, the morals, and the ethics that will be employed . . . in sum, *it controls the course of the individual's life.*

In the same manner, that which is sovereign *in the affairs of a nation* becomes the source of the flow of power and force that is *civil government* (civil control). That source defines the nation's policies. It sets its standards, prescribes the spirit and the letter of its laws, colors its regulations, and charts the nation's destiny.

Is all of this a valid thesis? Well, put it to the test.

When man sees *himself* as the ultimate authority—either alone or in majority, on what will he base his laws? What license will he issue, and to whom? What will he condone under the guise of liberty? By whom, or what, will he be governed? On what will he establish his restraints and contraints? On what scale will he measure the nature and quality and scope of civil government? To what purpose will that governance be employed?

By contrast, when man acknowledges the sovereignty of God, and knows God's laws to be supreme and binding, on what will he base his statutes and his regulations? By whom will he be governed? And, whom will he obey? What purposes and functions will he assign to government, self- and civil? And, on what scale will he measure the right and wrong and thus evaluate the duties and the conduct of those powers, church and state?

Through such a testing, and in the answers given, we find that that which is sovereign is, indeed, the source of the flow of the power and force that determines the nature and the quality of government.

WHEN GOD IS truly acknowledged as Sovereign, we seek to obey Him above all else; even knowing that in our fallen state we can only fall short of the mark. Yet, as His, we strive always toward that calling.

What does The Lord God demand, as Sovereign of men and nations? *This:*

> *"Therefore you shall love The Lord your God, and keep His charge, and His statutes, and His judgments, and His commandments, alway." (Deut 11:1).*

Obedience to God is proof that we know Him *(1 Jn. 2:3)*. It is proof that we love Him *(1 Jn. 2:5)*. We know He loves us; but, how does He know we love Him?

"If you love Me," said our Savior and our King, "(you will) keep My commandments." And, what is *the first and great commandment?* This:

> *"You shall love The Lord your God with all your heart, and with all your soul, and with all your mind." (Matt. 22:40)*

The nation that obeys the commandments of The Lord, that keeps His charge, and His statutes—that nation shall be blessed. But, the nation that does not obey His commandments, that nation shall be cursed *(Deut. 11:26, 27)*.

The nation that makes God its sovereign shall prosper *(1 Jn. 3:22)*. It will find favor in His sight *(James 1:25)*. It will gain the victory over its foes *(Pr. 16:7)*.

> *"Let us hear the conclusion of this whole matter: fear God, and keep His commandments: for this is the whole duty of man." (Ecc. 12:13)*

BEHOLD THE MIGHTY WORKS that come when a people acknowledge the sovereignty of God and seek to serve Him as King.

Consider the fruitage of that great *English reformation* of the 16th Century . . . that span of time when men on fire for God rose to remove the humanistic distortions that had encrusted church and

ON GOVERNING GOVERNMENT   337

state. It was this reformation that was used of God as the *potting shed for the tree of liberty* that was to be planted on America's shores—planted and nourished, preserved and protected in the spirit of His liberty.

With God as their King and The Bible as their great political textbook, the Pilgrims came to "advance the kingdome of The Lord, Jesus Christ." Through them, and through the other early American Christians, God formed a new nation conceived in Christ's perfect law of liberty and shaped and structured by the Christian methodology of self-government with unity . . . one body out of many members.

Governmentally speaking, the world of then was turned upside down *(Acts 17:6).*

Who, now, will stand and assert the unyielding primacy, the essentiality, of God's supreme sovereignty in the affairs of men and nations? Who, now, will work to prepare themselves to be used of God to turn the world *rightside up?*

"If the foundations be destroyed, what can the righteous do?"

They can *rebuild* the foundation! They can *restore* the land! They can *occupy* until He comes!

Salvation is a gift freely given, *Praise God!* But, life in Christ is not a free-ride. It is not a sometime affair. It is, it should be, a whole and Holy endeavor. We are to be His *stewards,* His *disciples,* His *soldiers* . . . going forth to teach men to observe all things whatsoever He has commanded. In *His* name. In *His* love. And, for *His* glory.

"There is another king, one Jesus!"

On Governing Government

"Therefore, my beloved brethren, be steadfast, unmoveable, always abounding in the work of The Lord, forasmuch as you know that your labor is not in vain in The Lord." 1 Cor. 15:58

BECAUSE SO MANY voices are now urging American Christians to political action—to participation in the affairs of civil government, perhaps some observations and suggestions are in order.

Christians have both *the right and the responsibility* to govern that which governs their civil affairs.

We do not drop to some alien status, we do not become second-class citizens, when we acknowledge Jesus Christ as Savior and King. In fact, since Christ is to be *King of all,* Christians must work for godly civil government.

(Is it not providential that early American Christians acknowledged and accepted such responsibility and were active participants in the founding of this republic?)

The Christian who neglects or denies such responsibility invites *the ungodly* to usurp the functions and powers of civil government. Politics, like nature, abhors a vacuum; *it is the lot of those who fail to govern government to be governed by those who do.*

And, do we not find ourselves in such situations in many areas of civil government today?

Man, in effect, holds God's *proxy* for civil government; we will be held to answer for the manner in which we exercise that proxy.

The purpose of government is to serve God! (Rom. 13:1-6)

Many Christians seem to overlook that Biblical fact. Inadvertently, they confuse *the reason for* civil government with *the purpose of* such government.

The reason for civil government (as ordained by The Lord God) was and is to protect human life ("in the image of God created He them") and the properties which are the extensions of that life.

The purpose of civil government (as established by The Lord God) was and is to cause man to live in obedience to God's laws.

Those who hold public office are to be *"ministers of God"* to the people for good. Those in power are to exercise that power in accordance with God's divine purposes and laws:

- to protect those who would lead a "quiet and peaceable life in all godliness and honesty" *(1 Tim. 2:2),* and
- to punish the evildoers *(Rom. 13:4; 1 Pet. 2:14).*

The early American Christians understood God's purpose and His instructions in this regard. *Mark their words!*

The Fundamental Orders of Connecticut (the first American Constitution, Jan. 14, 1638):

". . . well-knowing that where a people are gathered together

the word of God requires that to maintain peace and union of such a people there should be an orderly and decent government established according to God. . . ."

The *Great Law* of the Pennsylvania colony (April 25, 1682):

"Whereas the glory of Almighty God and the good of mankind is the reason and the end of government, and therefore government itself is a venerable ordinance of God. . . ."

And, again from *The Fundamental Orders of Connecticut,* these words concerning personal responsibility to The Lord in the election of public office-holders and the enactment of civil laws:

"The privilege of election which belongs to the people, therefore, must not be exercised according to their humors, but according to the blessed will and law of God."

In other words, this: Because government belongs to God, government must be governed according to His laws. Who but godly people will see that this is so?

CIVIL GOVERNMENT IS the fruit, the end-product, of self-government.
    The internal (self) is causative of the external (civil) *(Matt. 12:35).*
    If we are to change the character of civil government, so that it is godly, we must first change the character of our self-government, so that it is godly. The individual who cannot govern himself in such manner, is hardly fit or qualified to govern civil government (Pr. 25:38).
    FOR THE CHRISTIAN WHO WOULD BE GODLY, THEN POLITICAL ACTION BEGINS WITH SELF!
    It begins with the heart, with that "inner voice of authority." It begins as an "inside" job. If we would turn the world upside down for Christ *(Acts 17:6)* we must first ask Him to set our hearts right-side up!
    Some may be impatient with such order of priority on the grounds of "immediacy." They may object that "time is of the essence." But, whose time? Their time? Or, God's?
    Short-cuts that build structures without foundations are of man and of the moment. They do not stand. They are fleeting efforts that wash away with the tidess of passion; reactions that follow the siren calls of this world. Is it not all too evident that such short-cuts of the past have failed? *Where is their success?* Have they not, in fact, often resulted in a tarnished witness and an uncertain trumpet? In too many instances they have served not God, but man.

Men on white horses are but *humanistic substitutes* for The One Eternal King *(Pr. 25:26)*. God is to be our law-giver, our judge, and our chief executive *(Isa. 33:22)*.

BECAUSE GOVERNMENT BELONGS to God, and is to be governed by his laws, consider this to be the *bed-rock requirement for godly political action:*

The Holy Bible, the whole word—must be the Great Political Textbook for the Christian.

It was because early American Christians *studied and mastered* Biblical principles of self- and civil government that they were used of God to found this first and only Christian civil government. (It is, incidentally, a fact of American history that prior to the war for independence, God's Spirit swept the land with a *Great Awakening* that brought the colonists *back to The Bible.*)

When today's American Christians master and begin to apply Biblical principles of government, then we may realistically call upon The Lord God to heal our land and restore its foundations *(2 Chron. 7:14)*. And, it will be done not to glorify men, or groups, *but Him!*

There are now various plans and programs on Christian political action. Many deal mainly, or solely, with the techniques and tactics and media of the secular political world. There is some value in such effort *but generally it puts the cart before the horse.*

If such programs are truly to serve The Living God, and to bring honor and glory to His name, they must deal with—must concentrate on—basic Biblical principles and precepts of self- and civil government. God first—then come tactics and techniques.

In sum, then, this:

Government is God's. It is to be governed by His laws. It is to be guided by the Biblical principles and precepts His Book sets forth. As followers of Christ, those for whom He is both Savior and King, it is our task to strive toward that goal.

Where shall we begin?

In a sermon on Biblical principles of government, *Dr. James Singleton* (Tri-City Baptist Church, Tempe AZ), marked the starting gate:

"We start internally, always—*because every external problem starts internally.* What we find on the outside is a manifestation of that which is on the inside.

"We need to start with individual repentance of rebellion against God Who made us. We need to come back to The Book and we need to start to live by the principles that are found in The Book—and on which this nation was founded.

"We need to take these *Biblical principles* and start to apply them. We won't get them overnight. But, just realize that it all starts with 'me'—starts on the inside, starts with 'me' on my knees. it doesn't start with the White House, or the Senate, or the House of Representatives . . . it starts with 'me' saying *'Oh, God! Search me and know my heart. Try me, and know my thoughts.'*

"I know folks who are tired . . . who worked their heads off to get the 'right man' into office . . . and then he turned out to be just like the others who came down the pike. So, they are discouraged. I am not discouraged because I know it starts with me.

"I may not be able to do anything about Washington; that may be a little too big for me. But, I can start with me and, by the grace of God, I can rid my mind of all the humanism that has been planted there over the years—and the secularism and the ungodliness . . . and I can get my own heart right with God.

"THEN, IF ENOUGH PEOPLE DO THAT, OUT OF THE INTERNAL WILL COME THE RIGHT EXTERNAL!

"If we will only start to think in terms of *Biblical principles*—not in terms of expediency, not in terms of what it means to 'me', but in terms of Biblical principles—we can turn this nation back to God."

In such a way we serve The Living God!

And, is that not the purpose—the only proper role—for the Christian to become involved in politics?

Whom Shall We Obey?

"Then Peter and the other apostles answered and said, We ought to obey God rather than men." Acts 5:29

A Christian friend once informed us that if he had been around back in 1776, he would *not* have signed the Declaration of Independence.

Furthermore, he contended, the American Revolution was an *immoral* war and the Christians who fomented it and took part in it had *violated* the ordinances of God.

That brought to mind an article by a professor at a seminary a few years ago who had written much the same sentiments. Unfortunately both of these gentlemen are misinformed about the nature and the purpose of that war for independence.

The American Revolution was not an aggressive war. It was not an attack on England. The war for America's independence was, in every sense, a defensive war.

It was fought *to defend life, liberty and property;* fought *to defend religious and civil freedom.* It was fought *to defend the colonists against the encroachments of king and parliament.* It was fought *to defend the American Christians' right to obey God rather than man.*

The revolution of 1776 was not a precipitous, humanistic rebellion. For ten years, from 1765 through 1775, the colonists engaged in a *great constitutional debate*—among themselves and with the parliament—about *the defense of their God-given, "unalienable" rights* (rights, incidentally, that were supposed to be protected by the English constitution).

The prayer of the Americans, during those years, was that God would cause the king and parliament to see the errors of their excesses and relent so that the colonists could remain loyal to the crown. Their desire, indeed, was to be Englishmen. But, God had other plans; this land was to birth a new and independent nation. Through the 150 years of study in Biblical principles of self- and civil government, and through the Great Awakening, He was preparing those early American Christians for the separation that was to come.

If nothing else were to substantiate these assertions (and there are countless documents and manuscripts that do) the manner in which The Lord God moved so miraculously to bring *unity of purpose* among the 13 colonies, and the many instances of *His divine intervention* during the war-years . . . these speak more loudly than all the voices that claim the American Revolution was immoral or ungodly.

ONCE WE UNDERSTAND that the American Revolution was a defensive war, the question arises, *"Is a defensive war sinful?* Does it violate God's law?"

For the answer, we must turn not to men but to God's word:

Consider, for example, the patriarch, *Abraham.* That man of "true piety and pure religion" who was loved of God. When the four kings kidnapped his brother's son, Lot, what did Abraham do? Did Abraham's faithfulness to God prohibit him from defending Lot? No! Abraham gathered his forces, pursued the kidnappers, and rescued Lot.

And on his return, what greeting did Abraham receive from Melchizedeck, the priest of the most high God? Was he censured? *On the contrary!*

"Blessed be Abraham of the most high God, possessor of heaven and earth, and blessed be the most high God which delivered your enemies into your hand" (Gen. 14:18-20).

Such were the words of Melchizedeck, the brightest type of Christ. Who now presumes to have a conscience purer than his?

If defensive war is sinful in the eyes of God, what do we say about these servants of The Lord?

Moses, God's law-giver, who thought it not against God's will to defend the Israelites against the aggressions of the Amorites.

Or, David, sweet psalmist, a man after God's own heart, who defended Israel from her enemies.

Or, Joshua. And Gideon. And Jephtha. And Hezekiah. These "worthies of Israel" whom God blessed for their love and obedience to Him.

The Bible makes it clear: *defensive wars are sinless.*

THOSE WHO HOLD that the early American Christians sinned against God for taking part in the war for independence generally cite two passages of Scripture to support their contention. An examination of these Scriptures is especially important to American Christians of this day and time.

The first is Paul's discourse on government in *Romans 13:1-6:*

"Let every soul be subject unto the higher powers. For there is no power but of God: the powers that be are ordained of God. Whosoever resists the power, resists the ordinance of God: and they that resist shall receive unto themselves damnation. For rulers are not a terror to good works, but to evil. Will you then be afraid of the power? do that which is good and you shall have praise of the same: For he is the minister of God to you for good. But if you do that which is evil, be afraid; for he bears not the sword in vain: for he is the minister of God, a revenger to execute wrath upon him that does evil. Wherefore you must needs be subject not only for wrath, but also for

conscience sake. For this cause pay tribute also: for they are God's ministers, attending continually upon this very thing."

On the basis of this, our friend insisted that it is against God's will for Christians to disobey the civil authorities; that we must obey such power no matter how unrighteous the demands, no matter how ungodly the laws.

Is it not anti-Biblical, and totally illogical, to believe that Christians are to obey those who disobey God? How can we accept the proposition that we are to serve a righteous and perfect God by obeying the ungodly laws of unrighteous men?

The testing of such a proposition requires that we take it to its ultimate conclusion and examine the consequences.

If total submission to civil authority is obedience to God, what do we say about those who, down through the ages, refused to yield to the ungodly demands of the Caesars of their time? *Men such as Peter. And John the Apostle. And Paul, himself.* What of the *Christian martyrs* who gained victorious life through death rather than obey the evil dictates of civil authorities? Was that all in vain? The Bible assures us that our labors for Him are never in vain. Are these to be stricken from the Book of Life? The Bible tells us that those who lose their life for Him find life eternal.

What do we say about *The Great Reformation* that dared to stand against the authorities of that day—the power of State and church. Is that to be counted evil?

Who served God during Hitler's reign of terror and blasphemy? A *Corrie ten Boom* and a *Martin Niemoller?* Or the closet Christian who obeyed the Nazi while taking some twisted comfort in the "excuse" of *Romans 13:1-6?*

And, what of *those behind the Iron Curtain, in the prisons of Siberia,* who stand for Jesus? Are they a displeasure to The Lord? Does the cozening hierarchy of the State-controlled church find more favor in His eyes?

EVIDENTLY, THOSE WHO would stretch the Scriptures to cover total obedience to Caesar, or King George, or any unrighteous power, overlook *a central point:*

THE GOD WHO ORDAINED HUMAN (CIVIL) GOVERNMENT ALSO ORDAINED THE LAWS AND PRINCIPLES BY WHICH MAN IS TO GOVERN AND BE GOVERNED.

The "higher powers" of which Paul wrote—the higher powers "ordained of God"—can only mean *the "just, the good, the constitutional laws" that are in harmony with the Divine Constitution of the universe, the laws of God.* Such powers are to be binding on both the governed and the governors: it is the duty of each to obey those laws, *and to see that the other does the same.* These are the laws that God ordained for the protection and well-being of the individual, and his community.

Even a cursory study of *Rom. 13:1-6* establishes *certain criteria:* (1) those in civil authority are to be *"ministers of God" to the people for good* (three times Paul stresses that) and (2) those who do *good have no cause to fear* but those who do *evil should know God's wrath.* What is "good?" It is obedience to God's laws. What is "evil?" It is sin—the transgression of God's laws.

When these critera are not met, when the laws of men are out of harmony with the laws of God, then—as the great English jurist William Blackstone wrote—"such laws must be considered null and void."

THE SECOND PASSAGE of Scripture generally used to buttress the doctrine of hailing Caesar is *1 Peter 2:13, 14:*

> *"Submit yourselves to every ordinance of man, for the Lord's sake, whether unto kings as supreme, or unto governors, as unto them that are sent by him, for the punishment of evildoers, and for the praise of them that do well."*

As Rev. David Jones sermonized on July 20, 1775, "We cannot suppose that this text enjoins absolute submission to all laws that may be made in a land; for some are so wicked, so oppressive, and unjust in their nature and tendency, that the best of men have thought it their indispensable duty to disobey them."

If we were to accept the proposition that we must obey all laws, "every ordinance" of depraved men, what are we to say these "best of men?"

Shadrach, Meschach and Abednego—who went to the fiery furnace rather than obey the laws of Nebuchadnezzar that they worship his golden image.

Daniel—who went into the den of lions rather than obey Darius's law that he pray to Darius and not to The Lord God?

Or, the Hebrew midwives—who refused to obey the Pharaoh's law that they must kill all Jewish male babies?

Was it not Peter, himself, who proclaimed, *"We ought to obey God, rather than man!" (Acts 5:29).*

God did ordain civil government and the laws by which that government is to be governed. Some who have seized power or been entrusted with that power have been evil, tyrannical, and great offenders of God. Should they have continued with impunity, with the acquiesence of Christians? *God forbid!* Should that be the case now, or in the future? *God forbid!*

IT IS ESSENTIAL—*especially in these times*—that Christians view the two passages of Scripture under examination in the proper and tested light. Any suggestion that the cited words of Paul or Peter void such admonitions and teachings as *Deut. 11:1,* or *Mt. 5:19,* or *Col. 1:18*—yes, and *Acts 5:29,* are like unto *quicksand:* they can lead Christians into being *easy prey and submissive dupes of evil tyrants.*

Another Hitler, a future Caesar, an anti-Christ, would like nothing better than to have Christians "religiously" submit to their ungodly laws and evil powers. We must understand that obedience to the State is not absolute; *it is obedience only under God.*

Jesus is King! We are to advance His kingdom; not Caesar's!

On the Mandate for Christian Education

"Only take heed to thyself, and keep thy soul diligently, lest thou forget the things which thine eyes have seen, and lest they depart from thy heart all the days of thy life; but teach them to thy sons, and thy son's sons." Deut. 4:9

FOR THE GODLY Christian parent, that follower of Christ who seeks to know and obey The Word of God, the responsibility of educating his children is not a matter of debate or question: *it is a matter of Biblical mandate.*

"And thy children shall be taught of The Lord" (Isa. 54:13).
"Fathers, provoke not your children unto wrath, but bring them up in the nurture and admonition of The Lord" (Eph. 6:4).
"Lo, children are a heritage of The Lord" (Ps. 127:3).

Parents are responsible, and accountable, unto The Lord God for the care and education of those children He has placed within our care.

As godly Christians, then, we cannot—we must not—relinquish the education of the child to any individual, institution, or system, that is not firmly and totally founded upon and commited to the word of God. *God's word is the only acceptable guide for life; it is the only true foundation for right moral standards.*

Any system of education that is not based squarely on His work, any curriculum that does not hold to and hold forth His truth, His commandments, His principles and precepts, *must be held to be immoral.* The godly Christian will not—must not—permit his children to be educated in schools or teachings that are immoral.

> *"Know you not that to whom you yield yourselves: (or, your children) "to obey, his servants you are (and, are your children) "to whom you" (or your children) "obey; whether of sin unto death, or of obedience unto righteousness?" (Rom. 6:16).*

GOD'S WORD ADMONISHES us to be a peculiar people, a distinctive people, zealous of good works in and for Him. We are not to be of the world; we are not to be yoked with the things or the ways of this world. We are to be His alone, separate and apart. *And, we are to raise up our children so that they, too, are and will be separate and apart in lives that are consecrated to Him.*

How can we expect the child to grow up and be distinctive, zealous for The Lord, if we do not train them to do so? How can we expect them to stand firm in the faith, and to contend for the faith, if they are not trained in the faith? And, how can we work toward that end if we submit them and their education to institutions, instructors, and systems not of the faith but rather surrogates and advocates of an ungodly world?

> *"Be not deceived: evil communications corrupt good manners" (1 Cor. 15:33).*

TO UNDERSTAND CLEARLY the task of educating our children in today's world, consider the avowed purposes of education as espoused by the competing powers:

> *For the humanist,* the purpose of education is to educate the child to be *a servant of man*—either self, or others.
> *For the State,* the purpose of education is to prepare the child to be *a servant of the State.*
> But, *for the Christian,* the purpose of education is to train up the child to be *a servant of The Lord God!*

There we see the vast—the diametric—difference; and, there we see the root and the reason of the conflict between the humanist and the State, on the one hand, and the Christian parent: it is a battle for the soul, the mind, and the body of the child. In that battle, the Christain can give no ground, can make no compromise.

SOME, PERHAPS WITH good intention, may suggest that if the foundation of faith is built strong in the home, the child will withstand the onslaught in the State controlled and humanistic school. Perhaps some will; *but, many will not.* And, The Bible makes it clear that the parent is not to take such risk with the spiritual well-being of the children God has placed within his care. The parent is accountable *and may well be held culpable* should the child be thus separated from The Lord.

> *"But whoso offend one of these little ones which believes in me, it were better for him that a millstone be hanged about his neck, and that he were drowned in the depth of the sea" (Mt. 18:6).*

Yet, some may insist that it is acceptable to educate the child—in the home and church—in the things of The Spirit *while permitting the State to educate the child in the "dexterities" and "mechanics" of the world;* that while the parents and the pastor educate the soul, *the State may educate the mind.* (State-controlled education is by its nature stunted and distorted. No subject can truly be taught without recognition of God's sovereignty, law-order, and providence.)

Surely the godly Christian must realize that soul and mind cannot —must not—be separated; that which educates the mind affects the soul; that which conditions the soul influences the mind. *To fail to train both the soul and the mind in the word of God is to fail in the task The Lord God has mandated.* Are we to accept the suggestion that the soul belongs to God but the mind belongs to the individual, or to the State? Shall we say to the child, "God may direct your heart but the State will control your mind; you should render your soul to Christ but you may give your mind to Caesar?" *That, indeed, would be apostasy!*

> *"You shalt love The Lord your God with all your heart and with all your soul and with all your mind" (Mt. 22:37). "That you might be filled with the knowledge of His will in all wisdom and spiritual understanding; being fruitful in every good work, and increasing in the knowledge of God . . . That in all things He might have the pre-eminence" (Col. 1:9-18).*

The State-controlled system of secular education is *anti-Christian*. That which ignores, or denies, The Lord God—or seeks to place Him on a level with the gods of man, must be seen for what it is: *part and parcel of the anti-Christ.*

"Who is a liar but he that denies that Jesus is The Christ? He is the anti-Christ that denies The Father and The Son" (1 John 2:22). "He that is not with me is against Me" (Mt. 12:30).

For the godly Christian parent who seeks to obey The Lord, the education of the child must be *a total, all-encompassing spiritual process;* a complete and harmonious development of the soul, the mind, and the body. *All,* all must be founded on The Word of God; *all* must be purposed so that the child will mature into a faithful and competent servant of The Lord of Lords and The King of Kings.

THUS, OUR TASK is clear, and the responsibilities unalterable. We are to train up our children in the nurture and admonition of The Lord. *May we not, then, consider these as mandates?*

1. As parents we must zealously exercise our responsibilities for the spiritual, mental, and physical well-being and development of the children God has placed within our care. We are to help them build themselves in God, principle upon principle, precept upon precept, line upon line.

2. We are to do this in the home and in the truly Bible-based, Christ-centered church and school, working closely with the child, the pastor and the teacher so that the Christian education is a total effort and continuing process.

3. We must resist any attempts by any agency—private or public—to usurp or weaken or intrude upon our God-mandated parental authority and responsibility to bring up the child according to God's word and God's will.

4. We must not submit the child, or ourselves, to the dictates of any education or system of education—private or public—that is not founded on the word of God or that seeks to separate any part of the child's heart, mind, or body from the will of God and a life for God.

5. We must stand firm against any pressure or demand that we or our children lower our Christian standards to conform to the ways of this world, or that the child be subjected to any influence that denies, discredits, ignores, or in any way dishonors The Lord God or interferes with our freedom to worship Him.

Such a course of action—one that stands fast in The Lord and resists those powers that would place themselves above the auth ity of the Lord God — *is indeed Biblical:* it is a vital part of our co nant with Him. However, it must be taken in a godly manner thro lawful means, as befits servants of Christ. Christians are not a chists; we are not insurrectionists; *we are loyalists* — loyal in things to Him who is King of Kings and Savior of mankind.

We are instructed to render unto Caesar that which is his that we do willingly for that is God's will. But, He also teaches u render unto Him that which is His and it is clear and unassaila children belong not to the State, *but to God!*

THE CHRISTIAN CONGREGATION has the duty, the responsib to stand with the Christian parent in these matters of obedie concerning the godly education of the child. Thus, consider thes be essentials — *and one of the great missions* of the godly Chris church in America today:

1. Every Bible-believing and God-obedient Christian church sh seek to establish and operate a Christian school in conjunction wit ministry or strengthen and expand the school if it is already in be

If there is a truly *Bible-based* private Christian school in the area, parents may want to enroll their children there and the congregation might decide to help support that institution (through scholarships, grants, books, classroom equipment, faculty, etc.).

2. In those locales and circumstances where a single chu may find it impossible to operate a Christian school on its ow should seek out and join with a like-minded sister church to do Members who cannot assist financially can help in many way tithing their time and talents as teacher's assistants, office work in building and grounds maintenance, as phys-ed supervis through car pools, assisting in various fund-raising activities, prayer.

3. In those remote locations where it is extremely difficult for parent to take or send the child to a Christian school, enroll the c in a Christian home-study course of education, using the B based materials provided.

4. Should the Christian parent or church or school be challen by the State, the congregation should be prepared to stand fir behind the parents and/or the pastor, funding and employing e Biblical and legal means to seek the victory for The Lord.

5. The Christian school should strive for academic excellence thus to thwart the challenges of the ungodly (1 Pet. 2:15).

SOME MAY VIEW as sad and unfortunate the necessity to turn to the home and the church for the education of the child. *Not so! That is where The Lord God means it to be.* The ministry of the State is *not* education, *not* evangelism, *but justice* — and in the education the State now forces upon the people, there is little justice.

The excesses and the failures and, yes, the abominations of the State-controled school system have *awakened* many of God's people to their responsibilities and brought them back to *His* will, *His* mandate, and *His* purpose for education. *Thus, He is drawing firm and clear the line of separation, is that not so?* Rejoice, then! Rejoice and be exceedingly glad. And, be sure: *the victory and the glory shall be His!*

Our Christian Heritage

Hearken to me, you that follow after righteousness, ye that seek The Lord: look unto the rock whence you were hewn, and the quarry from whence you are cut." Isaiah 51:1

THERE ARE THOSE who deny, and those who belittle, the Christian foundations of the American Republic; those who seek to destroy the landmarks which our fathers set before us *(Pr. 22:28).*

William Foxwell Albright once observed that the writing of American history in the 20th Century was mostly *"a means of liberal propaganda"* (W. F. Albright, *From The Stone Age To Christianity*). James C. Malin put it in stronger terms: he saw the revisionisms as *"debasing history to the level of vicious propaganda in support of a social program being imposed upon a nation"* (J. C. Malin, *On The Nature of History*).

One of the major thrusts of the revisionists has been the denial, or the degradation, of America's Christian heritage: the attempt to discard as fantasy and fiction the facts of the influence and impact of Christian faith and presuppositions on early America and its foundational institutions and laws.

It is to be expected that those who would seek to raise the religion of humanism would attempt to deny the truths and undermine the appreciation of America's Christian heritage. And it is also understandable that those who would glorify Caesar and magnify his domain would do the same. (Before the tower of humanism could be erected, the facts of our Christian heritage had to be subverted. Thus, an important step in promoting humanism (or, advancing the gospel of Marx) was the effort to destroy the landmarks our fathers had set before us (Pr. 22:28). To those who worship man or Marx, such destruction was logical and for them the end justified the means.)

What is incredible is that such perversions and subversions of the record of America's Christian history could have taken root among journalists and theologians and educators in publications and seminaries and colleges that proclaim they are Christian.

Yet, the editor of one of the nation's leading Christian magazines wrote, *"America is not now and never has been a Christian nation."*

And, a professor of theology at a widely-known seminary asserted:

> "The largest religion in America is one that was established by our founding fathers; *it's the religion of humanism* . . .
>
> "You say, 'Well, I'm a little mixed up in my history, then, because I thought our founding fathers were Christians. I thought they were Bible-believing Christians and that this was started as a Christian nation.'
>
> *"That's a widely-believed myth; the sooner we put it to rest the better off we would be . . .*
>
> ". . . the founding fathers . . . were not born again Believers, they were not believers in The Bible as the word of God, they did not believe that Christ was The Son of God . . . they were really humanists."

Poor Samuel Adams. He would have been surprised—to say the least—to learn that he was not a Christian.

And, George Washington! He surely would have been upset to know that he did not believe that The Bible was the word of God!

And, *James Madison:* he who had been trained to be a minister of God. He would have been dumbfounded to find out that he did not believe that Jesus was The Son of God.

Then, there was poor *Reverend Jonathan Witherspoon,* that soldier of The Lord and activist in the founding of the republic. How would he have responded to the charge that he was "really a humanist?" He who insisted that the Declaration of Independence make it clear that "all men are endowed by their Creator with certain unalienable rights" and that the delegates pledge their lives, fortunes and sacred honor to support that Declaration "with a firm reliance on the protection of divine Providence."

And, John Quincy Adams, the fourth president of these United States! Did not President Adams proclaim:

> "The highest glory of the American Revolution was this: It connected, in one indissoluble bond, the principles of civil government with the principles of Christianity."

After an exhaustive research, Professor M. E. Bradford of the University of Dallas has clearly shown that 50, and perhaps 52, of the 55 framers of the Constitution of these United States were orthodox Christians of various denominations.

Some humanists, those founding fathers!

The myth is not that this republic was founded as a Christian nation. *The myth is that it was not.*

The facts of history are unyielding; those facts reveal the errors and deceptions of the revisionists who seek to deny America's Christian heritage.

Here, in brief part, is the record. It provides irrefutable justification for the claim that *these United States of America were* — in their pre-natal years, at their birth, and in their early days — *a Christian nation:*

c 1490-92 . . . Queen Isabella's commission to Columbus as he set out to find a new world was given *"for the glory of God."* According to his personal log, Columbus's purpose in seeking *"undiscovered worlds"* was to *"bring the Gospel of Jesus Christ to the heathens."* ". . . It *was the Lord who put into my mind . . . the fact that it would be possible to sail from here to the Indies"* "I am the most unworthy sinner, but I have cried out to The Lord for grace and mercy, and they have covered me completely. . . . No one should fear to undertake any task in the name of our Saviour, if it is just and if the intention is purely for His holy service." (from Columbus's *Book of Prophecies*). . .

1493 . . . "that which the unaided intellect of man could not compass, the spirit of God has granted to human exertions, for God is wont to hear the prayers of His servants who love His precepts even to the performance of apparent impossibilities. Therefore, let the king and queen, our princes and their most happy kingdoms, and all the other provinces of Christendom, render thanks to our Lord and Saviour Jesus Christ . . ." (Columbus's letter to Gabriel Sanchez, Spain's General Treasurer.)

APRIL 10, 1606 . . . *King James I, charter for the settlement of Virginia:* "to the glory of His divine Majesty, in propagating of the Christian religion to such people as yet live in ignorance of the true knowledge and worship of God. . . ."

MAY 23, 1609 . . . *Second charter granted Virginia:* ". . . because the principal effect which we can expect or desire of this action is the conversion and reduction of the people in those parts unto the true worship of God and the Christian religion."

NOVEMBER 3, 1620 . . . *King James I grants Charter of the Plymouth Council:* "in the hope thereby to advance the enlargement of the Christian religion, to the glory of God Almighty."

> "Language of similar import (that the colonies were established to "tend to the Glory of His Divine Majesty, in propagating of Christian Religion") may be found in the subsequent charters . . .
> . . . In language more or less emphatic is the establishment of the Christian religion declared to be one of the purposes of the grant." (*Opinion of the United States Supreme Court, Holy Trinity Church v. United States, October term, 1891, p. 466.*)

NOVEMBER 11, 1620 . . . *The Mayflower Compact:* Pilgrims aboard the Mayflower, in Plymouth Harbor, covenant "In ye name of God, amen . . . for the glory of God and the advancement of Christian faith . . ."

> "Our popular government lay in embryo on board the Mayflower . . . The idea born there, and embodied in civil constitution . . . grew with the growth of the colonies . . . *until finally it enthroned itself in the national mind, and then embodied itself in our national government.*" J. W. Wellman, *The Church Polity of The Pilgrims,* Boston, 1857.

1623 . . . *Colony of Virginia: legislation* enacted to require civil magistrates "to see that the Sabbath was not profaned by working or any employments, or journeying from place to place."

MARCH 4, 1629 . . . *The First Charter of Massachusetts:* ". . . and for the directing, ruling, and disposing of all other Matters and Thinges, whereby our said People . . . may be soe religiously, peaceablie, and civilly governed, as their good life and orderlie Conversacon, maie wynn and incite the Natives of Country to the Knowledg and Obedience of the onlie true God and Savior of Mankinde, and the Christian Fayth, which in our Royall Intencon, and the Adventurers free profession, is the principall Ende of this Plantacion . . ."

JANUARY 14, 1638 . . . towns of Hartford, Weathersfield and Windsor adopt the *Fundamental Orders of Connecticut* and ". . . enter into Combination and Confederation togather to mayntayne and presearve the liberty and purity of the Gospell of our Lord Jesus, which we now professe . . ."

AUGUST 4, 1639 . . . *Inhabitants of Exeter, New Hampshire:* "considering with ourselves the holy will of God and our own necessity, that we should not live without wholesome laws and civil government among us, of which we are altogether destitute, do, in the name of Christ and in the sight of God, combine ourselves together to erect and set up among us such government as shall be, to our best discerning, agreeable to the will of God . . ."

1641 . . . *Massachusetts Body of Liberties:* "The free fruition of such liberties Immunities and priveledges as humanities, Civilitie and Christianitie call for as due to every man in his place and proportion without impeacement and Infringement hath ever bene and ever will be the tranquilities and Stabilities of Churches and Commonwealths. And the deniall or deprivall thereof, the disturbance if not the ruine of both."

SEPTEMBER 26, 1642 . . . *"Old South Leaflets,"* Rules, and Precepts that are observed in *the College at Cambridge in Massachusetts Bay"* (now known as Harvard): ". . . Let every Student be plainly instructed, and earnestly pressed to consider well, the maine end of his life and studies is, to know God and Jesus Christ which is eternal life, John 17:3 and therefore to lay Christ in the bottome, as the only foundation of all sound knowledge and Learning. And seeing the Lord only giveth wisedome, Let every one seriously set himself by prayer in secret to seeke it of him. Prov. 2. 3."

(One hundred and six of the first 108 schools in America were founded on the Christian faith.)

MAY 19, 1643 . . . New England Colonies of Massachusetts, Connecticut, New Plymouth and New Haven adopt *Articles of Confederation:* "Whereas we all came into these parts of America with one and the same end and aim namely, to advance the kingdome of our Lord Jesus Christ, and to injoy the liberties of the Gospell in purities with peace."

APRIL 3, 1644 . . . *New Haven Colony* adopts charter: ". . . that the judicial laws of God, as they were delivered by Moses . . . be a rule to all the courts in this jurisdiction . . ."

1647 . . . *"Of Plimoth Plantation,"* by Gov. William Bradford: "Lastly, (and which was not least,) a great hope and inward zeall they [the Pilgrims] had of laying some good foundation, or at least to make some way thereunto, for ye propagation & advancing of ye gospell or ye kingdom of Christ in those remote parts of ye world; yea, though they should be but stepping-stones unto others for ye performing of so great a work. . . . their desires were sett on ye ways of God, & to enjoye his ordinances; but they rested on his providence, & know whom they had beleeved."

APRIL 21, 1649 . . . *The Maryland Toleration Act:* "Be it therefore . . . enacted . . . that no person or persons whatsoever within this province . . . professing to believe in Jesus Christ shall . . . henceforth be any ways troubled, molested (or disapproved of) . . . in respect of his or her religion nor in the free exercise thereof . . ."

APRIL 25, 1689 . . . *The Great Law of Pennsylvania:* "Whereas the glory of Almighty God and the good of mankind is the reason and the end of government . . . therefore government itself is a venerable ordinance of God . . ."

FEBRUARY 8, 1693 . . . England's sovereign, William and Mary, grant charter to *College of William and Mary,* Williamsburg, VA. ". . . to the end that the Church of Virginia may be furnished with a seminary of ministers of the gospel and that the youth may be piously enacted in good letters and manners, and that the Christian faith may be propagated amongst the Western Indians, to the glory of God."

NOVEMBER 11, 1701 . . . Trustees constitute the new (Congregational) college called *Yale:* "Whereas it was the glorious public design of our blessed fathers in their removal from Europe into these parts of America both to plant and under the Divine blessing to propagate, in this wilderness, the blessed reformed Protestant religion . . ."

AUGUST, 1752 . . . *The Liberty Bell,* State House, Philadelphia: "Proclaim liberty through all the land and to all the inhabitants thereof: *(Lev. XXV. 10).*

1772 . . . *Samuel Adams:* "The rights of the colonists as Christians . . . may be best understood by reading and carefully studying the institution of The Great Law Giver and Head of the Christian Church, which are to be found clearly written and promulgated in the New Testament."

SEPTEMBER 5, 1774 . . . *Continental Congress,* Carpenter's Hall, Philadelphia: With news just received that British troops had attacked in Boston, the minister opens the session by reading *Psalm 35:* "Plead my cause, Oh, Lord, with them that strive with me, fight against them that fight against me. . . ." (Congress also authorizes payment to chaplains to open its sessions with prayer.)

MAY 20, 1775 . . . *The Mecklenburg (NC) County Resolutions:* "We hereby declare ourselves a free and independent people; are, and of a right ought to be, a sovereign and self-governing association, under control of no power other than that of our God and the general government of Congress."

1775 . . . *John Adams* (who was to serve as the nation's second president, writes in a letter to his wife from the Continental Congress) "Statesmen may plan and speculate for liberty, but it is religion and morality alone which can establish the principles upon which freedom can securely stand."

1775 . . . *Continental Congress* issues a call to all citizens to fast and pray and confess their sin that The Lord God might bless the land.

MAY 17, 1776 . . . *Congress* appoints a day of fasting and prayer for the colonies so they might "by a sincere repentance and amendment of life, appease God's righteous displeasure, and through the merits and mediation of Jesus Christ, obtain His pardon and forgiveness."

JUNE 12, 1776 . . . *Virginia Bill of Rights:* "(Sec. 16) That religion, or the duty which we owe our Creator, and the manner of discharging it, can be directed only by reason and convictions, not by force or violence; and therefore all men are equally entitled to the free exercise of religion, according to the dictates of conscience; *and that it is the mutual duty of all to practice Christian forbearance, love, and charity towards each other.*" (Italics added for emphasis) Note: the Virginia Constitution—including its "Bill of Rights"—was "readopted/ re-ratified" in 1971.

(*George Mason,* author of that Bill of Rights, before the General Court of Virginia: *"The laws of nature are the laws of God,* whose authority can be superseded by no power on earth." It was in this context that the phrase, "the laws of nature and nature's God," was subsequently incorporated in the Declaration of Independence.)

JULY 2-4, 1776 . . . *Declaration of Independence:* ". . . the separate and equal station to which the Laws of Nature and of Nature's God entitle them . . . We hold these truths . . . that all men are created equal, that they are endowed by their Creator with certain unalienable rights . . . appealing to the Supreme Judge of the world . . . And for the support of this Declaration, with firm reliance on the Protection of Divine Providence. . . ."

("We have this day restored the Sovereign to Whom all men ought to be obedient. He reigns in heaven, and from the rising to the setting of the sun, let His kingdom come."—Samuel Adams, as the Declaration of Independence was being signed)

(An effort was started to have Hebrew made the official language of the new nation, "since it was the mother of languages, the key to The Scriptures and the cornerstone of education . . ." Commencement addresses at Yale and Harvard were delivered in Hebrew as late as 1817.)

(On July 4, Congress established three-man committee to design great seal for the United States. Committee members were Jefferson, John Adams, and Franklin. Jefferson proposed picture of Israelites in the wilderness guided by pillar of fire by night and cloud by day. Benjamin Franklin suggested the national motto be *"Rebellion to tyrants is obedience to God"* emblazoned on official seal depicting Moses parting the Red Sea for the exodus to liberty.)

1776 . . . *Delaware Constitution* prescribes this formal oath: "I, _____, do profess faith in God the Father, and in Jesus Christ, His only Son, and in the Holy Ghost, one God blessed forevermore; and I do acknowledge the Holy Scriptures in the Old and New Testament to be given by divine inspiration."

1777 . . . *Articles of Confederation:* ". . . on the fifteenth day of November in the year of our Lord one thousand seven hundred and seventy seven . . . and whereas it has pleased the Great Governor of the world to incline the hearts . . ."

SEPTEMBER 11, 1777 . . . *Continental Congress* directs its Committee of Commerce to import 20,000 copies of The Bible from Europe because the domestic supply was short. The Congress also authorizes chaplains in the Continental Army and General Washington moves to have chaplains appointed in each regiment.

NOVEMBER 1, 1777 . . . *Continental Congress* issues first proclamation of thanksgiving extending to all colonies: "Forasmuch as it is the indispensable duty of all men to adore the superintending Providence of Almighty God; to acknowledge with gratitude their obligation to him for benefits received and to implore such further blessings as they stand in need of . . . to smile upon us as in the prosecution of a just and necessary war for the defense and establishment of our unalienable rights and liberties . . . set apart Thursday, the eighteenth day of December next, for SOLEMN THANKSGIVING and PRAISE."

MARCH 2, 1778 . . . "The hand of Providence has been so conspicuous in all this, that he must be worse than an infidel, and more than wicked, that has not gratitude enough to acknowledge his obligation." *George Washington* comments on the fortunes of the United States' war for independence.

SEPTEMBER 10, 1782 . . . *The Congress of the United States* approves and recommends to the people The Holy Bible printed by Robert Aiken of Philadelphia (a "neat edition of the Holy Scriptures for the use of schools").

"Whereupon, RESOLVED THAT the United States in Congress . . . recommend this edition of the Bible to the inhabitants of the United States, and hereby authorize him to publish this recommendation in the manner he shall think proper."

JANUARY 16, 1786 . . . *Virginia Statute of Religious Liberty:* "Well aware that Almighty God hath created the mind free; that all attempts to influence it by temporal punishments or burdens, or by civil incapacitations . . . are a departure from the plan of the Holy Author of our religion . . ."

JULY 13, 1787 . . . *Northwest Ordinance:* (Article I) "No person, demeaning himself in a peaceable and orderly manner, shall ever be molested on account of his mode of worshipping or religious sentiments . . . *(Article III):* "Religion, morality, and knowledge being necessary to good government and the happiness of mankind, schools and the means of education shall be forever encouraged."

SEPTEMBER 17, 1787 (ratified May 29, 1790) . . . *The Constitution of The United States:* "(Preamble) We the people of the United States, in order to . . . *secure the Blessings of Liberty* to ourselves and our posterity . . ." (ART. I, Sec. 7) "If any Bill shall not be returned by the President within ten Days *(Sundays excepted) . . ."*

(Fifty, and perhaps 52, of the 55 men who framed the Constitution of the US were professing Christians. M. E. Bradford, *A Worthy Company,* Plymouth Rock Fndtn., 1982.)

(When the Constitution was adopted and sent to States for ratification, the population of America was about three and one-half million. The "Christian population" at that time was *at least two million.* About 900,000 were Scotch or Scotch-Irish Presbyterians, and an additional million held to basic Calvinistic beliefs. Thus, clearly, the fundamental presuppositions of the vast majority of Americans in 1787 were Christian.)

(Eleven of the first 13 colonies required faith in Jesus Christ and The Bible as basic qualification for holding public office.)

(The Constitutions of the several States acknowledge and call upon the Providence of God for the blessings of freedom: "We, the people of Kansas, grateful to Almighty God for our civil and religious privileges . . ." *(1863).* "We the people of the State of California, grateful to Almighty God for our freedom . . ." *(1879).* "We the people of Missouri, with profound reverence for the Supreme Ruler of the Universe and grateful for His goodness . . ." *(1945).)*

(In New Hampshire, until 1877, state senators and representatives were required to be of the "Protestant religion.")

1778 . . . *James Madison*, "architect" of the federal Constitution and fourth president "We have staked the whole future of American civilization, not upon the power of government, far from it. We have staked the future . . . upon the capacity of each and all of us to govern our-selves, to sustain ourselves, according to the Ten Commandments of God."

APRIL 30, 1789 . . . *Washington's First Inaugural Address:* ". . . my fervent supplications to that Almighty Being Who rules over the universe, Who presides in the councils of nations, and Whose providential aids can supply every human defect, that His benediction may consecrate to the liberties and happiness of the people of the United States a government instituted by themselves for these essential purposes . . ." ". . . we ought to be no less persuaded that the propitious smiles of Heaven can never be expected on a nation that disregards the eternal rules of order and right which Heaven itself has ordained."

MAY 1, 1789 . . . *United States House of Representatives* elects Rev. William Linn as its chaplain; $500 was appropriated from the Federal treasury to pay his salary.

MARCH 11, 1792 . . . "I am sure that never was a people who had more reason to acknowledge a Divine interposition in their affairs than those of the United States; and I should be pained to believe that they have forgotten that agency which was so often manifested in the Revolution." *President Geo. Washington*.

1794 . . . *Samuel Adams*, Lt. Gov., Massachusetts, addresses the state legislature upon the death of Governor John Hancock: "In the supposed state of nature, all men are equally bound by the laws of nature, or to speak more properly, the laws of the Creator:—They are imprinted by the finger of God on the heart of man. Thou shall do no injury to thy neighbor, is the voice of nature and reason, and it is confirmed by written revelation."

1799 . . . *Runkel v Winemiller 4 Harris & McHenry (MD) 429 1 AD 411, 417* (Justice Chase): "By our form of government, the Christian religion is the established religion."

1802 . . . *Judge Nathaniel Freeman*, in his charge to the Massachusetts Grand Jury: "The laws of the Christian system, as embraced by The Bible, must be respected as of high authority in all our courts and it cannot be thought improper for the officers of such government to acknowledge their obligation to be governed by its rule." "[our government] originating in the voluntary compact of a people who in that very instrument profess the Christian religion, it may be considered, not as republic Rome was, a Pagan, but a Christian republic."

MARCH 4, 1805 . . . *Thomas Jefferson:* ". . . I shall need, too, the favor of that Being in whose hands we are, who led our fathers, as Israel of old."

"The Bible is the source of liberty," *Thos. Jefferson.*

"Almighty God, Who has given us this good land for our heritage; we humbly beseech Thee that we may always prove ourselves a people mindful of Thy favor and glad to do Thy will. Bless our land with honorable ministry, sound learning, and pure manners.

"Save us from violence, discord, and confusion, from pride and arrogance, and from every evil way. Defend our liberties, and fashion into one united people the multitude brough hither out of many kindreds and tongues.

"Endow with Thy spirit of wisdom those to whom in Thy Name we entrust the authority of government, that there may be justice and peace at home, and that through obedience to Thy law, we may show forth Thy praise among the nations of the earth.

"In time of prosperity fill our hearts with thankfulness, and the day of trouble, suffer not our trust in Thee to fail; all of which we ask through Jesus Christ our Lord, Amen." (Thomas Jefferson, *"A National Prayer"*)

JUNE 4, 1805 . . . United States Senate ratifies *Treaty of Peace and Amity with Tripoli* after *repudiating and deleting* from it the phrase that the US "is not, in any sense founded on the Christian religion . . ."

1812 . . . *John Randolph, Speaker of the Virginia House of Delegates,* during debate on the War of 1812 with England: "We hold existence by charter from the Great God."

DECEMBER 22, 1820 . . . *Daniel Webster,* Plymouth, MA: ". . . let us not forget the religious character of our origin. Our fathers brought hither their high veneration for the Christian religion. They journeyed by its light, and labored in its hope. They sought to incorporate . . . and to diffuse its influence through all their institutions, civil, political and literary."

JULY 4, 1821 . . . *John Quincy Adams* (fourth president of the American republic): "The highest glory of the American Revolution was this: it connected, in one indissoluble bond, the principles of civil government with the principles of Christianity." "From the day of the Declaration . . . they (the American people) were bound by the laws of God, which they all, and by the laws of The Gospel, which they nearly all, acknowledged as the rules of their conduct."

NOVEMBER, 1828 . . . *Noah Webster* publishes the first edition of his *American Dictionary of the English Language.* Contains the greatest number of Biblical definitions given in any secular volume; thus demonstrating "the degree to which the Bible was America's basic text book in all fields." Webster believed "education useless without the Bible."

1833 . . . *Noah Webster:* ". . . the religion which has introduced civil liberty, is the religion of Christ and His apostles . . . This is genuine Christianity, and to this we owe our free constitutions of government. . . . the moral principles and precepts contained in the Scripture ought to form the bases of all of our civil constitutions and laws."

1836 . . . *William McGuffey* publishes the first edition of his *"McGuffey's Reader."* Between 1836 and 1920, 122 million copies are sold. Millions of American children learn to read and write from that "reader." In his foreword, McGuffey pens: "The Christian religion is the religion of our country. From it are derived our prevalent notions of the character of God, the great moral governor of the universe. On its doctrines are founded the peculiarities of our free institutions."

1841 . . . *Alexis DeTocqueville* (*Democracy in America*): "In the United States of America the sovereign authority is religious." ". . . there is no country in the world in which the Christian religion retains a greater influence over the souls of men than in America." Describing the American pioneer who made his way Westward, DeTocqueville writes, "[He] penetrates into the wilds of the New World with The Bible, an axe, and a file of newspapers."

JUNE 8, 1845 . . . *President Andrew Jackson* asserts "The Bible is the rock on which our Republic rests."

1851 . . . *Justice Joseph Story* (US Supreme Court, 1811-1845, and professor, Harvard Law School), writes in his *Commentaries on the Constitution of the United States*: "Probably at the time of the adoption of the Constitution, and of the first amendment to it . . . the general if not the universal sentiment in America was, that Christianity ought to receive encouragement by the state so far as was not incompatible with the private rights of conscience and the freedom of religious worship. Any attempt to level all religions, and to make it a matter of state policy to hold all in utter indifference, would have created universal disapprobation, if not universal indignation. . . ."

MARCH 27, 1853 . . . *Committee on the Judiciary, U.S. House of Representatives:* "Down to the Revolution, every colony did sustain religion in some form. It was deemed peculiarly proper that the religion of liberty should be upheld by a free people. Had the people, during the Revolution, had a suspicion of any attempt to war against Christianity, that Revolution would have been strangled in its cradle. At the time of the adoption of the Constitution and the Amendments, the universal sentiment was that Christianity should be encouraged—not any one sect. Any attempt to level or discard all religion would have been viewed with universal indignation. The object was not to substitute Judaism or Mohammedanism, or infidelity, but to prevent rivalry among the sects to the exclusion of others."

FEBRUARY 11, 1861 . . . *Abraham Lincoln,* farewell at Springfield, IL: "Unless the great God who assisted (Washington) shall be with me and aid me, I must fail; but if the same Omniscient Mind and Mighty Arm that directed and protected him shall guide and support me, I shall not fail . . . Let us all pray that the God of our fathers may not forsake us now."

"In regard to this Great Book (The Bible), I have but to say, it is the best gift God has given to man. All the good The Savior gave to the world was communicated through this book. But for it, we would not know right from wrong. All things most desireable for man's welfare, here and hereafter, are to be found portrayed in it." *A. Lincoln* (George L. Hunt, *Calvinism and The Political Order,* Westminster Press, 1965, p. 33)

MARCH 30, 1863 . . . *Presidential Proclamation:* "WHEREAS, the Senate of the United States, devoutly recognizing the Supreme Authority and Just Government of Almighty God, in all the affairs of men and of nations, has, by a resolution, requested the President to designate and set apart a day for National prayer and humiliation . . . I do . . . designate and set apart Thursday, April 30, 1863, as a day of national humiliation, fasting, and prayer . . . IN WITNESS WHEREOF, I have hereunto set my hand and caused the seal of the United States to be affixed." *Abraham Lincoln.*

1864 . . . *Maryland Constitution* requires citizens desiring to hold public office must have declared "belief in the Christian religion, or the existence of God, and in a future state of rewards and punishments."

MARCH 3, 1865 . . . *Secretary of the Treasury, Samuel Chase,* instructs U.S. mint to prepare a "device" to inscribe US coins with motto, "In God we trust." Congress gives its approval.

1884 . . . *U.S. Supreme Court* in reference to the individual's God-given rights "These inherent rights have never been more happily expressed than in the Declaration of Independence, *'we hold these truths to be self-evident'*—that is, so plain that their truth is recognized upon their mere statement—*'that all men are endowed'*—not by edicts of emperors, or decrees of parliament, or acts of Congress, but *'by their Creator with certain inalienable rights and that among these are life, liberty, and the pursuit of happiness, and to secure these'*—not grant them but secure them—*'governments are instituted among men.'*"

1891 . . . *U.S. Supreme Court,* Church of the Holy Trinity v. United States (143 US 457, 36 L ed 226, Justice Brewer): "Our laws and our institutions must necessarily be based upon and embody the teachings of the Redeemer of mankind. It is impossible that it should be otherwise; and in this sense and to this extent our civilization and our institutions are emphatically Christian." ". . . this is a religious people. This is historically true. From the discovery of this continent to the present hour, there is a single voice making this affirmation. . . . we find everywhere a clear recognition of the same truth . . . *this is a Christian nation."* (Emphasis added.)

> (In *1931,* US Supreme Court Justice George Sutherland reviews the 1892 decision and reiterates that Americans are a "Christian people.")

1909 . . . *Theodore Roosevelt* . . . "After a week on perplexing problems . . . it does so rest my soul to come into the house of The Lord and to sing and mean it, 'Holy, Holy, Holy, Lord God Almighty' . . . (my) great joy and glory that, in occupying an exalted position in the nation, I am enabled, to preach the practical moralities of The Bible to my fellow-countrymen and to hold up Christ as the hope and Savior of the world." (Ferdinand C. Iglehart, *Theodore Roosevelt—The Man As I Knew Him,* A. L. Burt, 1919)

1913 . . . *President Woodrow Wilson:* "America was born to exemplify the devotion to the elements of righteousness which are derived from the Holy Scriptures."

MARCH 3, 1931 . . . *U.S. Congress* adopts *"The Star Spangled Banner"* as our National Anthem: "(4th stanza) Praise the Power that hath made and preserved us as a nation. Then conquer we must, when our cause it is just. And this be our motto . . . 'In God is our Trust.' "

1943 . . . "Menaced by collectivist trends, we must seek revival of our strength in the spiritual foundations which are the bedrock of our republic. Democracy is the outgrowth of the religious conviction of the sacredness of every human life. On the religious side, its highest embodiment is The Bible; on the political side, the Constitution." *Statement issued by Herbert Hoover, Alfred Smith, Alfred Landon, Mrs. Calvin Coolidge, Mrs. Theodore Roosevelt, James M. Cox, John W. Davis, Mrs. William H. Taft, Mrs. Benjamin Harrison, Mrs. Grover Cleveland.*

1952 . . . *(US Supreme Court, Zorach v. Clauson, 343 US 307 313, Justice W. O. Douglas)* " . . . we are a religious people and our institutions presuppose a Supreme Being." "No constitutional requirement makes it necessary for government to be hostile to religion and to throw its weight against the efforts to widen the scope of religious influence. The government must remain neutral when it comes to competition between sects. . . . The First Amendment, however, does *not* say that in every respect there shall be a separation of Church and State."

1954 . . . *President Dwight D. Eisenhower:* " . . . the purpose of a devout and united people was set forth in the pages of The Bible . . . (1) to live in freedom, (2) to work in a prosperous land . . . and (3) to obey the commandments of God. . . . This

Biblical story of the Promised land inspired the founders of America. It continues to inspire us. . . ."

(June 14, 1954—Congress adopts phrase, "under God," to be added to the Pledge of Allegiance . . . "one nation, *under God,* indivisible, with liberty and justice for all.")

JULY 20, 1956 . . . *By Joint Resolution, Congress adopts bill,* by Rep. Charles E. Bennett (FL) providing that the national motto of the U.S.A. is "In God We Trust."

1958 . . . *Charles Malik,* Ambassador to the United Nations from Lebanon (President of the UN General Assembly); "Whoever tries to conceive the American word without taking full account of the suffering and love and salvation of Christ is only dreaming. I know how embarrassing this matter is to politicians, bureaucrats, businessmen and cynics; but, whatever these honored men think, the irrefutable truth is that the soul of America is at its best and highest, Christian."

1973 . . . *(Abbington v. Schempp, pp 21, 71):* "Secularism is unconstitutional . . . preferring those who do not believe over those who do believe . . . It is the duty of government to deter no-belief religions . . . facilities of government cannot offend religious principles . . ."

JANUARY 20, 1977 . . . *President Jimmy Carter:* ". . . Here before me is the Bible used in the inauguration of our first President in 1789, and I have just taken the oath of office on the Bible my mother gave me just a few years ago, opened to the timeless admonition from the ancient prophet Micah: "He hath showed thee, O man, what is good; and what does the Lord require of thee, but to do justly, and to love mercy, and to walk humbly with thy God" *(Micah 6:2).*

1980 . . . *President Ronald W. Reagan:* "The time has come to turn to God and reassert our trust in Him for the healing of America . . . our country is in need of and ready for a spiritual renewal . . ."

1980 . . . *(Kevin Walker v. First Orthodox Presbyterian Church, California State Supreme Court, 760-028.9):* "Freedom of religion is so fundamental to American history that it must be preserved even at the expense of other rights which have become institutionalized by the Democratic process."

OCTOBER 4, 1982 . . . As authorized and requested by the *Senate and House of Representatives* of the United States of America,

President Reagan designates 1983 as a national *"Year of the Bible"* . . . "in recognition of both the formative influence the Bible has been for our Nation, and our national need to study and apply the teachings of the Holy Scriptures." (Public Law 97-280 . . . "the renewing of our knowledge of and faith in God through Holy Scripture can strengthen us as a nation.")

JULY 5, 1983 . . . *U.S. Supreme Court* upholds time-honored practice of having chaplains open State Legislative sessions with prayer *(Marsh v. Chambers).* Said Chief Justice Warren E. Burger, "the men who wrote the First Amendment religion clause did not view paid legislative chaplains and opening prayers as a violation of that amendment . . . the practice of opening sessions with prayer has continued without interruption ever since that early session of Congress."

"I have lived, Sir, a long time, and the longer I live the more convincing proofs I see of this truth — that God governs in the affairs of men — And, if a sparrow cannot fall to the ground without His notice is it probable that an empire can rise without His aid?" *Benjamin Franklin,* June 28, 1787, at the Constitutional Convention.

SUGGESTED SOURCE & REFERENCE TEXTS: 1. VERNA HALL, *The Christian History of the Constitution of the United States of America,* Vols. 1 and 2; *The Christian History of the American Revolution,* (San Francisco, Foundation for American Christian Education, 1960, 1976). 2. RUS WALTON, *Fundamentals for American Christians,* Vol. 1; (Plymouth, MA, Plymouth Rock Foundation, 1978): *One Nation Under God* (Washington DC, Third Century Publishers, 1975, 1976). 3. M. E. BRADFORD, *A Worthy Company: Brief Lives of the Framers of The United States Constitution;* (Plymouth, MA, Plymouth Rock Foundation, 1982). 4. R. J. RUSHDOONY, *This Independent Republic;* (Tyler, TX, Thoburn Press, 1964). 5. ALICE M. BALDWIN, *The New England Clergy and The American Revolution;* (New York, Frederick Ungar, 1928) 6. JOHN W. WHITEHEAD, *The Separation Illusion;* (Milford, MI, Mott Media, 1977), *The Second American Revolution;* Elgin, IL, David C. Cook). 7. *American Historical Documents,* edited by HAROLD C. SYRETT; (New York, NY, Barnes & Noble, 1960) 8. EDWIN SCOTT GAUSTAD, *A Religious History of America,* Harper & Row, New York, 1974.

"The United States shall guarantee to every State in this Union a Republican form of Government. . . ." Article IV, Section 4, Constitution.

THE ROOTS OF OUR REPUBLIC

The roots of the American republic grew not from the glories that were Greece or the grandeur that was Rome. The roots of the American republic were planted at Mount Sinai.

The brilliance of our constitutional republic stems not from the gods of Mt. Olympus, not from the orators of the Roman Senate; it comes directly from the Holy Bible, the written word of the Living God.

Thus, as Rev. Louis DeBoer of the American Presbyterian Press, has written:

"Our national existence as a republic of free men is contingent on national faith, faith in the word of God, and presupposes the necessity of periodic reformation to bring us back to that word and its requirements."

What follows, then, is a brief consideration of the distinctions between the great Biblical principles on which the American constitutional republic was founded, and the malignant doctrine of "democracy" into which this nation has fallen and flounders.

"I pledge allegiance to the flag of the United States of America, and to the republic for which it stands; One nation, under God, with liberty and justice for all."

REPUBLIC

GOVERNMENT BASED ON GOD'S LAW

Bible is textbook of govt. Law based on God's law. Constitution guarantees individual freedom, defines proper functions of govt. Minority rights upheld. (Ex 20:1-17, 24:3; Dt 4:1-9, 17:18-19; Isa 33:22; Gal 5:1.)

REPRESENTATIVE GOVERNMENT

Power flows from God to citizen to representatives. People elect legislators, executives, judges. Officials accountable to electorate. Rights & due process upheld. (Ex 18:19-25, 19:5-6; Lev 19:15; Dt 1:13-16, 16:18-20; Rom 13:1-6; Tim 3:1-13.)

LIMITED GOVERNMENT

God is Sovereign; govt. His minister of justice. Citizens restrict govt. power; divide it between fed, state & local levels; erect checks & balances. (Num 16:1-3; Dt 10:12-14, 11:1; Josh 22:14; Ps 22:28; Acts 5:29, 17:7; Rom 13:3-4; 1 Tim 6:15.)

DEMOCRACY

MAN'S GOVERNMENT (Humanism)

State is "god," "vox populi" is sovereign. Majority rule, minority rights suppressed. God's law denied, humanism is state "religion." (1 Sam 8:7; 2 Chron 7:19-22; Isa 1:21-26; Mk 7:20-23; Rom 1: 21-25, 8:7.)

DIRECT GOVERNMENT (Mobocracy)

The people rule by emotion; legislate on impulse, judge by vote. No absolutes. Reason replace righteousness; majority decrees "justice." (Gen 11:1-9; Ex 23:1-2; Judges 21:25; Isa 59:1-15.)

CENTRALIZED GOVERNMENT (Tyranny)

Federal govt. unrestrained; local govts. mere appendages. Controls and bureaucracies sap nation's resources. Caesar is arbiter of morals, "truth" is what serves State. (1 Sam 8:14-18; Isa 3:1-15; John 19:15.)

REPUBLIC

DEMOCRACY

PROPERTY RIGHTS SECURE

All property is God's, entrusted to individuals as His vice regents. Man has property in self, in rights & estate. Govt's function is to protect person and property. (Ex 20:15-17, 22:3, 30:15; Lev 27:30-33; Num 5:6-8; Ps 24:1; 1 Cor 10:26.)

TAXATION (Confiscation)

Taxation an instrument of social control; citizens made servants of State. Personal property progressively taxed to support Caesar's excesses. (Lev 19:13; 1 Sam 8:11-18; 1 Kings 21:1-19.)

INDIVIDUAL LIBERTY (Freedom)

Liberty is gift from God to be exercised within His laws. Basic law of liberty is Ten Commandments, Mt 22:37-40, and to be conscientious toward God. (Ex 20:2; John 8:36; Acts 24:16; Gal 5:13; 1 Pet 2:16.)

LICENSE

Liberty licensed by majority; minority must conform. "Broad public policy" is "god;" constitutional guarantees give way to concensus and "divine right" of public officials. (2 Pet 2:17-19; Jude 4,5; Rev 17&18).

STEWARDSHIP (Free Enterprise)

God created man to glorify Him & to tend His earth. Man is God's steward; to be fruitful, to fulfill God's dominion charter and to obey His work rules. (Gen 1:19; 3; Lev 27:30-33; Dt 25:4; Mt 6:21,33; 25:14-20; Eph 6:5-9.)

COLLECTIVISM (Socialism)

Materialism is worshipped. Govt controls production & distribution. Man must serve State, not God. Property a privilege conferred or cancelled by State. (Lk 12:13-21; Rev 13:16-17.)

A Few Words About the Plymouth Rock Foundation . . .

The material in this book was originally published in the Plymouth Rock Foundation's periodicals: the LETTER FROM PLYMOUTH ROCK and the *FAC-Sheet*.

These publications are sent regularly to the thousands of Christian schools, churches and families in the United States and 14 foreign nations that comprise the Foundation's "Pilgrim Family." To date, more than 5 million copies of various *FAC-Sheets* and approximately 1 million copies of *Letters From Plymouth Rock* have been produced and distributed to and through that "Family."

In addition to those periodicals, Plymouth Rock also produces books and audio-visual materials (audio and video tapes, etc.) as part of its work for the reconstruction of America's Biblical foundations.

The Plymouth Rock Foundation is an uncompromising advocate of Biblical principles of self and civil government and the Christian world and life view. It is an expositor of the Bible-based principle approach to education in the Christian school and the Christian home and in that effort sponsors seminars for Christian educators and pastors. Also, the Foundation seeks to acquaint today's Americans with the blessings and facts of the nation's Christian heritage, thus to help undo and eradicate the harm that has been done by the uninformed and the revisionists who would discredit or deny the Biblical foundations of the American Republic.

Plymouth Rock is a non-denominational, non-profit, public foundation (Section 501 [c] 3). It was incorporated in the Commonwealth of Massachusetts in 1970, A.D. Financial support for its ministry comes solely from those who are led by The Lord to share with it some of that which He has entrusted to them. The United States Department of the Treasury has deemed such contributions to be tax deductible, should the donor be so inclined.

For further information concerning the Plymouth Rock Foundation and its programs and publications and other materials, please contact our General Offices in Marlborough, NH, 03455.

JOHN G. TALCOTT, JR.
President

RUS WALTON
Executive Director

Cover design by John Boatright, Memphis, TN
Set in Baskerville typeface by Thoburn Press, Tyler, TX
Printed and bound by Lithocolor Press, Inc.

Plymouth Rock Foundation
P.O. Box 425
Marlborough, NH 03455

Gentlemen:

I have your book *BIBLICAL PRINCIPLES concerning issues of importance to Godly Christians*. I would like to know more about your Foundation and its programs and publications and what it is doing "to advance the kingdome of The Lord Jesus Christ." Please send me an information packet and place me on your mailing list for a trial subscription to your periodicals, the LETTER FROM PLYMOUTH ROCK and the *FAC-Sheet*.

_____

name

_____

address

_____

city, state, zip

☐ I am also interested in knowing about FUNDAMENTALS FOR AMERICAN CHRISTIANS, your study course in Biblical Principles of Self and Civil Government.

☐ I would like to know about your seminars on the Principle Approach to Christian education.

☐ Enclosed is a tax-deductible donation to help meet expenses.

Miss Verna Hall
Foundation for American Christian Education
2946 Twenty Fifth Avenue
San Fancisco, CA 94132

Dear Miss Hall:

The Plymouth Rock Foundation, in its paperback book *BIBLICAL PRINCIPLES concerning issues of importance to Godly Christians*, suggests that I would be interested in your programs and publications. Please send me information on your organization and its work for The Lord God. Thank you!

_____

name

_____

address

_____

city, state, zip

☐ I am especially interested in information about your resource books on America's Christian history.

**THIS PAGE IS FOR
TEARING OUT AND
SENDING IN!**

WHY NOT DO THAT?

TODAY!!

Dr. Gary North
Institute for Christian Economics
P.O. Box 8000
Tyler, TX 75711

Dear Dr. North:

The Plymouth Rock Foundation, in its paperback book *BIBLICAL PRINCIPLES concerning issues of importance to Godly Christians*, suggests that I would be interested in the newsletters you publish. Please send me a free six month subscription to *Biblical Economics Today, Tentmakers, Christian Reconstruction,* and *Preface*. Thank you!

_____
name

_____
address

_____
city, state, zip

☐ Enclosed is a tax-deductible donation to help
  meet expenses.

_____

Rev. R. J. Rushdoony
Chalcedon
P.O. Box 158
Vallecito, CA 95251

Dear Rev. Rushdoony:

The Plymouth Rock Foundation, in its paperback book *BIBLICAL PRINCIPLES concerning issues of importance to Godly Christians*, suggests that I would be interested in the newsletter you publish. I want to sign up for a subscription to your monthly newsletter, *The Chalcedon Report*. Thank you.

_____
name

_____
address

_____
city, state, zip

☐ Enclosed is a tax-deductible donation to help
  meet expenses.

**THIS PAGE IS FOR
TEARING OUT AND
SENDING IN!**

WHY NOT DO THAT?

TODAY!!

John W. Whitehead, Esq.
Rutherford Institute
P.O. Box 510
Manassas, VA 22110

Dear Mr. Whitehead:

The Plymouth Rock Foundation, in its paperback book *BIBLICAL PRINCIPLES concerning issues of importance to Godly Christians*, suggests that I would be interested in the newsletter you publish which will keep me current on litigation in areas of concern to the Christian community. Please add me to your mailing list. Thank you!

_____
name
_____
address
_____
city, state, zip

☐ Enclosed is a tax-deductible donation to help
   meet expenses.

- -

American Vision
P.O. Box 720515
Atlanta, GA 30328

Gentlemen:

The Plymouth Rock Foundation, in its paperback book *BIBLICAL PRINCIPLES concerning issues of importance to Godly Christians*, suggests that I would be interested in the newsletter you publish. I want to sign up for a subscription to your free monthly newsletter, *Insight*, which deals with a Christian world-and-life view. Thank you.

_____
name
_____
address
_____
city, state, zip

☐ Enclosed is a tax-deductible donation to help
   meet expenses.

**THIS PAGE IS FOR
TEARING OUT AND
SENDING IN!**

WHY NOT DO THAT?

TODAY!!

Rev. G. W. Donnan
Caribbean Christian Ministries
P.O. Box 3018
Paramaribo, Suriname, South America

Dear Rev. Donnan:

The Plymouth Rock Foundation suggests that *Caribbean Christian Ministries* and its program to bring both The Gospel of Jesus Christ and Biblical principles of government to the Caribbean may be the most powerful weapon to save that area of the world from the tentacles of global Communism. Please send me some information on your ministry.

_____
name

_____
address

_____
city, state, zip

☐ Enclosed is a contribution to cover the cost of sending
   me the materials.

- -

Dr. W. David Gamble
American Reformation Movement
7341 Clairemont Blvd., Suite 106
San Diego, CA 92111

Dear Dr. Gamble:

The Plymouth Rock Foundation, in its paperback book *BIBLICAL PRINCIPLES concerning issues of importance to Godly Christians*, suggests that I would be interested in your programs and publications. Please send me information on your organization and its work for The Lord God. Thank you!

_____
name

_____
address

_____
city, state, zip

☐ Enclosed is a tax-deductible donation to help
   meet expenses.

**THIS PAGE IS FOR
TEARING OUT AND
SENDING IN!**

WHY NOT DO THAT?

TODAY!!